In 2002, Chrystopher J. Spicer became an Australian who was first when his acclaimed biography *Clark Gable* was published in the United States by McFarland to mark the centenary of Gable's birth. *Empire* film magazine observed that the biography had a 'meticulously researched and respectful approach'.

Spicer has been writing about Australian and American film and history for many years. He was a contributing editor of the former monthly Australian arts magazine *The Melburnian*, and has written for a number of magazines and newspapers in Australia and the United States. He was also a major contributor to the *Encyclopedia of Melbourne* (Cambridge University Press, 2004), the first encyclopedia of an Australian city to be compiled in this country.

Spicer teaches writing at James Cook University in Queensland.

CHRYSTOPHER J. SPICER

GREAT AUSTRALIAN WORLD FIRSTS

THE THINGS WE MADE, THE THINGS WE DID

ALLEN&UNWIN
SYDNEY • MELBOURNE • AUCKLAND • LONDON

COLL AV

Allen & Unwin
Sydney, Melbourne, Auckland, London
83 Alexander Street
Crows Nest NSW 2065
Australia

Phone: (61 2) 8425 0100
Fax: (61 2) 9906 2218
Email: info@allenandunwin.com
Web: www.allenandunwin.com

Cataloguing-in-Publication details are available
from the National Library of Australia
www.trove.nla.gov.au

ISBN 978 1 7423 76738

Cover images: top (clockwise from left): Jack Brabham, 1968; John Hoelscher and Lonnie Dupre, 2000;
envelope signed by Jessie Keith Miller, 1929; painting of Vida Goldstein by Phyl Waterhouse, 1944 (NLA
2292721); bottom (clockwise from left): Sutton car (courtesy Chris Clemons); Charlie Samuels (courtesy
Colin Tatz); Kay Cottee crossing finish line at Sydney Harbour, 1988 (© Newspix/Ian Mainsbridge);
original Angove wine cask (courtesy John Angove).

Set in 12/16 pt Bembo by Midland Typesetters, Australia
Printed in China at Everbest Printing Co

10 9 8 7 6 5 4 3 2 1

For Phil Pianta,
editor, friend and mentor

'What man can imagine, man can do!'
Jules Verne

CONTENTS

INTRODUCTION

Australians are so proud of the tradition that no one should do better than another within our culture that we've given a name to the practice of cutting down achievers: 'the tall-poppy syndrome'. We've assimilated this national harvest that reduces everyone to an equal shortness so thoroughly that it's become one of our great cultural excuses. As a nation, we have become so smug and self-satisfied in our lucky country that we would rather everyone lose equally than any individual win. We insist that students must not fail in the classroom because competition is too psychologically damaging, and then we decry the country's lack of business and political leaders when such leaders are forged in the heat of the race to win and honed by the cut and thrust of competition.

Unfortunately for our culture, reducing everyone to the same size in Australia hasn't meant raising everyone up to the same level; instead, traditionally the practice has been to cut everyone *down* to the lowest common denominator. Rather than stretch some student minds, for example, the entire class has to be taught at the pace of the slowest. Although Australia hasn't gone down the extreme paths of other countries that wanted everyone equal and so imprisoned their educators, scientists, talented artists and writers, it transports them instead to a cultural wasteland of inadequate funding, lack of interest and course cut-backs. Then we wonder why our children know nothing about their own country, let alone about reading and writing. We're far too civilised to sentence significant Australians to a gulag somewhere near Woomera, but every day we do something far worse and more lasting: we exile them from our collective national memory.

Australia as a country has a short cultural memory except when it comes to footballers and cricket scores. You don't think so? Alright then, shut your laptop and put away your mobile phone and answer from memory these three questions about Australians: Who was the first person to explore Antarctica from the air? Who was the first woman to circumnavigate the globe in a yacht non-stop and unassisted? Who was the first person to be awarded an Oscar for Best Actor after he died? If you answered all those questions correctly, you belong to a tiny and exclusive group of Australians. If you didn't, I can only point out that those are all twentieth-century people and rest my case. You see, we are all too ready to adopt Australian symbols, usually because television advertising tells us they're Australian, but we are too quick to forget the people.

Yet it is in the remembering of those people that we hold the history that defines our nation. Without it, we have no collective sense of who we are as Australian people. Those we remember as important in our history convey to us in the present our sense of identity, our sense of self. In remembering them, we honour not only their achievements but their values and their aspirations. By repeating their stories, we are conveying to the present generation the idea that these achievements, aspirations and values are important in the development of this country. In a way, we storytellers are carrying on the tradition of the classic bards and reciters of odes who have perpetuated since ancient times the memory of legendary heroes who set out into the unknown, met challenges head on, defeated their dragons and returned home victorious.

Australia has its own legendary heroes from many walks of life, not just cricket pitches, football fields or iron man competitions, and a select few have been the first in the world to achieve in their field.

INTRODUCTION

That's right—Australians have actually been the first in the world to fly distances, to explore the unknown, to build dreams like monorails and racing cars and television, to save lives with pacemakers and healing methods, to write books and to climb mountains. It is the tall poppies who, in the end, live on in our history and yet who have so often been denied recognition for their achievements within their own country.

This book contains just a few of their stories. This is by no means a definitive list; there are many more stories still to be told. No selection criteria were imposed for this particular group other than an attempt to be representative, that a first achievement was involved and that many of these people are largely unknown. I do realise that 'first' is often a qualitative term that is by no means definitive, and so I have often modified the term as 'first known' or 'first recorded' and I would always consider that is how the term should be considered. In the case of some inventive progressions, it can actually be quite difficult to say who was first, as many inventions rely on the preceding work of others and different patents are awarded in different countries. So I anticipate that some of these firsts may be a little controversial, but if that leads to discussion about aspects of our heritage, then it can only be good. To help with that discussion, I have added a section at the end of many stories to give the reader an idea of where this 'first' fits into the broader picture of development in that field.

Above all, I hope that this book encourages readers to learn more about people who are an integral part of Australia's cultural heritage, such as those featured here. Once you have finished reading it, I also hope that you will become involved in preserving and developing Australia's culture by passing these stories on to a younger generation who may thus be inspired to go into the future and achieve their own firsts. Let us change this country by growing more tall poppies rather than cutting them down.

Chrystopher J. Spicer
Cairns, Queensland, May 2012

PART I
ARTS

WAIF WANDER

Mary Fortune creates the detective before Sherlock Holmes

Firsts

- The first female writer of detective fiction
- Author of the longest-running nineteenth-century crime fiction series published in a periodical
- The most prolific known nineteenth-century crime writer

If you had been a reader of the popular magazine *Australian Journal* between 1865 and 1908, you would have been enthralled with the detective stories of a writer known as 'Waif Wander', or sometimes simply 'W.W.' If you were an avid reader of some of those 500 stories, then you might even have gone out and purchased a copy of that writer's collection of self-contained crime stories, *The Detective's Album: Tales of the Australian police*, published in 1871. Yet until well into the twentieth century, the author of these early detective stories was a complete mystery. Nobody knew who this writer was, or where they came from, or even their gender.

During the 1950s, the book collector J.K. Moir, realising W.W.'s importance to the history of crime writing, set out to solve the mystery of the writer's identity. In the course of his investigation, he found some manuscript poems and a letter addressed to a Minnie Furlong from about 1909, signed 'M.H. Fortune'. Then, in 1987, Lucy Sussex picked up Moir's magnifying glass and was able to prove that W.W. was indeed Mary Fortune, the first known female author of the detective fiction genre and the most prolific of any known nineteenth-century crime fiction writer. *The Detective's Album* series ran to some 500 stories published regularly for over forty years, the longest-running continuous series in the early history of crime fiction. By comparison, Arthur Conan Doyle's character Sherlock Holmes appears in only fifty-six stories and four novels published at intervals during a similar time period.

Mary Fortune was born Mary Helena Wilson around 1833 in Belfast, Ireland, to George, a civil engineer, and his wife, Eleanor. Mary would later write in her story 'How I Spent Christmas' that she 'never knew either mother or sister or brother', so it would seem that her mother may not have survived Mary's birth. After moving with her father to Montreal, Canada, Mary married a young surveyor, Joseph Fortune, on 25 March 1851 and the following year bore a son named Joseph George, who she called Georgie. By now, news of the discovery of gold in Australia had arrived and Mary's father quickly left for the goldfields soon after Georgie was born. In 1855, Mary and Georgie travelled to join her father, sailing onboard the *Bresias* first to England and from there to Melbourne where they arrived in early October.

In a time before you could simply pick up the telephone and make a call, Mary had to wait in Melbourne for some weeks while she advertised in the personal column of the *Argus* to let her father know she had arrived. She put the days to good use, making copious notes of her observations of life in the city that would later appear in her 1880s memoir known as 'Twenty-Six Years Ago; or, the Diggings from '55'. Eventually, she joined her father near Castlemaine on the Kangaroo Flat goldfields where he had become a general storekeeper, and she seemed to enjoy the tough life there.

A short time later, they abruptly moved to Buninyong, where Mary gave birth to another son in 1856; his birth went officially unrecognised for eight months. When he was finally registered, it was as Eastbourne Vawdrey Fortune and his father was listed as Joseph Fortune. As it is highly unlikely that Joseph had suddenly and mysteriously arrived from Canada, Mary seems to have used his name to conceal the identity of the real father to whom she might not have been married. So there may have been some good reasons why Mary would use a pseudonym such as 'Waif Wander' in an era when a woman's reputation had to be carefully protected.

When she left Canada, Mary had been commissioned to write a series of articles for *The Ladies' Home Companion* magazine, but she had to abandon that because it was just not economically viable. After all, fifteen shillings per article didn't go far when you had two young children to support. By 1858, Mary and her sons were living in Kingower and she would find this year in particular to be one of mixed sadness and joy. Her dear Georgie died in January, but in October Mary married the new local mounted police constable, Percy Rollo Brett, at Dunolly. Mary described herself as a widow on the marriage certificate but did not give the date of her husband's death, nor did she list the names of her children. Percy, for his part, overstated his age by four years at 24. Perhaps not surprisingly, their joy in this odd partnership was short-lived. Unfortunately, Percy was dismissed from the police force at the end of the year, apparently because he over-reacted to a comment about his stepson's parentage, and he promptly found himself in the uncomfortable position of being an unemployed cop in a small country town with a wife whose moral reputation was a little tarnished.

Their situation must have put a lot of pressure on their relationship, and it eventually broke down under the strain. Percy left town, and by 1862 he was working as a stock-dealer in Jerilderie in New South Wales. He eventually purchased farmland at Urana and married a prominent citizen's daughter, with whom he'd eloped, without obtaining a divorce from Mary.

Meanwhile, by 1865 Mary had moved to the Victorian mining town of Jericho (now Wehla) where a copy of the Melbourne magazine *Australian Journal* caught her eye one day; perhaps its strong crime flavour reminded her of life with Percy. Mary had already been writing for about ten years by now, submitting pseudonymous contributions to various goldfield newspapers such as the *Buninyong Advertiser*. However, she had found out from experience that it was not always a good idea to reveal her gender; the *Mount Alexander Mail*, for example, had once offered her a sub-editor's position after admiring her poetry only to withdraw the proposal in shock when they discovered their correspondent was actually a woman. So she sent in her first story to the *Journal*, for which she had fallen back on her knowledge of police procedure, under the pseudonym of 'An Australian Mounted Trooper', and to her delight it was published in late 1865 under the title 'The Stolen Specimens'.

Evidently the *Journal* liked Fortune's work; it quickly teamed her with one of their staff writers, James Skipp Borlase, to jointly produce the first detective series published in Australia. However, after nine stories together Borlase was dismissed for plagiarism so Fortune tried her hand at some other styles of serialised novel until the *Journal* decided in 1867 to renew the original series under the title *The Detective's Album* with Fortune as the sole author, using the pseudonym 'W.W.' According to Lucy Sussex's research, during the following year alone Fortune published three poems, fourteen short stories and three serialised novels—she also began a fourth. By Christmas Day 1868, she and her son were living in Melbourne and, despite being poor, she could write that she was independent and supporting herself through her writing—although, given the woeful rate paid for magazine stories in those days, she must have supplemented her income somehow, such as by taking in boarders. Her only book, published in 1871 as *The Detective's Album*, contained seven of the stories published under that collective title and was the first detective fiction book published in Australia.

A writer's life is an unpredictable roller-coaster, though, as Fortune was soon reminded. In 1871, the same year her book was published, her son Eastbourne was taken into custody as a neglected child and sent to the Industrial (Reform) School in Sunbury, later the Sunbury Lunatic Asylum and now part of the Victoria University campus. Unfortunately, and somewhat ironically given the subjects of Mary's stories, young Eastbourne became a regular guest at some of Her Majesty's more secure residences for a large part of his life, finally doing ten years after being sentenced for burglary in 1890. His arrest record reveals that within a short time Fortune had lost her independence to become a resident of the Melbourne Immigrants' Home, an institution that provided accommodation for the destitute, which explains why Eastbourne was running wild in the streets. In short, despite being one of Australia's most successful published authors, Mary Fortune was homeless.

Still, she kept on writing. Her last serialised novel, *The Bushranger's Autobiography*, appeared in the *Australian Journal* between 1871 and 1872. After that, her writing was devoted almost exclusively to the crime stories that appeared in virtually every issue of that magazine. For almost forty years, Fortune would write twelve short stories a year as part of the *Detective's Album* series, although some longer ones came closer to being novelettes, usually following the same format: a collection of mug shots through which Detective Mark Sinclair browses, reminiscing about criminals, cases and how they were solved. Fortune's work thus pioneers the form of crime writing that came to be known as 'police procedural'. Sinclair's lively and colloquial voice addresses the reader directly and, judging from some of her other writing, it seems to be very much Fortune's voice. She had a keen eye for character description and mannerisms, and for the particular styles of conversation and nuances of vocabulary used by various social groups.

No matter how much writing talent one has, though, a rate of production that intense eventually has to take its toll, and so it's probably not surprising that alcohol became Fortune's friend. After all, as the editor of the *Australian Journal* Ron Campbell observed in 1952: 'She wrote more, and doubtless got less for it, than any other Australian writer of the time.' Ironically, the only description of Fortune that has survived appears in a report in the *Police Gazette* of 10 February 1874, where she is recorded as being at that time aged 40, tall, pale and thin, dressed in a dark jacket and skirt and wearing a black hat and old elastic-sided boots. Even then, the report states, she was 'much given to drink and has been locked up several times for drunkenness'.

By the time she wrote the letter to Minnie Furlong that was located many years later by J.K. Moir, Fortune's failing eyesight had ended her writing career. She was living in poverty, reduced to wearing clothes that Minnie had given her, and her troubled Eastbourne had died in Tasmania two years previously. However, the *Australian Journal* continued to reprint her earlier stories and then maintained the *Detective's Album* series with stories by other writers. In a remarkable act of kindness, with perhaps a touch of guilt, the *Journal* sent the elderly Fortune an annuity until her death and then paid for her burial expenses. The date of her death and where she is buried remain Mary Fortune's last mysteries.

★

The rest of the world

Edgar Allan Poe became the first notable early detective fiction writer with his 'The Murders in the Rue Morgue' in 1841, the first of his trio of stories featuring the Parisian detective Dupin. Charles Dickens was responsible for Britain's first literary detective: Inspector Bucket in the 1852 *Bleak House*. The first Australian murder-mystery novel was *Force and Fraud: A tale of the bush*, written by Ellen Davitt, head of the Ladies Institute of Victoria school for governesses and a sister-in-law of Anthony Trollope, writing under the name Mrs Arthur Davitt. Her novel was serialised in *Australian Journal*, beginning in its first issue in 1865, but was not published in book form until 1993 and so is usually unrecognised for its significance. It did not feature a detective.

In England, Mary Elizabeth Braddon, whose brother Edward became a premier of Tasmania, was an early female mystery writer famous for her novel *Lady Audley's Secret* (1862). She later founded the *Belgravia Magazine* in 1866.

Catherine Louisa Pirkis wrote many short stories and fourteen novels after 1877 in England. These included stories published in *Ludgate Magazine* in 1894 featuring the professional detective Miss Loveday Brooke, who works for the Ebenezer Dyer detective agency, often undercover. Pirkis then abandoned her writing for work with the National Canine Defence League, which she had co-founded in 1891.

Although there were earlier suspense or mystery writers, the versatile Metta Victoria Fuller Victor, who used the name Seeley Regester, is the author of the first known American detective novel, *The Dead Letter*, which featured the amateur gentleman detective Mr Burton. Serialised in *Beadle's Monthly* in 1866, the chapters were published as a novel the following year by Victor's husband, Orville James Victor, head of dime-novel publishing company Beadle & Adams.

However, Anna Katherine Green is probably the best-known early American female detective fiction author, with her novel *The Leavenworth Case* published in 1878. Her father was a criminal lawyer who no doubt was the source of some inspiration. She was probably also the first female detective writer to feature leading characters who were female detectives: Violet Strange and Amelia Butterworth. The aristocratic Butterworth first appeared in 1897 in *That Affair Next Door*.

THE WONDERFUL, WONDERFUL CAT

Pat Sullivan and Felix

Firsts

- The first animated cartoon series starring an anthropomorphic animal character
- The first cartoon character to become a fully merchandised celebrity star
- The first cartoon animal to appear on television

If you had been driving around Los Angeles in the mid–1920s, you would probably have seen Chevrolet dealer Winslow Felix going by in his convertible painted with cartoons of the famous character Felix the Cat and perhaps with a giant Felix head sitting on the back seat. His briefcase was emblazoned with a Chevrolet logo and the words 'Order Yours from Felix'. Winslow was a friend of the Australian cartoon studio owner Pat Sullivan who, in exchange for a free car, had let him use the image of Felix as a marketing tool. In 1959, the W. Heath Company designed and erected a huge neon sign featuring Felix the Cat above the Felix Chevrolet dealership building on the corner of Figueroa Street and Jefferson Boulevard in Los Angeles, where it can still be seen today.

Long before then, Felix the Cat had become the most famous cat in the world. Not only could he be seen on the screen but also in books and newspapers, as dolls and figurines, on pencils, money boxes, bedroom slippers, ties, china, and even on Felix cigars. During World War II, British children's gas masks appeared with Felix on them. Having been revived in recent years, Felix is still with us, but what many people don't know is that his fame and creation were closely tied to an Australian: the artist, producer and animation studio owner Pat Sullivan.

Named after his father, well-known Sydney hansom cab driver Patrick O'Sullivan, the young Pat was born in Paddington in 1886, had a sound Catholic education and then studied art at night at the Art Society of New South Wales while working as a Toohey's Brewery gate-keeper. By way of earning some money on the side, he became a pianola demonstrator in Sydney and then toured a bioscope show with his brother Bill, while selling caricatures of sport celebrities in barbershops and even drawing a few quick portraits. When he was eighteen he found a regular job as an artist on the *Worker*, but by then the wider world was calling. O'Sullivan left Australia for England, where he found it convenient to appear less obviously Irish by dropping the 'O' from his name. It didn't help him find a job, though, and he was reduced to walking up and down Fleet Street knocking on newspaper doors looking for work and sleeping on park benches at night. Finally he found a job drawing for *Ally Sloper* and some other papers before even that came to an end with the death of King Edward VII in May 1910. Back in those more mannered times, the death of royalty meant extended public mourning, during which time publishing funny cartoons just wasn't the done thing.

Then fate stepped in, as she sometimes does. One day he went down to the docks to farewell some friends who were leaving for New York. Unfortunately, he'd had a little too much to drink and fell asleep on board. When he awoke it was to find the ship at sea and on the way to New York with him on it, but without enough money to pay for a return ticket. On arrival, he led a mule down the gangplank to distract the immigration authorities, but then he was on his own. He found freelance work drawing postcards and theatre posters before he finally landed a job with the McClure newspaper syndicate drawing comic strips with cartoonist William Marriner. The more he drew, the more he became intrigued by the concept of animating these figures.

When Marriner died in late 1914, Sullivan joined Raoul Barre's pioneering and successful film studio Animated Cartoons Inc. for a few months before opening his own studio at 125 West 42nd Street. Sullivan soon won advertising and entertainment contracts, and within two years his studio staff, including talented cartoonist Otto Messmer, were turning out films under his name, such as the 1916 Sammy Johnsin series. In 1954, the *Sydney Morning Herald* claimed that Sullivan had also introduced the first animated titles to the screen when he drew an elephant bursting into a kindergarten, throwing over a child's set of blocks to form the words 'Metro Pictures Presents'. On 3 March 1917, he released an animated feature titled *The Tail of Thomas Kat*, which proved to be the prototype of a much more famous cat indeed.

However, just when Thomas Kat hit the big time, Sullivan was convicted in 1917 of raping a fourteen-year-old girl and jailed for nine months. On the other hand, before they walked him into the Big House he just had time to marry Marjorie Gallagher, a pretty Ziegfeld Follies girl who was convinced of his innocence. His studio had to close while he was inside, but he had lots of time to practise drawing.

As soon as the prison door clanged shut behind him on his release, Sullivan lost no time in reopening his studio and creating new films, once again in partnership with Messmer. They went back to making animated short parodies of travelogues for Triangle Films, cartoons based on Chaplin's 'Little Tramp' character and cartoons that would accompany feature films in cinemas. One of these was the 1919 *Feline Follies*, once again starring Thomas Kat—or Master Tom as he was now known. By the end of that year, though, the cat was no longer on four legs but on two and his name had changed—to Felix.

There are different stories about how a cat named Felix became a cartoon star. In 1925, Sullivan claimed that he had been inspired when his wife, Marjorie, brought a cat into the office and on another occasion he said the idea came from Rudyard Kipling's poem, 'The Cat that Walked by Himself'. Fellow cartoonist and caricaturist Kerwin Maegraith wrote in the *Sydney Morning Herald* in 1954 that Marjorie found a stray cat with odd markings and a broken tail and brought it home, suggesting that it was Sullivan's good luck and he should draw it. According to Maegraith, Sullivan told her personally that he had at first drawn the cat solid black, modelling it after Peter Felix, the boxer and sparring partner of heavyweight champion Jack Johnson, but that he'd also been inspired by the term 'Australia Felix'. Latin for 'fortunate Australia', the name was coined by explorer Major Mitchell when describing central Victoria in 1836 and later used by the writer Henry Handel Richardson in 1917 as the title of a book.

However, controversy is also still raging across the Pacific as to whether Sullivan actually drew Felix personally or whether he was the creation of Sullivan's drawing partner, Otto Messmer. In 1967, by which point nearly all involved had passed on, Otto Messmer claimed that he had actually been the artist who created Felix, modelling the cat on the movements of Charlie Chaplin, who was a friend of Sullivan's. Because Messmer was working for Sullivan in his studio, he said, it had been Sullivan's name that went on the credits, not an unusual practice at the time. After all, Floyd Gottfredson drew the Mickey Mouse comic strips from 1930 to 1975, but as a Disney employee he was not allowed to sign his work.

On the other hand, it is quite probable that, as Sullivan himself said in an Australian interview in the *Argus* on 1 December 1925, he did the key drawings to indicate what the Felix plot line would be and Messmer, as chief animator, and his staff did the rest. Certainly, as New South Wales State Library curator Judy Nelson has established, the lettering in the 1917 film *The Tail of Thomas Kat*, which is copyrighted to Sullivan, is recognisably that of Sullivan, and a number of Felix's trademark features such as his removable tail are visibly evident in Thomas. Members of the Australian Cartoonist Association have also demonstrated that the lettering in the later 1919 *Feline Follies* also matches Sullivan's handwriting. Given the length of time that has passed, it is unlikely that anyone will ever know the full story.

Nevertheless, wherever and however the cat originated, *Felix* cartoons were certainly produced by Sullivan with outstanding success some years before another studio would bring fame to a talking mouse, thus making Felix the first cartoon animal character to be anthropomorphic—or given human qualities, such as speaking and walking on two legs. Although Krazy Kat, an earlier cartoon cat first seen in 1916, walked on two legs, it was never regarded as 'human'. It had no gender, spoke a barely recognisable language, and was even referred to by its creator as a 'sprite' or 'elf'.

Felix quickly became *the* animated cartoon star of the 1920s. Sullivan signed a contract with Famous–Players Lasky Corporation for one *Felix* cartoon a month, and in 1920 opened a bigger studio on 66th Street and Broadway. Even so, as often happens in stardust territory, both he and his producer soon had their problems. Sullivan was a heavy drinker and his reputation for being a difficult man to work with was only enhanced when Paramount dropped distribution of the *Felix* animated features in 1921. The story went around Hollywood that Sullivan had actually urinated on the desk of Paramount executive Adolph Zukor to express his feelings.

Still, while one door closed another one opened. When Sullivan unsuccessfully tried to interest Harry Warner (of Warner Bros) in Felix, Warner's secretary Margaret Winkler saw other possibilities and signed a contract with Sullivan in 1922, making her the first female producer and distributor of animated films. She also went on to become Disney's first distributor. By September, Winkler had secured distribution for Sullivan to 60 per cent of US and Canadian theatres and had negotiated for international distribution through Pathé. It was a very successful partnership; she got improvements in story, photography and animation quality from Sullivan and Felix made a huge profit for them all in return. There were thirteen *Felix* cartoons released in 1922 alone.

Felix's fans enjoyed films loaded not just with humour but with imaginative visual puns and spoofs. Demonstrating human intelligence, Felix dealt with problems by finding creative solutions, albeit often in ways that could exist only in the animation universe where there are no limits. By 1923, Felix's fame had developed to the point where King Features signed to syndicate a Sunday comic strip in America; within a few years it was appearing daily. There was even a hit Felix song in 1923 played by Paul Whiteman's band called 'Felix Kept on Walking'. That same year, Felix debuted in England's *Daily Sketch* newspaper and when the Sullivans were invited to England in 1924 for the British Empire Exhibition held at Wembley, London, they developed an industry in Felix dolls and toys. By then, Sullivan owned the rights to the Felix character and to over two hundred different Felix merchandising items. It was said that the royalties from Felix dolls alone at the exhibition were in the region of £250 000; even Queen Mary had a doll. In 1927, Felix was the first giant balloon to feature in New York's famous Macy's Thanksgiving Day Parade, and Charles Lindbergh took a Felix doll along with him on his historic flight across the Atlantic.

Educational Pictures took over the distribution of *Felix* cartoons from 1925 until 1928 with a deal of one cartoon short every two weeks. Over a hundred and fifty *Felix* feature films and shorts were made in total, using a studio production system pioneered by Sullivan and later copied and refined by Disney. However, it would be Disney's quick adoption of the new sound technology in 1928 for his talking mouse that proved to be Sullivan's and Felix's downfall. Despite urging by Educational Pictures, Sullivan refused to make the transition from silent to sound, and Educational refused to renew their contract. Only when Sullivan saw the success of Disney's *Steamboat Willie* did he change his mind and sign another contract with First National Pictures, but that didn't last and so he moved to Jacques Kopfstein and Copley Pictures. However, Sullivan still only seemed partially sold on sound and his first attempts consisted of just dubbing sound effects post-animation. It was Disney who proved to be the innovator in the long term with careful frame-by-frame synchronisation of animation with soundtrack, and the mouse began to draw audiences away from the cat.

Felix still had some tricks in his tail, though. In 1928, he became the first cartoon animal character to appear on television when RCA used a 33-centimetre-high papier-mâché Felix doll to provide a test image while the transmitted picture was monitored and adjusted during their first experimental broadcasts from station W2XBS in New York. Felix was chosen because of his sharp black-and-white tonal contrast and the doll's ability to withstand bright lights for extended periods. It was placed on a rotating record-player turntable and, with the use of a mechanical scanning disc, a 5-centimetre-tall image of Felix was broadcast to an electronic kinescope receiver for two hours every day. After a one-time payment to Sullivan, the doll remained on the turntable for nearly a decade as the station became part of NBC and moved to 42nd Street, where the company refined its attempts to attain high-definition pictures.

However, as the image of his cat became part of a new technology that would bring him to a wider audience than ever before, the ink of Sullivan's life began to run out. Kopfstein cancelled his contract with Copley Pictures and cartoon production stalled. Then, sadly, Sullivan's wife Marjorie fell to her death from their seventh-floor New York apartment in the Hotel Forrest in March 1932. Although in January the following year Sullivan signed a three-year contract with Paramount, reputed to be the most lucrative agreement signed between a cartoonist and a film company at that time, he never seemed to recover from the loss of Marjorie. Already ill from alcohol abuse, he died from pneumonia on 15 February the following year in a New York hospital.

After his death, it was found Sullivan had made no arrangements to carry on his studio's work, and it had to close down. In 1936, Amadee

Van Beuren of Van Beuren Studios obtained approval from Sullivan's brother to license Felix to his studio, but he reduced Felix to just another Disney-type funny animal character and the revival was short-lived. It wasn't until 1953, when Official Films purchased the Sullivan-Messmer shorts and added soundtracks to them for distribution to television, that Felix was seen again on screen by a substantial audience. Meanwhile, Messmer kept drawing Felix for Sunday comic strips and then for Dell Comics. In 1954, he retired and his protégé Joe Oriolo, creator of Casper the Friendly Ghost, struck a deal with Sullivan's nephew to begin a new television series. From 1958, a re-created Felix with his Magic Bag of Tricks starred in some 260 television cartoons, a series also remembered for the distinctive and catchy theme song sung by Ann Bennett.

Today under the management of Oriolo's son Don, the famous cat named Felix, created in the studio of Australian Pat Sullivan, is still being marketed and seen by audiences around the world. 'I made the cat,' Sullivan said in 1925 while visiting Australia, 'and the cat made me.'

★

The rest of the world

Sadly, Chevrolet dealer Winslow Felix died as a result of colliding with Australian actor 'Snowy' Baker in a polo game at the Riviera Country Club in May 1936.

The first animated animal star was probably Winsor McCay's Gertie the Dinosaur, who was part of his famous vaudeville act in 1914. Projecting the animated dinosaur sequence on a large screen, McCay created the interactive illusion of walking into the animation by disappearing behind the screen only to reappear on the screen, step onto Gertie's opened mouth and then climb onto her back for a ride.

John Randolph Bray's 1913 cartoon *The Artist's Dream*, or 'The Dachshund and the Sausage', is regarded as the first animated cartoon in the United States to be made using the 'cel' technique (later perfected by Disney), in which sequences of drawings painted on celluloid transparencies are photographed. Bray's 1920 cartoon *The Debut of Thomas Kat* is often credited as the first cartoon drawn in colour and also shot using a two-colour emulsion process.

The first Disney animal character to become famous and merchandised was not Mickey Mouse but Oswald the Lucky Rabbit, who featured in a series of twenty-six cartoons between 1927 and 1928. Animator Walter Lantz then took over Oswald, who became the first animated character for Universal, looking remarkably like competitor Mickey Mouse.

'I CAME TO LIFE WANTING TO PAINT'

Nora Heysen, an artist of war and peace

Firsts

- First commissioned female war artist in the Allied forces to work on the front line during combat
- First woman to win the Archibald Prize, Australia's major award for portraiture

As the army jeep slid to a halt in a cloud of dust outside the casualty clearing station in the New Guinea town of Finschhafen one day in mid-1944, an officer leaped out and barked a question at the first person he saw. 'Where can I find Captain Heysen?'

Following the direction of the pointing finger, he walked swiftly to the door of the officers' mess and jerked it open. As it slammed shut, he found himself in an oasis of stillness amidst the bustle of a front-line army camp. The long room was empty of people except for a uniformed woman standing in front of an easel, deeply engrossed in painting the boat-shaped vase of native flowers on the table before her.

'Captain Nora Heysen? My orders are to transport you to Lae immediately.'

The young woman turned with paintbrush in hand, looked with large, calm eyes for a moment at the young officer and then said quietly, 'Surely you can see that I'm busy here. I can't possibly leave now.'

With that, she turned back to add another layer of colour to some leaves. Nora Heysen might have been the first commissioned female war artist to work on the front line, but no one was going to tell her when she could and could not work, nor what she should paint.

Needless to say, her refusal to obey the order didn't go down well with army administration. Heysen was threatened with a court-martial and, even though that didn't eventuate, it was clear that the Officer-in-Charge of the Military History Section at the army headquarters in Melbourne, Lieutenant Colonel John Treloar, wanted this independent woman brought into line.

Nora Heysen was the fourth child of Sir Hans Heysen, one of Australia's great painters, and his wife, Selma. Born in 1911 and raised at The Cedars, the family home near Hahndorf in the Adelaide Hills, she experienced as a child the anti-German discrimination brought on by World War I, and it forged in her an early hatred of war. With her family heritage, there was no doubt in Nora's mind what she wanted to do. 'From four years old I was painting,' Nora said to author Scott Bevan, 'I came to life wanting to paint.' She learned all she could from her father, who constantly encouraged her, but she was more attracted to painting in oils than watercolours and to nature's smaller details in still-life groups and in people's faces. By the time she was a war artist, she was already an acclaimed still-life and portrait painter. One of her most frequent subjects was herself, and she may have painted more self-portraits than any artist except Rembrandt.

After studying at the School of Fine Arts in North Adelaide, she quickly gained recognition for her talent. By 1931, the state art galleries of New South Wales, South Australia and Queensland had all acquired her works. Nora held her first solo exhibition in Sydney two years later and was awarded the Melrose Prize for Portraiture for her painting *Ruth*. After travelling through Europe, she studied in London at the Central School of Art and met and was influenced by the post-impressionist painter Lucien Pissaro. After further travel, during which she studied the art of Cézanne and painted more works, she arrived back in Sydney in 1937. The following year, Heysen became the first woman to win the Archibald Prize, with her portrait of Madame Elink Schuurman, the wife of the Consul General for the Netherlands. Her award became mired in controversy when artist, theorist and teacher Max Meldrum criticised it, saying, 'If I were a woman, I would certainly prefer raising a healthy family to a career in art. Women are more closely attached to the physical things of life. They are not to blame. They cannot help it, and to expect them to do some things equally as well as men is sheer lunacy.'

When World War II broke out, Heysen immediately did what she could for the war effort, working for a while in a kiosk providing food for naval servicemen, but it wasn't enough for her. She knew what she was good at and wanted to become a war artist. However, the traditional place for any woman artist in wartime up until then had been at home. To achieve her goal, Heysen would have to change some prevailing military attitudes.

During World War I, in Australia, as in other Allied countries, various female artists had painted men leaving for war and arriving from it, but no official Australian female war artist had been commissioned during that conflict. However, two Australian women recorded the war in France unofficially: expatriate artist Iso Rae, who was living in the town of Etaples when war broke out, sketched activities at the large military encampment there where she was a volunteer and worker, as did Jessie Traill while she worked at the military hospital at Rouen. With the outbreak of war in 1939, there remained a profound reluctance to place women artists on a battlefield. The American military had no official female war artists, and out of a very small group of female British artists, only one, Evelyn Dunbar, was a full-time war artist employed by the Ministry of Information, and she was confined to recording the Women's Land Army in Britain.

So, even though Australian women's roles in military service had been opened up somewhat by the outbreak of World War II, no female artist had yet been offered an active part. Typically, when the authorities wouldn't come to her, Heysen took the fight to them. She persuaded her father to speak to Louis McCubbin, who had been an artist during World War I and was now director of the National Gallery of South Australia and a member of the Australian War Memorial Art Committee. He recommended Heysen to the committee in January 1943, and her appointment was approved in February. A few months later she met the man who would be her commanding officer, Lieutenant Colonel John Treloar, at the Melbourne headquarters of the Military History Section. Although Treloar also subsequently recommended her, it was most likely as an expedient political gesture. Heysen told Scott Bevan she had the feeling Treloar thought women should be supporting the fighting men through work on the home front, not exposing themselves to danger on the battlefront.

Before Heysen could enter the war, there was a battle over her pay and where she would work. If she was attached to the Australian Women's Army Service (AWAS), then she would receive a lower rate of pay than for the equivalent male rank, even as a commissioned officer. On the other hand, as a female war artist she was a specialist in her field, equally as qualified as a male war artist and thus entitled to the same rate of pay. The pay wrangle didn't go away until the war memorial offered to make up the difference between her female officer's pay rate and her 'male' war artist's rate, and in October the Minister for the Interior, Senator J.S. Collings, finally announced all war artists would receive equal pay. Then, the female head of the AWAS flatly opposed having her serve with them. However, if Heysen was attached to the AWAS she wouldn't be able to travel outside of Australia, which was not Heysen's plan in any case. She could not see herself sitting in a Melbourne studio painting war; she had to be there, to move among the men and make a personal record. Nevertheless, for a while she did have to be content with painting a series of portraits of distinguished women leaders in the armed services at home before finally receiving her commission, effective from 9 January 1944. It should have been an omen to the army that when Heysen was notified of her selection as a war artist in October and told to report to Canberra immediately, she replied that she had to go to Sydney first to arrange the framing and exhibition of some of her paintings.

Finally, because of a suggestion to Treloar by one of Heysen's portrait subjects, Colonel Annie Sage, matron-in-chief of the Australian Army Nursing Service, it was agreed that Heysen could travel to New Guinea to record the activities of the nurses there, who were closer to the front at that time than any other women. Now, a commissioned female war artist would actually be painting women at war at an overseas combat front with the sanction of the military itself, something that up until then had never occurred in the Allied armed forces. Just by walking into the previously all-male territory of the officers' mess at Allied headquarters in New Guinea, Heysen created history.

On 8 April, Heysen moved up to the front at Finschhafen to live with and paint the work of the nurses stationed there. To her surprise and chagrin, she found that the nurses resented her because of her rank and pay, compared to her lack of service experience, matters with which she'd really had nothing to do. She found herself ostracised to a tent by herself. None of this bothered her, though, because she preferred painting the men who were brought in or who were on rest leave. She sketched casualties, fever patients, the indigenous stretcher bearers (who she considered should be officially recognised for their work), various servicemen and, finally, the nurses.

By July, she had completed over thirty works that she forwarded to Treloar who, typically, was not impressed. He told her she had not covered enough of the activities of the nurses and the female medical service personnel. In his opinion, she had painted too many portraits while not creating enough historically relevant work and so she should return to Melbourne as soon as possible.

Heysen ignored him and stayed on in New Guinea for a while longer. After eventually obeying her orders and moving to Lae, she accompanied the nurses west to Madang and Alexishafen, continuing to paint them at their work, as well as soldiers and bulldozer drivers, flowers and insects, but Treloar remained unsatisfied. He was irritated no end by her attitude that she should paint the same subjects as male war artists; he wanted a female artist who would paint the activities of women. Finally, he ordered her home at the beginning of September, rationalising that the war memorial's art committee wanted more artists working shorter timespans to gain varied coverage.

By the time she arrived back in October 1944, Heysen's complexion was bright yellow due to the anti-malarial Atabrine tablets she had to take, and she was ill with tropical ulcers and severe dermatitis. After recovering at Hahndorf, she returned to Sydney to paint the women workers at the Blood Bank unit operating at the Sydney Hospital, which prepared blood for delivery to combat areas. Fortunately, she could also be near Captain Robert Black, a specialist in tropical diseases whom she had met in New Guinea.

She travelled to Melbourne to complete some of her paintings at the war artists' studios there, and then in the final days of the war she was transferred from the army to the air force. Appointed to the Medical Air Evacuation Unit at the Garbutt RAAF Station, Townsville, she worked at depicting the largely unrecognised work of the Women's Auxiliary Australian Air Force and the RAAF's nursing sisters, flying up and down the coast of Far North Queensland and even out to the island of Morotai in the then Dutch East Indies. She remained in Cairns after the war was over, depicting the malaria trials at the Medical Research Unit, until she flew home in November 1945, with boxes of artworks and materials that weighed more than 100 kilograms. Finally, she was discharged on 8 February 1946, having completed some 155 paintings and drawings.

In 1953 Nora married Dr Robert Black who became head of tropical medicine at the University of Sydney, (but they separated in

1972). Working from her Hunters Hill home and studio, 'The Chalet', Heysen continued to paint, exhibit and travel all her life, receiving the Australia Council's Award for Achievement in the Arts in 1993 and the Order of Australia for her service to art in 1998. Her works are held at the National Gallery, Australian War Memorial, National Library and National Portrait Gallery as well as by every state gallery. Her final exhibition was in 2000, when she was 89, at the National Library in Canberra. She died in 2003.

Just before she died, Nora Heysen, pioneer war artist, told Scott Bevan that she wished she could have contributed more.

★

The rest of the world

The first known female war artists in the Western world were the women who embroidered the Bayeux Tapestry depicting William of Normandy's conquest of England in 1066. Many centuries later, Lady Elizabeth Butler, née Elizabeth Southerden Thompson, was the first major female painter of war. While she certainly didn't go into the field, she ensured her paintings were meticulously accurate by interviewing soldiers who had fought in the Crimean and Franco-Prussian Wars and making detailed studies of uniforms and weapons. Her 1874 painting *Roll Call* became so popular it was taken on a national tour of Britain and was eventually purchased by Queen Victoria.

In 1916, the British government set up the first official war artists' scheme primarily for propaganda purposes but also as a way of creating an illustrated record. Only four women were eventually commissioned, compared to forty-seven men, and they all worked on the home front. However, there were official war artists who worked closer to combat, such as British Red Cross ambulance driver Olive Mudie-Cook. Australian-born artist Grace Evelyn Chapman painted French battlefields, especially Villers-Bretonneux, after the World

War I Armistice while she was in France with her father, who was attached to the New Zealand War Graves Commission. Canadian Mary Riter Hamilton, who had trained and exhibited in Europe, was privately commissioned in 1919 by the veteran magazine *Golden Stripe* to paint scenes of the World War I battlefields of Vimy Ridge and the Somme where many Canadians had fought. Over a three-year period, during which she lived alone in a hut in a countryside inhabited by ghosts, Hamilton produced over 350 pictures. Although highly decorated at the time by France in recognition of her work, she never achieved the recognition she deserved in her own country.

During World War II, a number of female British war artists painted scenes of the home front, but only three of those women were allowed to travel overseas and only after combat had ended. Molly Lamb Bobak was the first commissioned female Canadian war artist, enlisting in the Canadian Women's Army Corps in November 1942 and rising to the rank of lieutenant, but she too was not sent to European combat areas until after VE Day.

It wasn't until 1982 that Linda Kitson became the first officially commissioned female British war artist to accompany troops being sent overseas into combat. Commissioned by the Imperial War Museum, Kitson went with the Falklands Task Force during the British defence of those islands against Argentina. She was followed onto the battlefield by Arabella Dorman, who was the first officially appointed British female war artist in Iraq in 2006 and then in Afghanistan in 2009 and 2011.

The United States also does not appear to have officially commissioned any female war artists during the world wars. In 1967, the artist Chris 'Trella' Koczwara (now Professor Koczwara) was selected as a member of the US Marine Corps Combat Art Program and accepted an invitation from the US Navy to be a civilian combat artist at the New London Submarine base at Cape Canaveral. In 1970, she was invited to Vietnam by the US Marine Corps as the first official

American female civilian war artist in a combat area. Donna J. Neary was the first female commissioned combat artist in the US armed services, serving with the United States Marine Corps Reserve as a combat artist from 1978 until 2002 in many fields including Somalia, retiring with the rank of colonel. Her paintings can be seen in the Pentagon and the National Museum of the Marine Corps, among many other places, and over one hundred of her works are in the Marine Corps Art Collection.

In November 1943, fellow South Australian Stella Bowen followed in Nora Heysen's footsteps when she was granted a commission at the rank of captain and appointed to record in artwork the Australian forces in England, and in March 1945 Sybil Craig would be only the third woman appointed within a group of about forty Australian war artists. Neither Bowen nor Craig, though, would travel as far as Heysen.

MAD AS HELL AND NOT GOING TO TAKE IT ANY MORE

Peter Finch, actor

First

- First (and only) winner of a posthumous Best Actor Academy Award

The nine-year-old boy had been missing at Adyar in India, the home of the spiritual leader Krishnamurti, for three days when his grandmother begged Krishnamurti's tutor, Captain Richard Balfour Clarke, to look for him. Clarke found him in a dimly lit room clothed in yellow robes, his head shaven, holding a grass fan in one hand. When he told the boy of his grandmother's sorrow at his absence, he replied that he was a Buddhist monk now. Clarke took him by the hand and led him back to his grandmother. For the rest of his life, though, Peter Finch would remain in many ways faithful to his childhood vows.

Frederick George Peter Finch was born in London in 1916 to an English mother, Alicia Fisher, and her husband, Australian-born research chemist and mountaineer George Ingle Finch. Their marriage broke up shortly afterwards. Finch was to have partnered George Mallory on his ill-fated climb of Everest in 1924, but the Royal Geographic Society (RGS), sponsors of the bid, overruled the partnership because they deemed it unacceptable that an Australian, and a divorced one at that, be the first to climb Everest. Mallory refused to climb without Finch until the Prince of Wales personally appealed to his patriotism. Mallory and his partner never returned from the climb and their bodies were not discovered until 1999. Finch, who lived until 1970, was eventually made a fellow of the RGS in 1938 and received an MBE for his services to climbing. Ironically, Everest eventually was conquered in 1958 by a New Zealander and a Sherpa: Edmund Hillary and Tenzing Norgay.

Peter's parents divorced when he was two, and many years later he would discover that the cause of their separation had been his mother's affair with Wentworth 'Jock' Campbell, an Indian Army officer who was in fact Peter's biological father. Although George Ingle Finch gained custody of Peter, the boy was eventually raised by George's mother, Laura Finch, who was known for her salon of artists and musicians in Paris. In 1925, she took Peter with her to join the Theosophical community at Adyar, near Madras in India, and the following year he travelled with Theosophists to their headquarters in Sydney where he attended their school. Eventually he was located by George, who promptly sent him to live with his great-uncle Edward at Greenwich Point in Sydney. Meanwhile, Peter's mother married Jock Campbell.

After finishing high school, Peter started acting in small parts, then in vaudeville with Joe Cody, and with George Sorlie's travelling troupe. By 1939, he was working in radio drama with the Australian Broadcasting Commission, and was in demand because of his 'cultured' accent and resonant voice. He produced and compered radio shows, wrote scripts and, among a number of roles in radio plays, starred with Neva Carr-Glyn in a popular radio series, *Greyface*, as husband-and-wife detectives Jeffery and Elizabeth Blackburn.

Finch's first film role was a small part in the 1938 Australian film *Dad and Dave Come to Town*, which no one noticed very much, but he quickly moved on to larger parts in other Australian productions such as *The Power and the Glory* (1941). When World War II broke out, he saw active service in the Middle East before being posted to Darwin, where his impromptu performances for the troops led to his being granted leave to appear in Charles Chauvel's *The Rats of Tobruk* (1944). Meanwhile, in 1943 he had married Russian ballerina Tamara Rechemcinc ('Tchinarova'), a principal dancer with the Borovansky company. After the war, he was seen in one more Australian film, *A Son is Born* (1946).

In 1948, he was performing in Molière's *Le Malade Imaginaire* on the shop of floor of O'Brien's glass factory in Sydney when Laurence Olivier and Vivien Leigh turned up. The famous couple, touring Australia with their theatre company, persuaded Finch to come with his wife Tamara to London to appear in the Laurence Olivier Productions version of *Daphne Laureola*. Before long, Finch had fallen for Leigh.

While Finch was undoubtedly an excellent stage actor, most people didn't know that he suffered terribly from stage fright. Largely to give him a break from the consequent strain, he was persuaded by director Harry Watt to return to film at Ealing Studios in Watt's 1949 production of *Eureka Stockade* starring Chips Rafferty. Finch's wavy hair, penetrating eyes and strong square jaw soon became noticed by theatre audiences, and for a few years he successfully combined stage and screen careers, performing in such notable roles as the sombre, ruminative and determined Sheriff of Nottingham in Disney's *The Story of Robin Hood and His Merrie Men* (1952) and the master criminal who is so adept at disguise in *Father Brown* (1954). However, his international fame came with *Elephant Walk*, in which Vivien Leigh chose him to co-star with her after Olivier had turned down the role because he thought the film too slight. Once shooting of the film had got underway in Ceylon (Sri Lanka) at the end of January 1953, they both surrendered to the affair that had been waiting to happen. However, Leigh's fragile physical and mental state wasn't up to the strain, and she quickly became exhausted and prone to episodes of manic depression. Olivier flew out to be with her and, although he perceived what was happening, could find within himself no condemnation of Finch as he understood them both so well.

By March, when a million dollars' worth of location shooting had been completed, Leigh, Finch, Tamara and the Finches' daughter Anita were all back in Hollywood, living in the one house while shooting continued at the studio. It was an uncomfortable arrangement to say the least, and Leigh soon skidded into a breakdown. Found by David Niven and Stewart Granger wandering naked and distraught through the house, proclaiming lines from *A Streetcar Named Desire*, she was obviously in no condition to continue with *Elephant Walk* and was put into care while she was replaced on the film by Elizabeth Taylor. Under sedation, Leigh was taken back to the United Kingdom, where she spent three weeks in a mental hospital before returning home with Olivier. For a while, she and Finch would drift back into their particular kind of friendship at intervals, to which Olivier seemed rather resigned. However, in early 1956 Finch reached an agreement with Olivier to stop the affair, although the couple did eventually resume their friendship.

Finch's first lead film role was as Joe Harman in the 1956 film of Neville Shute's novel *A Town Like Alice*, for which he won the first of his BAFTA awards, followed by his sympathetic portrayal of the doomed German captain of the *Graf Spee* in *Battle of the River Plate* (1956). After that came other major roles, such as the swagman with child problems in *The Shiralee* (1957), Captain Moonlight in *Robbery Under Arms* (1957), his memorable Oscar Wilde in *The Trials of Oscar Wilde* (1960) and the doomed estate owner who kills for Julie Christie in *Far From the Madding Crowd* (1967).

However, Hollywood recognition didn't really arrive until his first Academy Award Best Actor nomination for his portrayal of the gay Jewish doctor in *Sunday Bloody Sunday* (1972). The story persists that Finch lost the Oscar to Gene Hackman in *The French Connection* that year because Finch's role involved a kiss between himself and actor Murray Head, the first kiss between two male gay characters in a mainstream motion picture.

Finch's marriage to Tamara did not survive his affair with Vivien Leigh. After their divorce, he married the young South African actress Yolande Turnbull (Turner) in 1959 in London, but that marriage did not last either. In 1964 he met singer Shirley Bassey while appearing in London's West End in a production of *The Seagull*, and they began what she later called 'an unbelievably beautiful affair'. She fell hard for this vibrant, energetic man who could discuss literature and philosophy. 'He was a knight in shining armour,' she recalled. 'He was so handsome, so knowledgeable. I would curl up and listen to him for hours.' All spring and summer their affair played out across London while an oblivious Yolande was in Italy on holiday with the children, but when tabloid reporters knocked on her door one day and asked her what she thought of it all, everything hit the fan. Yolande attempted suicide and Shirley Bassey's husband cited him as co-respondent in their divorce. Finch typically threw himself into work to take his mind off the mess his life was in, leaving for Israel to appear with Sophia Loren in *Judith*. The situation quickly became too much for Bassey, and shortly thereafter she flew to Israel to tell Finch their romance was over. A devastated Finch told one of his friends: 'I feel like those bones you see in the desert or on tropical beaches, absolutely bleached.' Divorced from Yolande in 1965, Finch eventually moved to Jamaica and in 1973 he married a multi-lingual and financially independent Jamaican woman, Mavis 'Eletha' Barrett.

Despite a lifetime of acting roles, many would argue that Peter Finch's greatest role was his last on the big screen, as television anchorman Howard Beale in the media-cynical *Network* (1976). After all, how many times have you heard someone repeat that line about being mad as hell and not taking it any more? Beale has become so disgusted with living, he predicts on air that in a week's time he will end his life in front of the cameras. Instead of public censure, his ratings go through the roof as he becomes the voice of the frustrated masses. What an intimation of the future direction of television!

Before he could publicly receive the forecast accolades for his role, Finch died suddenly in January 1977 after suffering a heart attack in the lobby of the Beverly Hills Hotel. Eletha accepted his posthumous Academy Award for Best Actor on his behalf. Although there have been other posthumous nominations and winners in non-acting categories, Finch remains the first and only person to receive an Oscar for Best Actor in the afterlife. And he was the only posthumous winner of any acting category Oscar until Heath Ledger's posthumous Best Supporting Actor award in 2009. One of the small group of actors who have won an Oscar, BAFTA and Golden Globe for the same role, Finch was also the first Australian to win an Academy Award as Best Actor.

★

The rest of the world

When she died suddenly in 1929 at the age of 39, Jeanne Eagels was the first person to be nominated posthumously for the Academy Award for Best Actress for her role as Leslie Crosbie in *The Letter* (1929). Since then, only six other actors have been nominated posthumously for Academy acting awards and the only winner apart from Peter Finch was another Australian.

James Dean was the first person to be nominated posthumously for the Best Actor Academy Award, in 1956 for his performance as Cal Trask in *East of Eden* (1955) and in 1957 for his performance as Jett Rink in *Giant* (1956). Thus he also became the only actor to receive a second, and consecutive, posthumous nomination for acting. Spencer Tracy was nominated posthumously in 1968 for Best Actor for his role as family father Matt Drayton in *Guess Who's Coming to Dinner* (1967).

Sir Ralph Richardson was the first person to be nominated posthumously in 1985 for a Best Supporting Actor award for his role as the Earl of Greystoke in *Greystoke: The legend of Tarzan* (1984). In 2009, Heath Ledger became the first person to win the Academy Award for Best Supporting Actor posthumously for his role as the Joker in *The Dark Knight* (2008).

PART II
INTERNATIONAL EXPLORATION

ABORIGINAL VOYAGER

Bennelong (Woollarawarre), ambassador and international traveller

Firsts

- The first Australian Aboriginal overseas ambassador
- The first Australian Aboriginal to travel from Australia to a European country
- The first Australian Aboriginal person whose name was given to an electoral division

Although the Sydney Opera House is undoubtedly an international architectural icon and a symbol of Sydney and of Australia itself, many people would not be aware that the point of land jutting into Sydney Harbour on which it is situated is named Bennelong Point because another Australian icon was once located there. Bennelong, or Woollarawarre as he was also known, was the most important Australian Aboriginal man in the early history of the colony of New South Wales. He was the first ambassador, albeit originally an unwilling one, between British and indigenous cultures in the colony, and the first known person born on this continent to ever travel on a journey of exploration to another country. He became the first Aboriginal Australian the people of England ever met on their own land.

The original inhabitants of the coast to the north and south of what is now Sydney Harbour were the Eora, pronounced *yura*, which meant simply 'people.' They were a coastal group who possessed a canoe (nawi) culture and lived on fish and seafood; the salt water was part of their natural habitat as well as the land. Although the Eora were initially afraid at the arrival of the First Fleet in January 1788, they quickly incorporated into their language these new canoes that were much larger than their own: they named the twenty-gun HMS *Sirius*, the biggest ship, 'mari nawi' or large canoe, while the smaller eight-gun brig HMS *Supply* was named 'narang nawi' or small canoe. Some Eora, like Bennelong, even eventually found that these larger canoes could help them cope with the new reality of a world beyond their horizon. With remarkable resilience and flexibility, they became guides, pilots, sailors, teachers, trackers and translators, some of whom travelled far from their homeland.

Within the Eora were a number of smaller family clans. Bennelong's clan was the Wangal and he was born about 1764 on the south shore of the Parramatta River in their country. With practically no points of reference to go by in terms of writing the pronunciation and spelling of Aboriginal words other than English phonetics, various writers of the time recorded his five names slightly differently but they are most commonly written as Woollarawarre, his own preferred name; Bennelong, said to mean 'large fish'; Bunde-bunda, meaning 'hawk'; Boinba, and Wog-ul-trowe. He had five sisters: Benelang, Warreeweer (or Wariwear), Karangarang, Wurrgan, and Munanguri. Warreeweer was married to Gnung-a Gnung-a from the Hawkesbury River area, the other great Aboriginal explorer who voyaged to Norfolk Island, Hawaii and North America aboard the HMS *Daedalus*.

When he arrived, Governor Arthur Phillip carried orders from George III to establish relations with the native inhabitants to enable a peaceful coexistence of indigenous people and settlers, but he wasn't able to communicate adequately because of the language barrier. As Aboriginal people did not come to the settlement, Phillip evidently despaired of achieving lasting communication with the indigenous people and felt he had no choice but to attempt that by force, through kidnapping someone to act as an educator, informant and go-between. However, his first kidnap victim died after only a few months, and so Bennelong became the second when he was abducted by a group of soldiers on Phillip's orders while fishing in Manly Cove in late November 1789. William Bradley, the lieutenant in charge of the capture that was carried out amid crying and screaming from women and children present at the time, recorded in his journal that it 'was by far the most unpleasant service' he was ever ordered to carry out.

Despite the involuntary circumstances of his arrival at the Sydney Cove settlement, Bennelong proved a quick student of English. In his mid-twenties at the time, muscular, witty and very intelligent, he soon demonstrated that he could be a shrewd and cunning politician who recognised some advantages in his situation. Phillip took him into his own house, and Bennelong in turn endeavoured to find a place for his new family within the framework of his traditional one, calling the governor his father and himself Phillip's son and exchanging names, as was his cultural practice. In many ways, he became exactly the link with his people that Phillip had wished for, as he attempted to explain the complexities of tribal structure and relationships, his vocabulary and place names, and also the horrors that smallpox had wrought among his people, who had no natural resistance to it. Half of the indigenous people that had originally lived in the area, he pointed out, were now dead.

Cultural ambassador he may have been, but the posting had after all been an involuntary one. Bennelong retained his independent spirit and in May 1790, he seized an opportunity and jumped the paling fence around the house, escaping back into the surrounding bush. Three months went by before he was sighted at Manly Cove again. Hearing the news, Phillip came down to join happily in the reunion when, without warning, his party was surrounded by Bennelong's people. Suddenly, one of them picked up a long spear and threw it, hitting Phillip in the shoulder. Despite the pain and shock of the attack, to Phillip's credit there was no retaliatory gunfire or later reprisals; instead, he seems to have recognised the likely significance of the action: a ritual and public payback for Bennelong's kidnapping that restored his honour and respect in front of his own people.

From then on communication between the settlers and the Eora people improved. Food, language and cultural knowledge were shared and goods were traded. In November 1790, Phillip built Bennelong a small brick house on a harbourside point of land, then known as Tubowgulle but that would later be named after its occupant. Although cultural coexistence might not mean everyone entirely agreed all the time, on the whole relations between settlers and indigenous people were friendly for the next two years. Of course, that didn't mean the settlers thought of the Aborigines as equals; these people were still generally regarded by the Europeans as 'savages', even if Phillip saw them in more of a romantic light as innocent and childlike.

Perhaps inspired by the voyage to Norfolk Island of Bundle, a fellow Eora man, with Captain Hill in 1791, Bennelong followed him later that year with his own first experience of the open sea beyond the horizon when he made the same journey with Lieutenant Commander Philip Gidley King aboard HMS *Atlantic*, accompanied by a young man from the same clan called Yemmerawanne who had become quite attached to both him and Phillip. Perhaps this trip opened Bennelong's eyes to new possibilities. By now he knew that the British occupiers were in desperate need of information about the Australian indigenous peoples, and he evidently saw a chance to improve his status within both cultures by becoming an ambassador between them. Certainly Arthur Phillip saw him in a similar role, writing to his friend Sir Joseph Banks in 1791 that if he could take Bennelong to England, much information would be obtained because he was very intelligent. Phillip hoped that by educating Bennelong and Yemmerawanne further, and giving them experience with British social and language skills, they could become ambassadors for their people and thus conduits for knowledge and understanding between the two cultures. At the same time, though, Phillip was also indulging in a long-standing tradition, established in the sixteenth century, of bringing back to England indigenous peoples and animals from newly explored or colonised lands.

On the morning of 11 December 1792, the *Atlantic* sailed out of the Heads bearing into another world Phillip, Bennelong, Yemmerawanne, four kangaroos and some dingoes. They reached Rio de Janeiro by 7 February 1793, crossed the equator in early April, dodged a French privateer that fired on them, and docked at Falmouth in England on or about 21 May 1793. From there they travelled to London where they lived in lodgings while Phillip ordered identical sets of Regency-style clothes to be made for the two men, including coats, waistcoats, knee-breeches, silk stockings, under-waistcoats and shoes. Over the next few months, their wardrobes expanded to include a dozen shirts and cravats, hats, buckled shoes, and brushes and razors.

Although Phillip's intention may have been to gain them an audience with George III, as had been customary with earlier indigenous visitors from other countries, there is no evidence that one actually took place. In fact, in comparison with the public gawking and intense media attention attracted by those earlier indigenous visitors, Bennelong and Yemmerawanne were largely ignored by both the public and the newspapers.

In July they moved into the residence of a Mr Waterhouse in Grosvenor Square, in the middle of the fashionable West End. They had their own servants, and reading and writing teachers were supplied by Phillip. To help with their English cultural education, they toured the sights of London in horse-drawn carriages, travelled up the Thames by boat, went bathing, and were taken to the theatre and to Parkinson's Museum of natural history. This London museum, originally known as the Leverian, existed until 1806 and held displays of most of the cultural artefacts brought back to England by Captain Cook from his three voyages of discovery. One can only imagine the horror that went through the minds of Bennelong and Yemmerawanne as they gazed upon the two heads of warrior chieftains included in the collection.

Then, during September, Yemmerawanne became ill. Doctors were called in and evidently a recommendation was made that some fresh country air was needed, for by the end of October they were living in what was then the rural Kentish village of Eltham under the care of Mrs and Mr Phillips, the steward of Thomas Townshend, first Viscount Sydney, who lived nearby on the vast Frognal estate. As Home Secretary in the Pitt Government, Sydney had been largely responsible for the plan to settle convicts at Botany Bay and Phillip had been his choice of governor, so it's really no surprise that Phillip named Sydney Cove and the ensuing town after him. In one of the great historic ironies, the two Aboriginals regularly visited with the man whose plans to give convicts the opportunities of redemption and freedom in a new country had removed those possibilities from the very people, their own people, who were already living there.

In late November they returned to London, but by now winter was setting in. Despite the best medical care available, Yemmerawanne's condition deteriorated. Bennelong had to leave him there when he returned to Eltham and his friends for Christmas festivities. He returned in early January to continue his theatre and social outings and, despite his condition, Yemmerawanne accompanied him on some of these, which included an excursion to a civil trial, in order for them to observe an example of British justice in action. By then, plans were already being formulated for their journey back to Australia later in the year with the new governor, John Hunter.

However, a few days after they had returned to Eltham, on 18 May 1794, Yemmerawanne passed away, aged only nineteen—the first Australian Aborigine known to have died in England or indeed in any country other than Australia. With his death recorded in the local register, he was given a Christian funeral and buried among the local residents in the churchyard of St John the Baptist Parish Church at Eltham. Even in death, he was treated with respect by those with whom he had lived in this foreign land. For many years, it was an annual custom for children of the village to lay flowers at his headstone on his anniversary.

From then until he left for Australia, Bennelong remained in Eltham in the care of Mr and Mrs Phillips. On 22 July, he journeyed to Chatham and boarded HMS *Reliance* which, along with the *Supply*, was being fitted out for the long voyage to New South Wales. However, by the time the ships moved to Spithead two months later, orders were yet to arrive from the Admiralty for his passage home. Not only that, there were still not enough crew members to man the ships adequately. By the end of January the following year, the ships had sailed no further than Plymouth Sound. Poor Bennelong, who would have thought on boarding the ship that he would soon see his own land, had been trapped in this nautical prison for six months and it was now mid-winter. Needless to say, his health deteriorated. If that wasn't bad enough, *Supply* broke free from her moorings during a storm and was grounded. She had to be completely unloaded and dry-docked for her bottom to be inspected to make sure she would survive the voyage south. It was not until February 1785 that the two ships left Plymouth as part of a convoy.

As it happened, naval surgeon and future explorer George Bass was on board the *Reliance* for this voyage and made it his mission to restore Bennelong to health. In return, Bennelong taught him as much indigenous vocabulary as he could—which would stand Bass in good stead on later exploratory voyages of his own.

Finally, on 7 September 1795, Bennelong set foot on the land of his birth once again. He'd been gone nearly three years; by now his wife was living with someone else. It's really no surprise he wrote to his friends back in England that, now he was home, he never wanted to see England again.

Quite understandably, Bennelong probably saw little future in continuing to act as an ambassador. After all, it had cost him a wife and some good friends, and had taken him away from his beloved homeland for a long time. So, soon after coming ashore, he left his

English clothes and education behind and returned to live with his people, only occasionally visiting Sydney and Governor John Hunter. Eventually, Bennelong found a new partner with whom he had a son, Dicky, who was placed in the Native Institution at Parramatta in 1816. Five years later the boy went to live with the family of the Methodist missionary Reverend William Walker, who taught him to read and write and publicly baptised him as Thomas Walker Coke in 1822. Only a year later, he died aged only nineteen.

Although the story persists into the present day that Bennelong was rejected by his clan, Keith Vincent Smith convincingly demonstrates in his essay, 'Bennelong among his people', that he returned to a respected position as an elder and clan leader within the Eora from whom he had been forcibly taken. In fact, Bennelong was known to have officiated at the last recorded Aboriginal initiation in the Port Jackson area. On 3 January 1813 he died as a result of illness at his home on the property of the brewer James Squire, on the north shore of the Parramatta River at what is now known as Kissing Point. An insulting obituary in the *Sydney Gazette* accused him of being a drunk who had refused all attempts to civilise him; it made no reference to any of the diplomatic assistance he'd rendered to the early colony to aid cultural coexistence. Bennelong was buried between his last wife Boorong and another Aboriginal elder in the Squire orange orchard on the banks of the river that divided the country where he lived from that where he had been born.

While his significance to Australian history might be largely forgotten, Bennelong's name still lives on. Apart from Bennelong Point, Bennelong Lawn in the Royal Botanical Gardens, the Bennelong Society and the Bennelong Medal, there's also a 58-square-kilometre Bennelong electorate on Sydney's lower north shore that includes Ryde and some of Hornsby and Parramatta city council areas. It gained a place in political history in 2007 when John Howard, who had represented it for many years, became only the second prime minister to lose both government and his own seat in an election.

Created in 1949, it was the first electoral division to be named after an Australian Aboriginal person.

When the Sydney Opera House was opened in 1973, Bennelong appeared at the official ceremony in the form of Aboriginal actor Ben Blakeney, who delivered an oration from the peak of the tallest roof shell. The man who stood between two changing cultures had come home.

★

Other early Aboriginal post-settlement explorers

Bennelong and Yemmerawanne were the first known named Aboriginal people to travel so far, and they were followed by a number of others.

Bundle (or Bondel) was an Aboriginal orphan who was cared for by Captain William Hill of the New South Wales Corps. When Hill was ordered to Norfolk Island in 1791, Bundle went with him and thus became the first known Australian Aboriginal person to sail east over the horizon from their country. During 1821–22, he would also circumnavigate Australia and visit Mauritius aboard the survey ship HMS *Bathurst,* commanded by Phillip Parker King.

In 1793, Gnung-a Gnung-a Murremurgan sailed across the Pacific aboard the storeship HMS *Daedalus* to Norfolk Island, Hawaii, Nootka Sound (Vancouver) and the Californian coast before returning to Sydney the following year. Aboard the *Britannia*, Tom Rowley visited Calcutta, Madras and New Ireland between 1795 and 1796.

Tristan Maamby jumped ship in Rio de Janeiro in 1807, aged seventeen, rather than continue a voyage to London with his guardian Samuel Marsden. He didn't return to Sydney for seven years.

Bungaree sailed with Matthew Flinders on HMS *Investigator* between 1802 and 1803 to Timor, and was the first indigenous

Australian known to have circumnavigated the continent. His eldest son, Bowen, would sail to San Francisco in 1849 aboard the brig *William Hill* in time for the beginning of the California gold rush, along with fellow Aborigines Bill, Callaghan, Cranky and Dick.

Daniel Moowattin, a collections assistant for botanist George Caley, was in 1810 the third Australian Aboriginal person to reach England. After accompanying Caley to Norfolk Island and Van Diemen's Land (Tasmania), he reached England aboard HMS *Hindoostan;* he lived there for a year before returning to Sydney.

'I WORSHIPPED THEIR BEAUTY'

Emmeline Freda Du Faur, mountaineer

Firsts

- The first woman and the first Australian to climb and reach the summit of Aoraki/Mount Cook, New Zealand's highest peak
- The first person to summit and name Mount Nazomi and Mount Cadogan, in New Zealand; a member of the first team to summit Mount Dampier
- The first person to summit all five of New Zealand's highest peaks and to summit seven of the highest ten peaks
- With guides Peter Graham and David Thomson, Du Faur was the first to completely traverse all three peaks of the summit ridge of Aoraki/Mount Cook (the Grand Traverse) and the first (with guides) to traverse New Zealand's Mount Sefton

If Freda Du Faur's family background was anything to go by, then she was the lady least likely to climb mountains. On her father's side she was descended from an aristocratic French lineage that could be traced to the mid-fourteenth century and whose family seat was the Chateau de Pibrac near Toulouse. Her great-great-grandfather had emigrated to London in the mid-1700s in search of intellectual freedom as part of the Huguenot exodus and had there begun an English family; her great-grandfather was an explorer who narrowly missed being executed during the French Revolution. Freda's father, Eccleston Frederic Du Faur, had come out to Australia in 1853 in search of adventure during the gold rush and became a surveyor and explorer who was instrumental in setting up the New South Wales Academy of Art in 1871, the forerunner of the Art Gallery of New South Wales. Her mother, Blanche, was a graceful and sensitive woman, a pianist whose father was the Reverend Dr John Woolley, friend of poet William Wordsworth and professor of classics and principal of the University of Sydney.

Emmeline Freda was born in 1882, preceded by two brothers, and named after Blanche's older sister, but it was quickly apparent that she was too much of a tomboy for that first feminine name and so it was soon forgotten. As she grew up in and around the family's house in Ashfield, Sydney, she learned to ride, played tennis and became competitive with her brothers, who were quick to make fun of her if she couldn't keep up or showed any weakness. She became everything a father could have wanted in a son—intelligent, articulate and physically courageous.

By the time Freda was eight, her father's pastoral and land investment company was proving successful enough for them to move into a large new home in the northern suburb of Warrawee; named 'Pibrac', it had been designed by the renowned American architect John Horbury Hunt. But Eccleston became enamoured of a new project to turn the 14 000 hectares around the nearby Cowan Creek and up the Hawkesbury River into a national park, and at the end of 1895 they moved into a smaller Horbury Hunt house, 'Flowton Hall', on the slopes above Ku-ring-gai Chase. Although she missed the bigger house, the move allowed Freda more time in her beloved great open spaces instead of having to abide by etiquette and be a suitably feminine candidate for a good marriage. Her mother and aunt, who were firmly on the side of social mores, combined forces to combat the situation by sending

Freda off to the recently established Sydney Church of England Girl's Grammar School. However, on her afternoons off, Freda would visit her independent Aunt Emmeline, who lived with Ethel Pedley, later renowned as the author of the Australian classic *Dot and the Kangaroo*.

By the end of the century, Freda was eighteen, finished with school and back home, helping her father in his involvement with the Chase and spending a lot of time escaping into its valleys and scaling the rock walls under the excuse of cataloguing wildflowers and trees. There, away from the eyes of a society that would have thought such pursuits little suited to the apt development of a young lady, Freda gained her first experiences in rock climbing, developing her self-reliance, physical skills and sense of adventure. Conscious that she wanted in some way to help her fellow human beings, though, Freda became a probationary nurse at the Sydney Homeopathic Hospital in 1903 when she was 21. Her work was so highly regarded that in February the following year she was promoted to full nurse on a pound a week, but the hospital's lack of qualified staff in the face of high patient demand meant she was working long hours, often at menial labour instead of actual medical care. Depressed and discouraged by the situation, she left the hospital only a month later.

Then her life took an unexpected turn. In November 1906, Freda accompanied her father on a trip to the New Zealand International Exhibition of Arts and Industries in Christchurch. He wanted to exhibit photos he'd commissioned of Ku-ring-gai Chase and the Blue Mountains, and also to purchase paintings for the National Art Gallery of New South Wales. It was Freda's first visit to the South Island, and her first exposure to the beauty and grandeur of the Southern Alps as portrayed in photographs and paintings at the exhibition. She became so fascinated by the mountains, in fact, that she remained behind when her father returned to Sydney in December and purchased a train ticket that would take her south.

On her way there, she became friends with two fellow travellers, Heinrich von Haast and his wife, Nellie. Heinrich was the son of

Sir Julius von Haast, who in 1862 was the first recorded explorer to ascend and describe the Mount Cook range. The group left the train at Timaru and continued on by coach and horses around lakes and up into the foothills towards the Hermitage at the foot of the Mueller Glacier, the only hotel at Mount Cook. As her eyes filled with the vistas of the mountain ranges, Freda could barely contain her longing to touch their snows and climb their heights and to feel herself at one with the mighty forces around her. 'From the moment my eyes rested on the snow-covered alps,' she wrote of this moment, 'I worshipped their beauty.'

While she was staying at the Hermitage, Freda became acquainted with the chief mountain guide, Peter Graham, and persuaded him to teach her to climb. He was impressed by her ability; she had a vision of being a mountaineer, of conquering her fears and the limitations society placed on her as a woman. Freda also befriended another of the guests, explorer and biologist Professor Walter Baldwin Spencer, who would encourage her climbing career. But then her visit was cut short by news that her mother had fallen ill; although she set off for home immediately, by the time Freda reached Sydney Blanche had died.

During the following year, Freda looked after her family while remaining in touch with Peter Graham. Then in March 1908, her Aunt Emmeline died and left her a substantial inheritance, for those days, of £2000 plus interests in some property investments. She was now an independent young woman, reliant on no one for whatever path in life she chose, and the one she could see ahead of her led to one particular mountain.

Later that year, she heard from Professor Spencer that he and his daughter were returning to the Hermitage and they invited Freda to join them. There, she resumed her training with Peter Graham as her guide and mentor. In those days before crampons, the only way to ascend through ice and snow was to cut steps with long-handled ice picks, work usually done by men rather than women (who climbed in skirts)—even a woman as physically fit as Du Faur. After only a week, she and Peter made a ten-hour traverse of Mount Wakefield and Mount Kinsey at the southern end of the Mount Cook range. As a result, Peter was convinced Du Faur could be a future mountaineer. In turn, Du Faur expressed her resolve to soon be the first woman to reach the summit of Mount Cook (now known as Aoraki/Mount Cook). She left for home and further practice in the Chase, promising Peter that she would return for more training in higher altitude ice and snow.

Du Faur lived up to her word, returning to the Hermitage in December 1909 with top-end climbing equipment for those days such as hob-nailed boots and manila hemp rope. She was superbly fit, confident and ready for any challenge. When she announced to the guests that she and Peter would have to camp out overnight on their way to ascend Mount Sealy, her first challenge proved to be a social one. The women pleaded with her not to ruin her reputation by spending the night alone with a strange man merely for the sake of climbing a mountain. Du Faur tartly pointed out that camping in the snow in a tiny tent with only a burner for heat was not conducive to passion, but in the end she had to relent to moral order and hire a porter who would also act as a chaperone. Nevertheless, their climb was a success and Peter was full of praise for Du Faur's ability. They went on to climb the Nun's Veil and then in the New Year made the first ascent of the west ridge of Mount Malte Brun, crossing the Cheval ridge to be only the second party at the 3176-metre summit. A few days later, accompanied by Peter and Professor Spencer, Du Faur was the first woman to climb the 3065-metre Minarets, which had been climbed only once, thirteen years previously. Now, if only the weather would allow her, Du Faur felt ready for Mount Cook.

However, it was poor weather that the mountain was renowned for, a mountain that even today jealously protects itself. Like most major peaks, to indigenous people it's a sacred place, moody and dangerous with a temper. After the first trio of climbers were turned back by the weather in 1882, it had taken twelve years of attempts before

New Zealanders Tom Fyfe, George Graham and Jack Clarke reached the summit on Christmas Day 1894. It would take more than one try for Du Faur, too. Her first attempt with Peter on 21–22 January 1910 proved a lesson in logistics; although she was equal to the task in ability, the diminutive Du Faur simply wasn't tall enough or powerful enough physically to help Peter out of difficulty or to assist him adequately in problematic climbing situations. They would need a third member of the party next time. A bitterly disappointed Du Faur had to return to Sydney in February without having achieved her ultimate goal, knowing that she was surely running out of time. Other women climbers would soon reach Mount Cook's summit if she didn't.

To increase her physical fitness still further, Du Faur began the Edwardian female version of 'working out'. The Dupain Institute gave exercise lessons to women, using two female personal trainers: Jeannie Dupain, sister of the institute's founder, and Muriel Cadogan. Muriel soon had Du Faur on a healthy diet and undergoing an exercise regime that would not only strengthen muscles but build up her lung capacity to help her cope with climbing at a high altitude. Like Du Faur, she was an independently minded woman who was not afraid to say what she thought. The two women found they complemented each other and formed a close friendship that soon developed into a relationship.

So, later that year in November, the 28-year-old Du Faur sailed for New Zealand ready for the challenge of her life. She was at the peak of her physical and mental fitness. This time she also brought along her camera, with which she would become one of the most skilled alpine photographers of her time. Arriving at the Hermitage, she and Peter quickly began warming up on various small climbs, including Mount Annette and Mount Mabel, before they were joined by Peter's brother Alex, the third member of the team. They set out in clear weather on 2 December 1910, and made camp at the end of that first day above the Hooker Glacier. Leaving camp at 2 a.m. after a few hours' sleep, the trio quickly reached the summit of Mount Cook at 3754 metres on 3 December in a record time of six hours (a total of fourteen hours return). Du Faur had found her path to be one with the universe.

When her achievement was announced, Du Faur instantly became famous. Interviews appeared in newspapers all over New Zealand, although back in Australia she was virtually ignored. Nevertheless, she became an inspiration to women everywhere, especially climbers. On 12 April 1912, Australian Annie Lindon became the second woman to climb Mount Cook, and on 13 December 1915, Muriel Graham (Peter's wife) became the first New Zealand woman to reach the summit.

Naturally, having conquered the tallest New Zealand peak, Du Faur turned her attention to Mount Tasman, which at 3498 metres is the second tallest. It had been climbed only once before, in 1895. On 16 December Freda and the Graham brothers set off to climb Mount Tasman but were defeated by ice and bad weather, having taken the time to summit the 3279-metre Silberhorn on the way. Instead, on 30 December, Du Faur and two other guides became the second team to climb the 2842-metre Mount Green at the head of the Tasman Glacier, and a few days later the first team to climb Mount Chudleigh.

In February 1912, Du Faur returned to the Mount Cook area complaining that she was unfit. Even so, she and Peter set out to climb a virgin summit that would take her name: Du Faur Peak. This was followed by a very difficult climb up Mount Sebastopol that nearly stranded them. Then, on 14 March, they climbed another virgin peak of 3002 metres, which Du Faur named Nazomi, 'heart's desire' in Japanese. Although the weather was closing in as the season grew late, Du Faur and the Grahams decided on another attempt on Mount Tasman. They finally reached the summit on 24 March in conditions so bad it had taken them five hours to climb the last 180 metres. Hearing other climbers were about to tackle the unclimbed 3440-metre Mount Dampier, Du Faur, Peter and fellow guide Charlie Milne added that peak to their list of first summit achievements on 30 March. They went on to summit the 3201-metre Mount Lendenfeld, the fourth highest peak in the Alps, which had only been climbed once, in 1907. When they finally returned to the Hermitage, Du Faur had become the first person to summit all three of the highest peaks in the Southern Alps.

By then, Du Faur and Muriel were planning to move to Europe, lured by the possibilities of mountaineering there and the need to get away from the demands of their respective families. But Du Faur still had two more New Zealand goals: to traverse all three peaks of the 1.6-kilometre-long summit ridge of Aoraki/Mount Cook (now known as the Grand Traverse) and the first east–west traverse of the 3157-metre Mount Sefton—climbs that most mountain guides considered impossible. At the beginning of December 1912, Du Faur returned to the Southern Alps. As a warm-up climb, she and Peter Graham climbed and named Mount Pibrac and then, on 1 January 1913, they set off to tackle the Grand Traverse with Darby Thomson as the second guide. From the Hooker Valley, they reached the lowest southern peak at 7 a.m. on 3 January and then traversed the ridge to the middle peak, which included two hours of step-cutting on a 60-degree angle in hard ice. They then ascended a knife-sharp ridge across treacherous ice cornices to reach the highest summit by 1.30 p.m. before carefully descending to the Tasman Valley via the Linda Glacier. It had taken them some twenty hours to make a traverse still considered the greatest alpine climb in New Zealand, but Du Faur later tended to downplay her remarkable achievement, saying they had all been very lucky and that future climbers would need much patience and good weather.

It was the weather that kept them from Sefton, a mountain renowned for its steepness, avalanches and exposure; it rained for sixteen days but finally, on the morning of 9 February, Du Faur, Peter and Darby left the Hermitage for their attempt on the Sefton traverse. They endured avalanches, ice walls and violent gusts of wind that threatened to blow them off ridges just 60 centimetres across. For much of the climb, only one climber could move at a time while the others anchored, and when they reached the saddle between the peaks the wind forced Du Faur to her hands and knees before they reached the summit. By the time they were descending, a snowstorm had reduced visibility and they became temporarily lost, then trapped in camp for two days by bad weather, before finding their way back to the Hermitage to the relief of all there. Before leaving her beloved mountains, Du Faur and Peter climbed one last unnamed peak, which Du Faur called Mount Cadogan in honour of Muriel, and then they climbed Aiguille Rouge in the Malte Brun Range, which had not been attempted again since the first climb in 1909.

Du Faur returned home to begin work on what would become her book, *The Conquest of Mount Cook and Other Climbs*, and to plan other projected climbs in Europe, the Himalayas and perhaps even Canada. But she suffered from recurring bouts of influenza, and she was also losing confidence, all too aware that, now over 30, she was not the young woman at the peak of fitness that she had once been.

Then there was the matter of recognition. While she had been accepted for membership by the Canadian Alpine Club because of her climbing achievements, the English Alpine Club traditionally refused women membership and Du Faur proved no exception. Nevertheless, Du Faur and Muriel left Australia in June 1914 for England. There they found the freedom to live together as they pleased, establishing a home in Pinner on the outskirts of London. In 1915, Du Faur's book was finally published, but it was not the success she had hoped.

After the war, having visited Australia briefly in 1919, Du Faur and Muriel moved to Bournemouth and then later into a large house in nearby Christchurch, where Muriel gradually slipped into depression over the next few years. Du Faur did everything she could, but despite this Muriel became delusional. In early 1929, Du Faur brought Muriel to hospital, thinking they would be able to share a room there while Muriel received care. Instead, she found herself imprisoned and drugged for three weeks while Muriel was taken to another facility where she was subjected to electric shock treatment and what later became known as 'deep sleep therapy', probably because doctors considered that being gay was a mental illness from which you could be cured. When Du Faur was discharged from the hospital, she was not allowed to see Muriel again except to say goodbye. After fifteen years together, they were forcibly separated and Muriel was sent back to Australia. She died on board ship before she reached her destination.

A distraught Du Faur was never able to discover Muriel's exact cause of death. However, many years later during the 1960s, a number of people died in Sydney as a result of the same kind of deep sleep therapy that Muriel had received. By 1930, Du Faur herself had begun to hear voices, possibly due to the side-effects of her own therapy. She returned to Sydney in 1933, but her condition deteriorated and, anyway, she was too independent and justifiably mistrustful of doctors to seek help. Having already made her will, Du Faur packaged her possessions one night in September 1935, turned on the gas in the oven, knelt down and rested her head inside. It was two days before anyone found her, and she was buried in an unmarked grave.

Thankfully, that injustice has now been rectified. A headstone of greywacke from the South Island's Mackenzie Country, along with a plaque, was finally installed on Du Faur's grave in 2006. The centenary of Du Faur's summiting of Aoraki/Mount Cook was marked over the weekend of 3–5 December 2010 by Freda Du Faur Centenary Celebrations, hosted by the New Zealand Alpine Club held in the Aoraki Mount Cook Alpine Village and in the national park in her honour. On Australia's highest mountain, the 2228-metre-high Mount Kosciuszko, she was recognised on the same weekend by the Freda Du Faur Kosi Climb, in which some forty women participated. However, outside of a few mountain-climbing groups, Australians remain largely unaware of their first female mountaineer.

★

The rest of the world

The first recorded summit climb of a major peak by a woman was that of the 4810-metre Mont Blanc on 14 July 1808 by Maria Paradis, a young woman from Chamonix who ran a souvenir stall at the foot of the mountain. Like other women in the town, her boyfriends were guides and porters, and they persuaded Paradis that her business would benefit if she could claim to be the first woman on the mountain. She set out with a group of them and was eventually dragged and carried to the summit after suffering from exhaustion. Although she did become famous, Paradis never went up a mountain again.

Still, thirty years later when the second woman, Henriette d'Angeville, reached the same summit, Paradis personally congratulated her when she returned. D'Angeville's climbing outfit was made up of layers of silk, a black velvet mask, a large fur hat and a black fur boa, and the food list for her party included two legs of mutton, two sides of veal, twenty-four fowl, eighteen bottles of wine, and a cask of wine for the porters. She would forge on to make another twenty-nine ascents of other peaks and found a museum of mineralogy, refusing to retire until she was 69. Because Paradis suffered from exhaustion and was carried to the Mont Blanc summit, d'Angeville is often referred to as the first woman to reach a summit by her own strength and unassisted. In 1854, when Mrs Hamilton with her husband and guides became the first British woman to climb Mont Blanc, they were also the first recorded husband and wife climbing team.

Anne 'Gentleman Jack' Lister, lesbian, diarist (4 000 000 words), colliery-owner and mountain climber, was the first English climber to ascend the 3355-metre-high Mont Perdu (or Monte Perdido), the third highest peak in the Pyrenees, and in 1838 was the first foreign climber to reach the summit of the 3298-metre Grand Vignemale, the highest peak of the French Pyrenees In 1871 the experienced English climber Lucy Walker achieved the summit of the Matterhorn after the first attempt by Félicité Carrel had been halted 100 metres below the summit when her crinoline blew over her head. Over twenty-one years, Walker would make some ninety-eight climbing expeditions, becoming one of the founding members of the Ladies' Alpine Club in 1907 and its second president in 1912. The first president and founder of the club was Mrs Aubrey Le Blond whose alpine climbing career extended over twenty years. During the 1880s and 1890s, the petite Kathleen Richardson, often climbing with Mary Paillon, made 116 major alpine ascents, six of them the first by anyone and fourteen the first by a woman.

Soon, however, European peaks were not enough. Fanny Bullock Workman with her husband and three guides claimed an ascent of Pyramid Peak in the Karakoram in 1903 and the 6930-metre-high Pinnacle Peak in Kashmir three years later. Her competitor for the women's altitude record was American mountaineer Annie Smith Peck who climbed a number of South American peaks, one of which was named in her honour. In 1934 Hettie Dyhrenfurth became the first woman to climb beyond 7000 metres but it was not until forty years later that three Japanese women climbed beyond 8000 metres. In 1975, Junko Tabei of Japan made the first female ascent of Mount Everest.

On the negative side, mountain climbing is a dangerous and frequently lethal sport. If the toll figures were made public like road tolls, though, people would become afraid to climb and a lot of tourist economies would plunge, so you never hear numbers. However, women die up there as well as men so by way of remembering them I will mention three climbers. The first British woman to reach the summit of K2, Julie Tullis, died on the descent in 1986. Wanda Rutkiewicz of Poland, the third woman in 1978 to summit Everest, the first woman to climb K2 (without supplemental oxygen), and who summitted the highest mountain to be climbed by a woman, was last seen alive in 1992 ascending the north-west face of Kanchenjunga. She had reached the summit of eight mountains of more than eight thousand metres. Finally, Lilliane Barrard of France, who in 1984 had been the first woman to summit the 8125-metre-high Himalayan peak Nanga Parbat, perished with her husband descending K2 with Rutkiewicz in 1986.

'I FELT LIBERATED'

Sir Hubert Wilkins, polar explorer and photographer

Firsts

- The first person to traverse the Arctic Circle, cross the Arctic Sea, and fly over the Arctic ice cap in an aeroplane (with pilot Carl Ben Eielson)
- The first person to fly over Antarctica (with Eielson) in an aeroplane and to explore and map areas of that continent from the air
- The first person to take a submarine to the Arctic ice cap
- The first person to film actual combat in progress from the ground and the air as a cinematographer and official war photographer
- The first person to discover the Wilkins's Bunting (or Wilkins's Finch)

With a sharp crack, the featureless expanse of ice suddenly fractured as a massive black steel pillar thrust its way through it, sending large blocks of ice tumbling over the long, humped hull of the nuclear submarine USS *Skate*. As Commander James Calvert looked out from the bridge through a howling gale into the dim twilight, he could barely see the featureless expanse of ice around him. From here, 90 degrees north latitude, every direction was south. While Calvert and his crew could celebrate that they were the first submarine to surface at the North Pole, they were also there for a more personal reason: to honour a fellow submariner and visionary explorer who had attempted the same voyage before them. Sir Hubert Wilkins, once described by General Sir John Monash as the bravest man he'd seen, was an extraordinary man who during his life was a war correspondent, polar explorer, naturalist, geographer, climatologist, aviator, war hero, secret agent, submariner, navigator, author and journalist. He made some thirty-three expeditions to polar regions, and was knighted by the king of England and honoured by the leaders of a number of nations; yet, to this day, he remains largely forgotten in his own country.

George Hubert Wilkins's home was a long way from any ice and snow in a lonely South Australian stone homestead sitting in an open expanse of red dirt and rock behind Mount Bryan East, near Hallett, about 150 kilometres north of Adelaide. His birth occurred on Halloween 1888, and he was the thirteenth and youngest child, born when his mother was 50. His grandparents, William Wilkins and Mary Chivers, had arrived in South Australia on board the brig *Emma* in 1836, one of the nine ships bearing the first two hundred settlers. It's highly likely that his father, Henry, who was born only three days after the settlement's proclamation, was the first surviving settler child born in the colony. After spending some time on the Victorian goldfields as a teenager, Henry became a successful drover and married Louisa Smith. Eager to find land where they could establish a profitable sheep and cattle farm, the family piled their possessions on a bullock cart and travelled 200 kilometres inland to take up land in the Mount Bryan area. Unfortunately, Henry's land was beyond what would be known as Goyder's Line, the invisible line surveyed a few years later by George Goyder beyond which there is insufficient rainfall for successful agriculture. Wracked by successive droughts and the deaths of children, the family's venture was fated from the outset to be one of hardship.

George Wilkins grew up helping his father and brothers on the property, learning from an early age how to become self-sufficient in a savage climate and an empty land. He formed friendships with the local Aboriginal teenagers, camping and living with them, learning how to hunt and live off the land and taking a great interest in their spiritualty and mysticism. Such empathy with indigenous people would later save his life in a far different place. Although he had some schooling, he was largely self-taught, reading voraciously during the day while out ploughing vast paddocks alone with just the horse and dog for company or at night by kerosene lamp in the homestead. Given the importance of the weather in his family's life, it is really not so surprising that George Wilkins became fascinated as a young teenager by long-range forecasting and the sources of weather patterns, about which very little was known in those early days of the twentieth century.

After years of struggle in an unforgiving geography, the final straw for the Wilkins family was the great drought of 1901. Four years later, Henry was forced to sell the 400-hectare farm to pay the debts, and they moved to Adelaide. George was apprenticed to electrical engineers to pay for his study at the Conservatorium of Music, from where he moved on to learn mechanical engineering at the University of Adelaide and electrical engineering at the South Australian School of Mines. Then one day, while he was installing lights in an Adelaide theatre, a man from a travelling picture show asked him for help with a faulty generator. When they offered him a free seat in thanks, Wilkins stayed to watch the movies and never left. During the next eighteen months he travelled around the country with them, discovering a passion for photography and cinematography.

By 1911, Wilkins was working in film studios in Sydney when he was offered a job with the Gaumont newsreel company in London. According to Wilkins, while on his way there he was kidnapped in Tunis by gun-runners from whom he escaped with the help of a young Arab girl who arranged to smuggle him to safety. Eventually reaching London, Wilkins went to work as a cameraman for Gaumont and also as a reporter for the *London Daily Chronicle*. During the next eighteen months he travelled through twenty-seven countries on assignments throughout Europe, including the 1912 Turko–Bulgarian War (or First Balkan War) in which he became the first official war photographer to shoot actual combat footage, mostly on horseback while dodging bullets, and the first to fly over a front line in an aeroplane. He photographed massacres, helped bandage the wounded and was very nearly executed after being arrested as a spy. It was during his time with Gaumont that he met the famous pioneer English aviator Claude Grahame-White, who inspired George to learn to fly.

While on assignment in Trinidad, Wilkins was asked by Gaumont to join the Canadian Arctic Expedition of veteran polar explorer Vilhjalmur Stefansson as official cameraman, cinematographer and journalist. An extended mission to explore 100 000 square kilometres of the Arctic from the Alaskan border to the Beaufort Sea, this would be the largest and best-equipped polar expedition to venture into the region, but it would still eventually cost a number of lives. Aboard the old, square-rigged, retired whaler *Karluk*, Wilkins went north with Stefansson and between 1913 and 1916 captured in some 1200 photographs and 3000 metres of motion picture film the Arctic mammals, birds and plants, as well as the indigenous peoples and their way of life. His and Stefansson's party became separated from their ship, which was later crushed by the ice, and had to trek for three weeks across the ice with dog teams to Point Barrow; Wilkins's facial frostbite was so severe it took a year to heal and he nearly lost his sight due to snow blindness. His film footage was the first to be shot in the central Arctic and his photographs of Banks and Melville islands were the first taken there. In recognition of his efforts on behalf of the expedition, Stefansson promoted him to second-in-command of the Northern Party and during long periods sheltering from storms together, the two men often debated whether aeroplanes or submarines could be the ideal future methods of polar exploration. But, events had overtaken the debate; when the men finally emerged from their frozen isolation in 1916, it was into a world in the grip of war.

When he returned to Australia, Wilkins was accepted into the Australian Flying Corps as a Second Lieutenant in 1917 despite being colourblind. However, he didn't become a pilot. Possibly because of the influence of his friend and fellow cameraman Frank Hurley, Wilkins was appointed instead as a war photographer to the Australian War Records Section in London headed by historian C.E.W. Bean. During World War I, Wilkins took around 3000 still photos and many hours of motion picture film. Working frequently with Hurley, he soon gained a reputation for his charmed life while taking photographs under fire. Blown off his feet by shells, nicked by bullets and shrapnel, gassed and nearly run down by tanks, he was wounded nine times yet never carried a gun. 'It seemed like a trip into Hell,' he once remembered. In June 1918, he was awarded the Military Cross for rescuing wounded soldiers during the Third Battle of Ypres. He was then promoted to captain and became Commanding Officer No. 3 (Photographic) Sub-section of the Australian War Records unit, work that often took him into the thick of combat. During the Battle of Hindenburg, Wilkins temporarily took command of a company of American soldiers whose officers had all been killed in action, for which he was subsequently awarded a Bar to his Military Cross.

When it was all over, Bean and Wilkins led one last photographic mission to Gallipoli in 1919 to gather and record evidence of that disastrous campaign. Then, although still officially in uniform, Wilkins returned to flying and journalism. Still talking of exploring the North Pole by air, he joined the Royal Navy's Lighter–Than–Air Command and learned to navigate airships. When Prime Minister Billy Hughes announced a prize of £10000 (around $2.8 million today) for the first crew to fly the 18000 kilometres from England to Australia in 1919, when an aeroplane was yet to cross any major ocean, Wilkins just had to be in the race as navigator in a plane called the *Blackburn Kangaroo*, only to be forced to retire from the contest after they crashed in Crete.

The following year, Wilkins became involved with the ill-starred British Imperial Antarctic Expedition that, although touted as a grand five-year exploration of the continent making use of twelve aeroplanes, turned out to be little more than a con man's fantasy. Wilkins quickly left for New York, where he was contacted by Sir Ernest Shackleton to join his Antarctic circumnavigation expedition aboard the *Quest* as a naturalist and cameraman. When they were forced into Rio de Janeiro for repairs, Wilkins sailed on ahead at Shackleton's suggestion to the island of South Georgia where for six lonely weeks he photographed and recorded the flora and fauna. His joy when the *Quest* finally arrived there was crushed by the news that Shackleton had died suddenly the night before. After burying the great explorer on the island, they all agreed that Shackleton would have wished the expedition to continue, and so they sailed on to explore some of the least-known islands on Earth, including the Tristan da Cunha group. There on tiny Nightingale Island, occupied by more than three million pairs of birds, Wilkins discovered some of only one hundred pairs of a rare finch now known as the Wilkins's Bunting (*Nesospiza wilkinsi*), and that brought him to the attention of the British Natural History Museum.

On his return to England, Wilkins resumed his advocacy of aerial polar exploration and of polar weather monitoring stations that would make daily radio transmissions of their observations to an International Bureau of Meteorology. While his prescient plans were being considered by the Royal Meteorological Society, Wilkins was engaged by the Society of Friends to write about and film their famine relief program then in operation in Soviet Russia. After two years of drought during which an estimated five million people had died, Lenin had finally been forced to appeal to the international community for help, and organisations such as the American Relief Administration, the Red Cross and the Quakers were now feeding millions every day. Not only the Quakers wanted information, though; the British government quietly asked Wilkins to supply them with information on just how bad the situation was within the new Communist country. It was worse than bad. As Wilkins and his Quaker companions travelled from Moscow across the Volga and out onto the vast steppes, they found a barren wasteland of the dead and dying where Wilkins was once more reminded of the havoc that weather could wreak. In the Samara region alone, 10 000 people were dying a month. Wilkins recorded it all in four films for the Quakers, collectively known as *New Worlds for Old*. On the way back, he met with Lenin in his private apartments at the Kremlin. He told him what he had seen; an already-ill Lenin admitted that he may have tried to bring civilisation to the Soviet Union too quickly.

In June 1921, the Natural History Museum in London received a plea for help from their colleagues in Australia. The flora and fauna of Northern Australia were at risk, they heard, along with the indigenous inhabitants. If they didn't do something now to record what was left, it could all be gone in a few years as advancing European settlement enforced its toll. Still involved with analysing Wilkins's collection from the *Quest* voyage, and aware of his Australian background, the museum considered him the ideal choice to lead an expedition to his homeland that would journey through central New South Wales to Cape York and the Gulf of Carpentaria and even out to the Torres Strait islands. So from early 1923 into 1925, the Wilkins Australia and Islands Expedition travelled by boat and truck, on foot and on horseback through some 4000 kilometres of desert, jungle and coral island collecting over 5000 specimens, discovering mammals never before recorded. He wrote about this expedition in his first book, *Undiscovered Australia* (1928), controversially criticising Australians for their deforestation, destruction of native wildlife, racism and murders of local Aborigines. To his amazement, Wilkins found Australians generally unconcerned about the havoc they were wreaking on their landscape and its animal and native inhabitants; it was to them then, as it is now, an inevitable product of progress. The situation was, he wrote as a man recently returned from famine-stricken Russia, 'perhaps the most sadly depressing of any that I have experienced'.

Understandably, Wilkins couldn't wait to get back to the Antarctic. He dearly wanted to use the money he had received in payment from the British Natural History Museum to mount an expedition that would make use of the relatively new aviation technology to photograph and map the mostly unknown southern continent. In 1925, he proposed the Australasian Polar Pacific Expedition to fly from the Ross Sea across King Edward VII Land to Graham Land, but discovered only a profound lack of interest in Australia to funding such a venture.

So with the help of his old friend Vilhjalmur Stefansson, Wilkins turned to the United States for assistance with a different project. He eventually inspired the *Detroit News* and the Detroit Aviation Society, a group that included Edsel Ford, son of Henry Ford, among its members, to sponsor him for a flight across the Arctic ice cap. Among other things, the flight would settle the question of whether there was land out there, a possibility that had excited potential explorers for centuries. The *Detroit News* even instigated a successful penny drive involving thousands of local school children as a publicity event to raise money. As Wilkins was primarily a navigator, Stefansson introduced him to expert bush pilot Carl Ben Eielson. Known to the Inuit as 'Brother to the Eagle', Eielson had only four years earlier flown the first air mail in Alaska and made his living flying daily over the treacherous Arctic landscape. Between them, Wilkins and Eielson came up with a plan to be the first to fly from one side of the Arctic Circle to the other, and with the money raised, Wilkins purchased a pair of Fokker tri-motor planes for the expedition. By now, although Wilkins had never claimed to be attempting to reach the North Pole, he was in a race with retired American naval flyer Richard E. Byrd, who desperately wanted to be the first to fly there, as well as veteran explorer Roald Amundsen and his sponsor, millionaire Lincoln Ellsworth, who were planning to reach the pole in the Italian airship *Norge*.

The following year, Wilkins was farewelled from Detroit by thousands of people lining the streets. Palmer Hutchinson, a special correspondent for the *Detroit News*, travelled with them to file reports. One of the planes was christened the *Detroiter*, to recognise the paper's contribution, while the other was christened *Alaskan*. However, essential supplies failed to arrive at their Point Barrow, Alaska, departure point, and the planes proved too heavy and mechanically difficult, crashing one after the other. Tragically, Hutchinson was killed when struck by a propeller. They had every reason to quit right then, but Wilkins wouldn't hear of it. For three weeks they struggled to repair the planes until the *Alaskan* could be put back in the air, ferrying gasoline between Fairbanks and Barrow. Although Wilkins hoped that the weather might clear over Barrow to enable him to explore the Arctic from the air, it favoured Richard Byrd instead who claimed to have flown to and circled the North Pole on 9 May 1926, a claim still debated to this day. Nevertheless, Byrd's flight still didn't settle the issue of whether there was land in the Arctic, and that left the way open for Wilkins.

Despite not having achieved his initial objective, Wilkins still returned to the United States a hero for attempting it all in the first place, and in early 1927 the *Detroit News* sponsored the *Detroit News–Wilkins Arctic Expedition*. Wilkins even received a message of support from President John Calvin Coolidge. So in February Wilkins and Eielson returned to Alaska with two Stinson planes and a new team. Using skis fitted to the planes, Wilkins's main aim this time was to land on the ice, which no one had yet achieved in an aeroplane, in order to take depth soundings of the Arctic Ocean to discover whether land lay just under the ice cap. Taking off on 29 March, they were five hours and 700 kilometres from the Alaskan coast over a featureless frozen wasteland when the engine stopped dead. Reacting quickly, Eielson managed to turn it over just enough in order to skilfully come down safely on the ice. While Eielson worked on the engine, Wilkins hacked a hole in the ice, lowered in a detonator and set it off. It took seven seconds for the sound to bounce off the seabed and reach his echo-sounder. Contrary to scientific opinion that the Arctic Ocean was shallow, the two explorers and their plane were standing on a thin sheet of ice 5625 metres above the floor of a very cold sea. Wilkins was the first person to prove just how very deep it was, deep enough in fact to sail a submarine under the ice.

On their return journey, the engine died again and they had to land on the ice once more, this time in the dark. Before they could take off, the weather closed in and imprisoned them in the plane cabin for five days. With no choice left but to strike out for the coast on foot if they wanted to live, they staggered and crawled for thirteen days through blizzards across 200 kilometres of frozen crevasses and giant blocks of ice before they arrived at the Beechey Point trading post on the northern tip of Alaska to find that the outside world had given them up for dead.

Back in the warmth of California, Wilkins sold the *Detroiter* to two Australian flyers, Charles Kingsford Smith and Charles Ulm, who renamed it the *Southern Cross* in which they would make the first flight across the Pacific Ocean. Wilkins was still planning his own flight across an ocean: once again he and Eielson would attempt to cross 3500 kilometres of Arctic Ocean from Point Barrow in Alaska to Spitsbergen in Norway, literally on the other side of the world. With the money from their aircraft sale, Wilkins bought a Vega monoplane built especially for him by the newly formed Lockheed Aircraft Corporation, which added extra fuel tanks, windows in the cabin floor for weather observation and shortwave radio. Painted bright orange so it could be easily seen against the ice, Wilkins's Vega was only the third aircraft Lockheed had built. On 15 April 1928, Wilkins and Eielson finally achieved their successful traverse of the Arctic in the Vega in twenty hours and twenty minutes over mostly uncharted territory, landing with empty tanks during a blizzard on Dead Man's Island at Spitsbergen. Once again they were trapped in their plane cabin for five days until the weather lifted sufficiently for them to fly to Green Harbour to become the first aviators to cross the Arctic Ocean and the Arctic Circle.

This pioneering journey, recounted by Wilkins in his second book *Flying the Arctic*, made him internationally famous. He was awarded the gold Patrons Medal of the Royal Geographic Society and was the first recipient of the gold Samuel Finley Breese Morse Medal of the American Geographic Society, never awarded since it had been established in 1902 for achievements and pioneering in geographical research. He and Eielson were granted an audience with the King of Norway on their arrival there, cheered by 10 000 people in Germany, and in England Wilkins was personally knighted by King George V as Sir Hubert Wilkins, because he would not presume to use the King's name. During celebrations and a ticker-tape parade in New York, Australian singer and actress Suzanne Bennett greeted him with a bouquet of flowers. Although she claimed not to know the difference between the Arctic and the Antarctic, they found enough in common to subsequently marry in 1929. Bennett would later estimate that in the first eight years of their marriage they spent a grand total of three months together, but they loved each other all their lives.

Wilkins was now in a position to attempt a realisation of another dream: to become the first to fly across the Antarctic continent from the Antarctic Peninsula to the Ross Sea. Although he pointed out that such an expedition would give Australia territorial advantages and enable the country to establish valuable meteorological stations there, a typically short-sighted Australian Federal government once again declined to become financially involved in his proposed expedition. Fortunately the Americans were not as hesitant, and newspaper magnate William Randolph Hearst offered $40 000 for exclusive press and radio rights and another $10 000 if Wilkins was first to the South Pole. Once again, Wilkins would unwillingly find himself in a race with Richard Byrd to another pole.

Planning to base his operations on Deception Island in the South Shetlands, Wilkins hoped to fly from there across the Weddell Sea to the Antarctic mainland where he would establish fuel depots to enable him to make the flight across the continent. He intended to use the same plane as he'd flown in the Arctic, renamed *Los Angeles* in honour of Hearst, who lived on the outskirts of Los Angeles at San Simeon, plus a second Vega named *San Francisco* as a back-up aircraft. This time, Carl Ben Eielson would be chief pilot seconded by another experienced ice pilot, Joe Crosson.

On 22 September 1928, the Wilkins–Hearst Expedition left New York for Montevideo in South America. Once there, they loaded their supplies and the two aircraft onto the whaling ship *Hektoria* and sailed for the Falkland Islands in October. Meanwhile, the Foreign Office in London had become concerned that Byrd might be planning to make American territorial land claims in Antarctica. Wilkins would be the nearest person to fly the flag for England, and so when he landed at the Falklands he was promptly given the job of ensuring he establish a British sovereign claim in Antarctica first.

The *Hektoria* dropped anchor at Deception Island on 4 December and Wilkins, Eielson and the rest of the team began to assemble the aircraft. Only about 100 kilometres off the Antarctic coast, Deception is the nearest of the South Shetland Islands to Antarctica, and its flooded volcanic caldera has provided a favourite shelter from the weather for shipping since the nineteenth century. Wilkins's ultimate goal was to use one plane to refuel the other at various depots as they made their way across the continent to the Ross Sea. On 16 November, Eielson took off in the *Los Angeles* from the sandy beach by the whaling station for twenty minutes, making the first aeroplane flight in Antarctica. Ten days later, both planes took to the air: Eielson in the *Los Angeles* lifted off from the ice out in the bay and Crosson in the *San Francisco* from the beach. However, as it touched down to land, the *Los Angeles* skidded off the edge of the ice nose-first, up to its wings in the water. It took eighteen hours to pull the plane back out.

But then, unexpectedly, the December weather remained warm and the bay ice refused to thicken. In order for the planes to land on their way across the continent to refuel they would need to be fitted with skis but if the ice did not thicken, the planes would not be able to take off with the skis attached. With so many seabirds in the vicinity, they wouldn't be able to take off on floats from the water either, so there was nothing for it but to clear the beach landing strip of large rocks for 700 metres by hand. With the help of some whalers, the team worked for thirty-six hours straight but, unfortunately, the runway was still not long enough for a take-off with sufficient fuel to reach the Ross Sea. Nevertheless, they filled the tanks of the radio-equipped *San Francisco* with enough fuel for a flight of over 2200 kilometres and loaded emergency rations of biscuits, pemmican, chocolate, nuts, raisins and malted milk tablets to last two months, or an 800-kilometre walk, in case they were forced down. Then early on the morning of 20 December 1928, with Eielson at the controls and Wilkins navigating and operating the radio, they took off into the Antarctic sky and pointed the nose of their small aircraft south, the first men to explore Antarctica from the air.

Crossing Bransfield Strait, they flew around the 1200-metre peak of Trinity Island and then parallel to the mountains along the Antarctic Peninsula's western coast until they climbed over the mountain range at an altitude of 3000 metres, the only people to have ever seen the summit plateau of Graham Land. 'I had a tremendous sensation of power and freedom—I felt liberated,' Wilkins would later recall to his biographer Lowell Thomas. Only a few years earlier, it had taken three months for him to map a small section of the magnificent landscape spread out below them. As they now followed the curve of Graham Land's eastern coast, Wilkins saw beneath them so many fjords and channels that he mistakenly thought they were flying over an island archipelago rather than a single peninsula. Over this unknown land, Wilkins attempted to fill in the blank spaces on his maps as he charted their progress, making notes and taking photographs with two movie cameras and a hand-held Kodak. He named a number of features, including the Stefansson Strait and Hearst Island, and the Wilkins Coast and Wilkins Sound now commemorate his exploration of the region. Finally they reached the Antarctic mainland, but by now they were threatened by storms. Reluctantly taking note of fuel gauges that read half-empty, Wilkins dropped the Union Jack and a British territorial claim document from the plane before they turned for Deception Island, having covered some 2000 kilometres, nearly 1600 of which was over previously unknown territory. A few days later, they made a second flight along much the same route to look for a suitable base site for a flight south to the Pole, but saw only sheer walls of ice and deep crevasses occupying any potential landing sites. So, they dismantled the planes, stored them at the whaling station and, early in January 1929, sailed back to New York and civilisation.

On his return from the Antarctic, Wilkins was invited by Hearst to join the largest airship in the world at that time, the *Graf Zeppelin*, to report on the technical aspects of the first around-the-world flight to be made by an airship. Then, having gathered much publicity and financial support due to the success of the first expedition, Wilkins returned to the Antarctic aboard the factory ship *Melville* in late November 1929, with a second Wilkins–Hearst Expedition. The British government donated the services of the research vessel *William Scoresby*, on which Wilkins shipped the first car brought to the Antarctic: a Baby Austin fitted with eight wheels connected by chains. Wilkins and his pilots Al Cheesman and Parker Kramer made a number of successful flights between December 1929 and January the following year, discovering that Charcot Land on the west shore of the Peninsula was in fact an island. However, they were saddened to hear news over the radio that Eielson, who had remained behind to establish Alaskan Airways, had been killed when his plane had crashed on a fog-shrouded Siberian hillside while on a mercy mission. He and Wilkins had flown together over more than a million square kilometres of the Earth's surface that had never before been charted. Sailing south to about longitude 100 degrees in the vicinity of Peter Island, Wilkins's expedition reached the most southerly point achieved by any known ship. He and Cheesman then took off across the sea in the Vega for one short flight before bad weather closed in and forced them to return to the ship. Although in the end not able to achieve his dream of traversing Antarctica from the air, Wilkins was the first to fly there and had travelled a greater distance in polar airspace than anyone else.

Finally, he and his wife Suzanne were able to have their belated honeymoon in Switzerland during the summer of 1930, staying for six weeks at the luxurious Schloss Lenzburg owned by their wealthy friend Lincoln Ellsworth. While they were there, Wilkins and Ellsworth began discussing whether it was possible to take a submarine under the ice of the Arctic Ocean in order to pioneer the gathering of scientific and meteorological data. It was an idea Wilkins had been considering ever since his days with Stefansson. They drew up plans for a grand voyage from New York to London to Norway, under the Arctic ice cap to Alaska, then down the West Coast of America to the Panama Canal through which they would sail to the East Coast and back to New York. At that time, such a journey was the equivalent of going to Mars. The 14 000 000 square kilometres of the Arctic Ocean, its currents, temperature and depth were still a mystery; no ship had been within 800 kilometres of the North Pole and returned to tell the story, and Wilkins was proposing to sail *under* it! When the plan was announced, the general public perception was that too much time on the ice had affected his mind.

This would be no cheap expedition to mount: Ellsworth, Hearst, the Woods Hole Oceanographic Institute and Wilkins himself all contributed to the bill of around $200 000. Wilkins entered into partnership with pioneer submarine designer Simon Lake and former submarine officer Commander Sloan Danenhower to lease the decommissioned, 53-metre, WWI-vintage American submarine O-12 for one dollar a year for five years from the US government. Originally designed by Lake in 1918, the O-12 could dive to 60 metres with a crew of twenty. For this expedition, it was insulated against the temperature and custom-fitted with a scientific laboratory, a cushioned bow-sprit and reinforced bow for collision protection, two ice drills that could cut a tube through 30.5 metres of ice to supply air for the diesel engines and for the crew and also provide ice-core samples, and a third hollow drill 61 centimetres in diameter that could cut through 4 metres of ice and provide access to the surface for the crew. Even the periscope was modified so that it folded like a jackknife in order to prevent any contact with ice. There was an on-board machine shop for repairs and a diving chamber to enable divers to enter and exit under water. Lake renamed the submarine the *Nautilus*, and Jean-Jules Verne, grandson of Jules Verne who wrote the book *20,000 Leagues Under the Sea* that featured the original *Nautilus*, attended the boat's christening on 4 March 1931 by Lady Suzanne Wilkins under the Brooklyn Bridge, watched by some 800 people. Because of Prohibition, a bucket of ice had to be used rather than the traditional champagne. Perhaps someone should have reminded Lake about the traditional bad luck associated with renaming ships.

As with first expeditions anywhere, this one was fraught with dangers and experts both naval and polar were not slow to point them out. The submarine could get caught beneath ice so thick the drills would not be able to penetrate it, for example, leaving the crew and engines to run out of air; it could be damaged in a collision with ice or be crushed between ice floes; battery power could be discharged more rapidly than it could be replaced; or they could simply become lost beneath the ice. One and all chorused that the expedition was too hazardous and some even declared it suicidal.

After a series of trial runs and practice dives, the Wilkins–Ellsworth Trans-Arctic Submarine Expedition of 1931 set sail across the North Atlantic on 4 June, only to become stranded halfway when the engines broke down. After being towed to Ireland and then England for repairs, the *Nautilus* finally reached Bergen, Norway, on 5 August where they picked up the six-member scientific team and then headed north for Spitsbergen. Nine days later they reached the edge of the pack ice and spent a few days making scientific observations. According to Wilkins, it wasn't until 22 August when they planned to begin dive tests that they realised the stern diving planes were no longer attached to the boat, and he along with others aboard would later blame sabotage. With no means of controlling the *Nautilus* once submerged, diving under the ice was no longer possible but they remained for a few more days carrying out experiments. They took ice-core samples, recorded bathymetric data, determined the temperature and salinity of the sea at various depths and collected plankton. By 31 August, Commander Danenhower had worked out a method by which he could take the submarine partially under the ice, trimming her two degrees down at the bow so that he could nose the submarine under some large ice floes. His first test run was a success, although the noise of the ice against the hull was terrifying, and so on a second run Danenhower went further under the ice. Disappointingly, the large ice drill mechanism failed and they had to back out, but they had been the first submariners to prove that sailing under polar ice was possible. Finally, they had to turn back to Bergen. On the way they ran into a fierce storm that damaged the *Nautilus* so severely that by the time they limped into port a safe return home could no longer be guaranteed. After gaining permission from the US government, Wilkins had the old submarine towed offshore and scuttled.

Wilkins returned home to criticism for an expedition some labelled foolhardy but for which many also praised him. He continued to partner with Ellsworth as second-in-command of the Lincoln Ellsworth Antarctic Flight expeditions, visiting the Arctic region four more times during the 1930s. In 1937, Wilkins joined the search for the lost Soviet Polar Expedition commanded by Sigismund Levanevsky, spending seven months as leader of the Alaskan–Canadian section. Despite no trace of the expedition ever being found, Wilkins was personally invited by Stalin to Moscow where he was decorated for his efforts.

At the outbreak of World War II, Wilkins offered his services to the Australian government who rejected this proposal as they had consistently rejected him. Wilkins just shrugged and went off on undercover missions for British Intelligence and the American Office of Strategic Services before becoming the resident expert on military survival skills and equipment at the United States Quartermaster Research Command. In 1957, his early predictions concerning the importance of meteorological observations at the poles were validated by the International Geophysical Year, during which twelve nations established fifty research stations in Antarctica, leading to the setting up of the Antarctic Treaty of 1961. Naturally, Wilkins was there for a South Pole circumnavigation.

On 5 August 1958, after two unsuccessful attempts, the nuclear submarine USS *Nautilus* became the first vessel to sail under the North Pole, crossing the Arctic Ocean following much of Wilkins's earlier aerial route across that same ocean. Only a few days later, the USS *Skate* skippered by Commander James Calvert became the second submarine to sail under the North Pole and the first to surface in the Arctic through polynyas, or gaps in the ice. Familiar with Wilkins's book *Under the North Pole* and his predictions about surfacing there, Calvert invited Sir Hubert to visit him on board when they returned. The two explorers had much to share during that afternoon, Wilkins advising Calvert that to truly conquer the ice he should break through it in winter. When Wilkins died only a few weeks later, Calvert agreed to take his friend on the one voyage he was not able to complete in life. In winter, on 17 March 1959, the USS *Skate* became the first submarine to break through the ice at the geographic North Pole. There, under the flags of Australia, England and America, two dozen crew members formed ranks on either side of a table on which sat a small bronze urn. As several men held flares to light the darkness, Commander Calvert read a short speech before walking with a burial party a short distance away from the boat. There he read the committal while the ashes were sprinkled into the wind. A rifle was fired three times in salute.

Eight years later, a memorial was unveiled in honour of Wilkins at Hallett, and in 2001 the restored family homestead at Netfield was officially opened. Wilkins Island, Wilkins Sound, the Wilkins Ice Shelf and the Wilkins Runway near Casey station in Antarctica have all been named after him. He is honoured in the United States as one of the great men of the twentieth century, but in his homeland which erects bronze statues to football stars there are none for Sir Hubert Wilkins.

★

The rest of the world

It was nearly thirty years before another USS *Nautilus*, the first nuclear-powered submarine, became the first to reach the North Pole on 3 August 1958, sailing under the ice on a course identical to the one planned by Wilkins and conclusively confirming Wilkins's theory that such a voyage was possible.

In September 2005, the original *Nautilus* was rediscovered by Dr Stewart Nelson and Dr Hans Fricke of the Max Planck Institute and their research team. Using a JAGO two-person submersible, they carried out four dives while photographing the wreck in detail, clearly locating the submarine's distinctive modifications and confirming the vessel that had truly gone where no-one had gone before was still in excellent shape.

A TROPICAL QUEENSLANDER ON ICE

John Hoelscher's circumnavigation of Greenland

First

- The first known person, with American team-mate Lonnie Dupre, to circumnavigate Greenland by non-motorised transport

Sometimes, accidental meetings lead to more important events. After spending four years working on Antarctic research bases, John Hoelscher travelled to the United States in 1993 to be with twenty-two sled dogs from Mawson Station in Antarctica that had been relocated because of the implementation of the Madrid environmental protection protocol that no introduced species could remain in the Antarctic. The dogs were being taken to new homes in northern Minnesota where they could still work, and it was there in Ely that Hoelscher first met Lonnie Dupre, who knew immediately on meeting Hoelscher that his experience, competence, attention to detail and love of the polar regions would make him the ideal partner in a future expedition.

Born in 1963 and raised in Brisbane, John had moved north to the beachside town of Yeppoon with his parents when he was sixteen, developing interests in surfing, diving and fishing while he was completing his electrical apprenticeship in Rockhampton. His love for the sea led him to take a job on Heron Island Resort on the Great Barrier Reef, where he could sail out around the surrounding islands in his free time, learning more about the reef and its bird and sea life. Working within a close-knit community in an isolated environment proved ideal training for his next job.

Looking for new adventures, John discovered that his qualifications were suitable for work at the Australian research stations in Antarctica. After enduring the lengthy application process, he was accepted and went to Casey Station in 1989 for the Australian Antarctic Division as part of Australian National Antarctic Research Expeditions (ANARE). He enjoyed it so much that he remained on the ice for seventeen months in the challenging position of station maintenance electrician. He returned to Australia in the autumn of 1991. While working at Casey in Antarctica, he'd become interested in sled dogs and so, discovering that they were still actively used at Mawson, he reapplied and within six months was working on the rebuilding of the station there. Established in 1954, Mawson is Australia's oldest working Antarctic research station and huskies had been bred and used continuously there, enabling early research expeditions to explore and travel new routes. In 1992, there were twenty-eight dogs at Mawson, cared for and loved by Hoelscher and the other station members. Soon Hoelscher was learning from previous expeditioners the skills needed to efficiently and practically run with and handle the teams on the ice while travelling long distances, camping with them along the sea ice and up in the plateau.

During that summer of 1992, Hoelscher and his colleagues learned that this would be the last year for the dogs. The new international protocol for Antarctic environmental protection that had been signed in Madrid meant that no introduced species could remain, even including sled dogs that had been there. They would all have to be taken out of Antarctica, so Hoelscher and three others undertook one last research expedition with the dog teams, travelling the tough 300 kilometres west along the sea ice in freezing spring temperatures with eighteen dogs to successfully document the three emperor penguin colonies including the Kloa rookery.

When the icebreaker RSV *Aurora Australis* arrived, Hoelscher helped load twenty-two dogs for the journey to the United States. New homes had been found in Minnesota, where they could still do the work for which they had been bred at the Voyager Outbound School and Wintergreen Outdoor Adventures.

A few months later, Hoelscher went back to Minnesota to make sure they had settled in and gather more dog-team experience from the 'mushers'—people who travel in sleds with dog teams—in the area. He ventured further afield to experience mushing adventures in the Brooks Range of Alaska and in Canadian Ellesmere Island, where he helped train adventurers travelling to the North Pole with some of the relocated Australian Mawson huskies. He also spent months travelling to other parts of the Canadian Arctic, visiting remote Inuit communities and researching the lives of these Arctic people. It was during this time that he met Lonnie Dupre in Ely. They quickly became friends and promised to stay in touch.

Dupre had been raised in Minnesota and had always been fascinated by the Inuit and the Arctic. After his first low-budget trek in Alaska in 1983—a 73-day backcountry journey that he christened the Brooks Range Experiment—he was hooked. He raised and trained sled dogs and thought of places to take them. In 1989, he had been invited to be part of the Bering Bridge Expedition, a joint Russian–American 1900-kilometre crossing from Siberia to Alaska. Three years after that, he'd raised enough money to launch a project of his own, the Northwest Passage Expedition. In mid-winter, Dupre and three others had set out by dogsled from Prudhoe Bay, Alaska, headed for Churchill, Manitoba, some 4800 kilometres east, but they had run into trouble in appalling weather that had stalled their travel speed. Their supplies had nearly run out and unfortunately some of their dogs had died before the group was eventually rescued, dramatically demonstrating the unpredictability of the polar environment and how unforgiving it can be.

Nevertheless, Dupre kept on exploring. It was in the summer of 1995, during a 402-kilometre dog-team expedition with his wife, Kelly, across Banks Island, in the footsteps of earlier explorers Vilhjalmur Stefansson and Hubert Wilkins, that they began to plan a similar venture on a larger scale: the first circumnavigation of Greenland, the world's largest island, using only traditional Arctic transport—dog team and kayak. Not only would the expedition be an adventure in itself, but they would be able to educate the outside world about indigenous cultures that still strive to maintain their traditional way of life based on achieving a balance with nature.

Now, only a person who loves ice and snow very deeply would think of Greenland as a place to spend some time kayaking. Lying north-east of the Canadian Arctic and two-thirds within the Arctic Circle, and with only 60000 people, Greenland has the lowest population density on earth. The largest island that is not a continent, it's about 2650 kilometres long and 1200 kilometres wide with its northernmost point lying only some 740 kilometres from the North Pole. About 81 per cent of Greenland's surface is covered by an ice sheet up to 3500 metres thick at its deepest point, second only in depth to Antarctica's ice. Much of the island is ringed by high mountains through which the ice flows as glaciers down valleys to coastal fjords. Eric the Red gave the country its ironic name as a public relations gesture so that people would be motivated to colonise it. They needed a lot of motivation; during the long, dark winters, cyclonic winds drive snow sideways and temperatures drop to well below −50 degrees Celsius.

Still, when Dupre called Hoelscher at Mawson later that year to ask whether he'd like to do a little sledging in Greenland, Hoelscher didn't hesitate to accept; he knew in his heart that he had always wanted to travel and learn from traditional dog team experts. He was excited to be able to partake in a long expedition which would encompass both sea kayaking and dog sledging, knowing it would enable them to travel by traditional transport through, and document life in, this challenging and remote Arctic nation. So, in early 1996, he joined

Dupre in Minnesota to help plan and raise sponsorship for the expedition, and to develop and test equipment. By about September, the International Greenland Expedition was finalised.

Hoelscher would be the communications person, hauling a laptop, satellite phone, two radios, specialised polar transmitter, video camera and emergency rescue beacon, plus a portable wind generator and solar panels for recharging all those batteries. After a lot of hard canvassing over many months, they managed to raise support from about eighty sponsors. Dupre calculated the expedition would cost around US$400 000, of which they had about half in cash. The biggest single cost, about $68 000, would involve air and sea drops of 816 kilograms of food for Dupre and Hoelscher and 3402 kilograms of food for the dogs, packaged in 168 boxes that would make up the thirteen supply depots along the route, along with spare sled parts. Each depot would contain food, fuel and gear that was calculated to last the team fifteen days until they reached the next depot. In some locations, the supplies would have to be tucked inside polar-bear-proof cages of heavy-duty metal grating. These boxes would have to travel by ship from Minnesota to Reykjavík in Iceland where they would be loaded onto charter planes and boats to be deposited around the ice-capped coast. A bowl of oatmeal with milk and nuts was going to cost Dupre and Hoelscher about $10.

Then there was the small matter of communication in a land with no mobile phone towers; in fact, Greenland doesn't even have a road system. To go anywhere, they would have to either fly, hitch up the dog team or get in a boat. Hoelscher and Dupre could borrow a $20 000 satellite phone, but it would cost $4.95 per minute to use and, in any case, that far north all they would hear would be static. So they invested in a satellite transmitter, allowing Dupre to file weekly diary entries with his website designer in Minneapolis and occasionally chat with sponsors. They also took out a $5000 rescue insurance policy, in case a helicopter had to fly in and lift them off a drifting ice floe.

They initially planned to make the attempt between May 1997 and September 1998. They would leave the settlement of Paamiut on the south-west coast in two specially designed 5.2-metre kayaks and travel 2414 kilometres north during the summer along the island's west coast, which would be free of ice but still exposed to violent and freezing weather. They could resupply in villages along the way, hopefully reaching Qaanaaq in north Greenland before the autumn storms arrived, after which they would live with the local Inuit people for five months while they purchased and trained dog teams. (Importing their own trained teams into Greenland was forbidden, to guard against any diseases being introduced to the native dog population.) Then, once the sea ice was well established in winter, they would set out with dog teams pulling 3.6-metre sleds along 4184 kilometres of the north-western, northern and eastern coasts that, remote and primarily uninhabited, would be an entirely different story from the west coast. This is where they would have to be supplied by the thirteen dropped-in supply depots.

Having reached the village of Ammassalik, on the south-east coast, by spring, they would switch back to travelling in a tandem 5.8-metre kayak for the final 4497 kilometres along mostly uninhabited coast, carrying all their supplies in the kayak. Rounding the southern tip of the island, they would eventually return to Paamiut in August of 1998. It would probably take, they estimated, about fifteen months to travel the 7725 kilometres. A car trip of comparable distance in the United States would run from Miami to Manhattan and then on to San Francisco before doubling back to Denver. Along the way they could expect calving and rolling icebergs, swells the size of two-storey houses and winds that could induce frostbite—and that was just while kayaking. While crossing the icy landscape in a dogsled, they would have to be on the lookout for bottomless crevasses hidden by fresh snowfall, winds of 160 kilometres per hour, hungry polar bears and temperatures that could well hover around −50 degrees Celsius.

On 16 May 1997, they paddled away from Paamiut and headed north in their two single polyethylene kayaks joined together like a catamaran and rigged with sails. They had concluded that this would be a safer configuration than travelling separately, one that would carry them across exposed bays and protect them from the dangers of capsizing in frigid waters. Just in case that happened, they wore one-piece dry suits as protection against hypothermia. For the next eighty-four days during the Greenland summer, they travelled 2000 kilometres across open water and through pack ice, sudden squalls, sleet, heavy seas and huge waves caused by calving icebergs. Given the shortness of the summer there, they had to make 25 kilometres per day, preferably after 10 p.m. during the glow of the midnight sun when the water was calmer. This meant at least nine to twelve hours of paddling per day, and on two days they had to paddle for seventeen hours before finding a suitable campsite. Sometimes fog would settle on the water, bringing visibility down to 10 metres. They floated alongside whales, through pods of seals and by calving glaciers accompanied by seabirds until on 8 August they reached the village of Kullorsuaq near Melville Bay, having made the longest kayak voyage in Greenland's history. There they learned that hazardous pack ice blocked the way north to the next settlement, Savissivik. The only way to reach the Qaanaaq area would be with local hunters by *umiatsiaq*, the small Inuit open powerboat used for hunting and fishing.

Setting out by *umiatsiaq* on 21 August, they finally reached Savissivik after a sixteen-hour journey through pack ice during which they had to replace a propeller broken on ice. A few days later they finally reached Qaanaaq. While Dupre returned home for part of that time to take care of sponsorship and logistical commitments, Hoelscher remained in Qaanaaq for the next five and a half months, assembling their two dog teams and training them. The Inuit named him Ujuut. On 26 October, the sun disappeared below the horizon for four months of polar night, not to reappear until 17 February. Even so, it's not necessarily a time of total darkness. On clear nights, the light of the moon and stars reflecting off the snow and ice can provide enough light by which to read. Inuit sled dogs are not pets and can be dangerous enough to attack you if they sense vulnerability. One of the team lead dogs was christened Holyfield and the other one was called Tyson after it tried to bite off Hoelscher's ear while he was harnessing the dog. During winter while working, the dogs needed a high-calorie diet and to be fed every day, preferably seal or walrus meat and skin when it was available. When Dupre returned in early January of 1998, he and Hoelscher began making long training runs.

On the cold and windy morning of 14 February, Dupre and Hoelscher set out with their dog teams hauling two heavy wooden sleds about 4 metres long and 1 metre wide laden with the supplies that would help them survive for the month it would take them to reach their first supply depot at Rensselaer Bay. Six days later, they were enduring 160 kilometre per hour winds, huddled in tents on their way up the Clements Markham Glacier. After being trapped for five days, they had to retreat back down to the shelter of a hut. Finally the storm blew out and they were able to ascend the glacier, cross the plateau and descend to the hut at Rensselaer Bay, which they reached in early March. They then crossed the Kane Basin in −50 degree Celsius temperatures, struggling through 5-metre-high ridges of pressure ice and dodging polar bears. After being faced with impenetrable gorges and icy waterfalls, they reached the Kennedy Channel after travelling 523 kilometres. Faced with endless pressured pack ice and with 201 kilometres still to go to their next depot, they realised they would run out of food before they reached the depot and had to retrace their steps to Siorapaluk and Qaanaaq. Their dogsled attempt on the northern and eastern coasts of Greenland was officially over.

The melt season came on a month early, and so in May of 1998 Hoelscher and Dupre arrived at Ammassalik on the south-eastern coast of Greenland just below the Arctic Circle to begin training for the last leg of their circumnavigation: the 1496-kilometre kayak journey around the southern tip of the island to Paamiut. By then it was light twenty-four hours a day and temperatures were climbing past 10 degrees Celsius, but the warmth also meant that large ice floes and bergs were calving from glaciers and ice shelves further north and drifting down towards them, choking the waterways. On 9 July in their tandem kayak loaded with 80 kilograms of food, fuel and equipment, they paddled out of Ammassalik into the worst pack ice the locals could recall. The kayak had been shipped in aboard the resupply vessel *Kista Arctica*, which had been trapped in floes for over a week.

After the last village, Isortoq, they paddled for 830 kilometres to reach the next habitation, the Prince Christian Sound weather station. They had allowed for thirty days of supplies for this part of the trip. At night they could hear the thunder of bergs calving in the distance. Within two days, they were stopped by compressed packs of ice floes and had to resort to pulling themselves along between them with gaff hooks or, where the ice proved impenetrable, climbing out and hauling the kayak over the ice, even occasionally using it as a bridge between floes. Meanwhile, they had to keep a constant lookout for piteraq winds, which could funnel down from the ice cap through fjords and out to sea, reaching speeds of more than 300 kilometres per hour, and for polar bears when camping. Every day they were aware they could easily die out there.

Having taken twenty-six days to cover the 834 kilometres, Hoelscher and Dupre navigated through dense fog by the sound of a generator to surprise the six Danes manning the Prince Christian Sound weather station at the southern end of Greenland's east coast. After a good meal and some travel advice, they set sail again through the sound, a narrow 64-kilometre-long waterway between 1524-metre cliffs that connects the east and west coasts and provides a safer alternative to rounding Cape Farvel at the southern tip.

Finally, thirty-two days and 890 kilometres after leaving Ammassalik, they pulled up on the shore at Aapilatoq at the southern end of Greenland. Hearing that the weather was deteriorating, they left Aapilatoq after only a few hours. For five days, conditions deteriorated so severely that they were making no progress and they were forced to concede that they would not be able to reach their destination of Paamiut, their original starting point in May the previous year. Of the seventeen days it took them to travel a few kilometres of coastline, ten were spent huddled in their tent as the autumn storms descended with brute force. When they finally struggled into Qaqortoq on 21 August, it was the end of the expedition. They had travelled over 5100 kilometres on their odyssey, reaching Qaqortoq after paddling, sailing and pulling their kayak 1207 kilometres from Ammassalik in forty-three days. The danger of their journey was abruptly brought home to them a few days later when they learned that experienced Danish kayaker, journalist and dogsled expeditioner Lone Madsen, who had left Ammassalik on 1 August to follow their route, had perished on the way.

Undaunted, Dupre and Hoelscher were determined to finish what they had begun, and over the next few years they embarked on another two expeditions by dogsled and kayak to complete their journey around the island. In February 2000, they returned to Greenland on the Thule 2000 Expedition and with fourteen huskies they travelled another 2900 kilometres over ninety-five days on the longest dogsled journey in Greenland's history. Leaving Constable Point, near Ittoqqortoormiit on the east coast on 18 February, they mushed north to reached Qaanaaq on 30 May. The following year they returned in April on the Second Thule Expedition, this time travelling south from Qaanaaq to reach the village of Savissivik on the north side of Melville Bay. Finding they were unable to cross the bay because of thin ice and blizzards, they left the dogs and equipment at the village and went south with kayaks to paddle the small coastal section from Paamiut to Qaqortoq that bad weather had prevented them from completing in 1998. Then, in mid-June, they returned north to cross Melville Bay.

Finally, they tackled the most dangerous section of their circumnavigation: the 1110-kilometre stretch of mountainous east coast from Constable Point to Ammassalik where 1000-metre peaks rise vertically from the water's edge and icebergs calve from glaciers with a roar into the sea. They battled for days through ice fields, fog, freezing gales and huge swells that at one point capsized them, and they encountered whales and polar bears; then at last, on 5 September 2001, they arrived at Ammassalik, completing their circumnavigation of Greenland that had taken over twenty-three months of elapsed travel time.

In calendar time, though, it took over four years for Lonnie Dupre and John Hoelscher to complete the 10 486-kilometre first circumnavigation of Greenland using dogsled and kayak. To do so, they had formed three expeditions and had travelled approximately 5538 kilometres by dog team and sled and 4948 kilometres by kayak. About 8153 kilometres made up the actual circumnavigation and the remaining 2333 kilometres were cultural journeys by dogsled throughout the lands of Kane Basin, Nares Strait and villages of the Polar Inuit.

When they arrived back in the United States on 9 September 2001, news of their incredible achievement was swamped by the tragedy of the September 11 terrorist attack on the World Trade Center. It's only recently, with the publication of Dupre's book *Greenland Expedition: Where ice is born*, that Hoelscher and Dupre's circumnavigation has begun to receive the public recognition it deserves.

During the period of their expeditions, Hoelscher never saw summer as he moved between the Arctic and other expeditions in the Antarctic. He has now worked at all the Australian Antarctic stations, including Davis Station and Macquarie Island, journeyed to Siberia to assist Dupre with the One World Arctic Ocean Expedition in 2005, and returned to sail along the Greenland coast aboard the Greenpeace ship MV *Arctic Sunrise* and assist glaciologists. He still lives near Yeppoon, and he and Dupre remain close friends.

★

The rest of the world

Eric the Red, a Viking from Iceland, was the first to explore the southern end of Greenland in 982 AD and then four years later led a group of settlers back there.

In 1888, a party of six led by Fridtjof Nansen of Denmark, who would later become famous for his expedition towards the North Pole aboard the *Fram*, accomplished the first land crossing of Greenland. Their party took forty-nine days, travelling on skis while hauling sleds, to cross southern Greenland from Umivik Fjord on the west coast to Nuuk on the east coast. One hundred years later, American polar explorer and Arctic preservation advocate Will Steger led the 1600 mile south–north traverse of Greenland in 1988. It was the longest unsupported dogsled expedition in history.

American Robert Peary explored the north of Greenland by dogsled in 1886 and 1891, establishing that the northern coast stopped well short of the North Pole with the discovery of Cape Jesup at the northern tip of the island.

The only other known attempt to circumnavigate Greenland was in 1993 by the Russian polar icebreaker *Kapitan Khlebnikov*. She became trapped and had to be freed by another icebreaker.

'IT'S EVERYONE'S WORLD'

Kay Cottee and Blackmores First Lady circumnavigate the globe

Firsts

- First woman to complete a single-handed, non-stop circum-navigation of the world by sea, and thus the first woman to circumnavigate non-stop west to east travelling south of the five southernmost capes: Good Hope, Leeuwin, South East Cape (Tasmania), South West Cape (Stewart Island, NZ) and Cape Horn
- First woman to spend that length of time—189 days and 32 minutes—alone at sea
- First solo woman to cover that distance at sea—22 100 nautical miles—non-stop and unassisted

After 188 days at sea, Kay Cottee was only 33 nautical miles from home and five hours from sighting the South Head Light at Sydney Heads. She would be the first woman to have sailed non-stop, single-handed and unassisted around the world, battling seas that had knocked her boat flat more than once with only her lifeline to prevent her being washed away. As she thought about the implications of reaching safe harbour, Kay realised that those 189 days at sea might have been easier to deal with than what lay ahead. 'The idea flashed through my mind,' she wrote later, 'how easy it would be to turn the wheel slightly, to head east and go round again . . .'

Kay and her three sisters were born into a family dedicated to sailing. When they were little, her mother, Joy, would tie them all to the mast of their yacht on short leashes for safety when she and her husband, Jim McLaren, went sailing. By the time Kay was nine, she and the family were crewing on *Joy Too*, the 11-metre timber yacht that Jim had built in the backyard, during races across Sydney Harbour. Occasionally the girls were also allowed to participate in longer ocean races, except when Jim was sailing a Sydney to Hobart race. Two years later, she was sailing her own VJ dinghy and spent most of her time in high school dreaming she was sailing over the horizon out across the oceans.

Married at eighteen, she found herself working for her father-in-law in the office of their family plumbing business on weekdays while at night and on weekends she and her first husband built, fitted out, sailed and sold a number of yachts. Within a year Cottee was operating her own yacht charter business full time. However, she never lost sight of her ultimate goal: to one day build and own an ocean-going yacht in which she could be the first woman to sail solo, non-stop and unassisted around the world.

By 1985, Cottee and her friend Shirley King were running her yacht charter fleet seven days a week. Needing a break, she sailed a friend's yacht back from Lord Howe Island solo; by the time she reached home, Cottee knew in her heart that this was what she really wanted to do. Within a couple of months she had sold the business and begun fitting out the hull of an 11.3-metre Cavalier 37 yacht designed by New Zealander Laurie Davidson in the front yard of her garden flat. She originally named it *Jimmy Mac*, after her father.

In March 1986, Cottee successfully sailed her yacht, now sponsored by Blackmores Limited and re-christened *Cinnamon Scrub*, in the Transfield Two-handed Trans-Tasman race to New Zealand with friend Linda Wayman, and then Cottee sailed back to Australia alone in the Solo Trans-Tasman Race. Before that race was over, Cottee was planning her circumnavigation voyage. Having glued a broken tooth back together with epoxy pipe-jointing compound en route, sucking mints to combat the awful taste, the experienced yachtswomen was confident of handling whatever the ocean could throw at her.

As well as achieving her own dream, Cottee also wanted to raise money for a worthwhile cause. Once again, she had the full support of Marcus Blackmore of Blackmores Limited, not only for the voyage but to help in raising money for the Reverend Ted Noffs' Life Education Program (LEC), which educates schoolchildren about the dangers of drug and alcohol abuse. Cottee eventually raised over $1 million for the charity. Her yacht was renamed *Blackmores First Lady* and a departure date was set for mid-November, so that hopefully Cottee would be back before the worst of the Southern Ocean winter.

Before she left, there were medical checks, dental checks, psychology checks, self-defence classes and checks on the strength of the yacht. The hull around the keel was strengthened; two water-tight crash bulkheads were installed, a strobe-light attached to the mast-head, and a radar and radar-detector fitted. Cottee had fibre-glassed two extra floors into the hull in case of an underwater collision, strengthened the mast-step with a steel beam, and installed bracing columns in the cabin in case the boat was hit by a sudden hard wind gust or huge wave and suffered a 'smack-down', laid flat on its side in the water, or was rolled completely over under the water and righted itself.

In the days before laptops, the internet, satellite communication and the web as we know it, there were no such things as blogs, webcam diaries, tweeting or playing computer games to keep your mind occupied out on the sea alone. All communication on *Blackmores First Lady* was via an old-fashioned two-way radio. Among many other things, Cottee took dozens of books to read, crossword puzzles to work on, needlepoint and knitting, storybook and music cassettes to listen to (no iPods in those days either) and a Spanish language course to work on. Before leaving, she also studied sea safety and rescue methods, even flying to Canberra to meet members of the national sea rescue teams who would possibly have to look for her if she encountered major trouble in Australian waters.

On 24 April 1895, Joshua Slocum had set out in his wooden 37-foot (11.3-metre) sloop *Spray* on the first solo circumnavigation of the globe. He left Boston at noon not to return home for a little over three years. Ninety-two years later, likewise at noon, Cottee sailed out of Sydney Heads in a light north-easterly breeze on Sunday 29 November 1987. Hundreds of people were there to see her off. As they faded into the distance, Cottee knew that for many months now her only contact with people would be—weather permitting—through the two-way radio with its attached telex machine, the first small-boat telex installed in Australia.

Four days out, she was knocked flat by a massive wave that destroyed the wind generator that charged her batteries, and from then on she was reliant on charging batteries with her small diesel generator and the limited solar panels whenever the weather allowed. On 9 December, Cottee sighted Stewart Island's South West Cape as she rounded the south of New Zealand; as she did so, dozens of dolphins played around her. It was her first outward-bound marker.

When Christmas Day dawned, Cottee was running with a storm jib before a 60-knot gale with only two hours' sleep, but she managed a small Christmas dinner after baling out the bilges. By New Year's Day, she was out of radio communication with land and her only contact was with the radio operator on board a container ship.

Then in early January, only 1400 nautical miles from Cape Horn, Cottee was knocked flat again by a cross sea—a wave from the side rather than the bow—that cracked the boom. This was serious; if the boom completely snapped, it would take months longer to complete the journey. After temporarily splinting and strapping it, Cottee began cutting up sections of aluminium spinnaker pole during the next few weeks, opening them out and bashing them with a hammer into plates that shaped around the boom and over the crack. Then over a number of days, working during occasional breaks in the weather, Cottee drilled holes in the plates and the boom, tapped threads and then bolted and glued the plates into place.

She approached Cape Horn through squalls of rain under bare poles, sails furled tightly, in a 55-knot wind. She had to tow a sea anchor to slow the boat down in order to round the cape between weather lows. At one point, Cottee looked astern to see the anchor that was being towed on some 80 metres of chain and line bouncing down the face of the wave above and behind the one they were riding. Looking up from her cockpit, she estimated the height of the approaching wave to be 20 metres; she could actually see the colours of the sunlight reflecting through the peak. But then the wind dropped as she rounded the towering black cliffs of the cape on 19 January 1988, and she could celebrate with a meal of bread with crab and mayonnaise, washing it down with some Grange Hermitage. A congratulatory telegram from Prime Minister Bob Hawke was relayed to her over the radio. Then she turned to run north along the east coast of South America to cross the equator and so reach her halfway point; it would be 4000 nautical miles across the Atlantic to her next cape.

On 23 January, fifty-three days since she had last seen a human being, she was met by the Stanley Harbour pilot boat as she passed the Falklands. The three fisheries officers circled her, calling out questions while a photographer clicked away. Then she threw them some mail, and they waved farewell and turned back for the harbour. Cottee was alone again, but definitely not idle. She celebrated her birthday with chocolate cake on 25 January; she was still working on the boom repairs, the auxiliary engine had to be fixed and a constant lookout had to be kept for ice floes and bergs. The wind would gust between 40 and 70 knots and sails had to be set and reset amid huge seas.

By early February, the weather was hotter and humid, and the sea calmer. Finally able to finish repairing the boom, Cottee could now wash and dry clothes as well as carry out other maintenance.

Completely absorbed in her life on the sea now, Cottee felt the rest of the world fading away. She crossed the equator on 25 February, and two days later rounded her halfway marker, the Sao Pedro and Sao Paulo Rocks, amid an audience of dolphins and whales. Now it was south to the Cape of Good Hope.

A month later she was back in the Southern Ocean, beating up to the cape with the wind gusting up to 50 knots and waves of 12 metres. By the beginning of April the weather was deteriorating, and she was moving south of the cape to try to avoid the worst of it. The boat had already fallen off three huge waves during one afternoon when suddenly, as she was sitting below deck at around seven at night, she felt the bow rising vertically as a massive freak wave lifted it into the air. As the boat's arc flattened out, she knew the whole boat was completely out of the water and free-falling through the air towards the trough. She leaped to her feet, braced her hands against the roof and wedged her feet either side of the saloon bunks as the *First Lady* crashed into the trough. Amazingly, Cottee and the boat both survived to round the Cape of Good Hope, passing 360 nautical miles to the south on 4 April.

A week later, still sailing in the same atrocious weather conditions, they were knocked completely flat to starboard during the night by another rogue sea. With the mast under water, for several minutes Cottee stood on a bulkhead until the *First Lady* righted herself. She grabbed a bucket and began bailing, but before the water was down more than a few centimetres the *First Lady* was knocked flat again to the port side. Cottee landed on her back with her feet in the air among the entire contents of the cabin. Once more, the *First Lady* struggled upright, but by the time Cottee disentangled herself and climbed on deck, the boat was travelling through a 75-knot gale and 18-metre waves at over 20 knots. Desperately trying to slow the boat, Cottee looked up only to see a huge ship bearing down on her. She turned on all her lights, trained the spotlight on her mast and lit a white flare; finally the ship saw her in time and lumbered by with only 300 metres between them. The next minute, the *First Lady* was knocked flat again and Cottee was in the water, secured only by her harness lines, until the boat righted and she was washed back on board by another wave. Exhausted, bruised from head to foot and shaking badly, she fell into her bunk in her wet clothes for a rest before going back on deck to try to slow the boat down.

Thankfully, the sailing was never that rough again. On 8 May, she passed 400 nautical miles south of Cape Leeuwin, only 2300 miles from Sydney. Civilisation arrived in the shape of an RAAF Orion, which flew in low over her. Cottee began reading *Why Do I Think I'm Nothing Without a Man?* On 25 May, she rounded the fifth and final cape in the Southern Ocean: South East Cape, the southern tip of Tasmania.

Kay Cottee and *Blackmores First Lady* crossed the finish line in Watsons Bay, Sydney, at 1232 hours on 5 June 1988, to an incredible reception from an estimated 100000 people on shore and hundreds of water craft. Hazel Hawke, the prime minister's wife, officially welcomed Cottee home and Sir Eric Neil, Commissioner of the City of Sydney, presented her with the key to the city. Three days later, she and the *First Lady* were given a parade through the main streets of Sydney. On 26 January 1989, Cottee was named the Bicentennial Australian of the Year. She later received, among many other honours, the Officer of the Order of Australia award, the Inaugural Spirit of Australia Award and the Advance Australia Award.

Cottee and her husband, Peter Sutton, now own Yamba Marina on the Clarence River in northern New South Wales. They have built a home further up the river where Cottee can work on her paintings of seascapes and marine and life-study sculptures. She is currently restoring an old yacht to go cruising with family and friends when her son finishes school.

'I was brought up believing there is no such thing as a man's world or a woman's world,' she once said. 'It's everyone's world.'

★

The rest of the world

The first recorded circumnavigation of the globe was completed in 1522 by the few surviving members of Ferdinand Magellan's expedition in search of the Spice Islands.

Joshua Slocum's 1895 voyage, including his encounter with the ghost of the pilot of Columbus's *Pinta*, is told in his fascinating book *Sailing Alone Around the World*. Sailing westbound via the Strait of Magellan, he achieved what was then a momentous and unheard-of undertaking.

It would be nearly fifty years before Argentinian Vito Dumas repeated that feat in 1943, travelling eastbound via Cape Horn and stopping only once. The first non-stop circumnavigation was completed by Sir Robin Knox-Johnston from the UK in 1969 in *Suhaili*, also travelling eastbound.

In 1981–82, Western Australian sailor Jon Sanders was the first person to circumnavigate Antarctica (and thus the globe), passing south of capes Horn, Good Hope and Leeuwin—and he did it not once but twice, becoming in the process the first single-handed (solo) sailor to remain continuously at sea twice around the world and for that distance. In 1986–87, he went one better by completing a triple non-stop solo circumnavigation to establish a new non-stop solo voyage record of 71 023 nautical miles, taking 658 days, twenty-one hours and fifteen minutes. This is still the longest trek in human history—on land or sea.

Krystyna Chojnowska-Liskiewicz from Poland was the first woman to sail single-handed around the world, though not non-stop. Leaving the Canary Islands on 28 February 1976, she returned there on 21 April 1978, sailing westbound via the Panama Canal (thus not technically a completely ocean sail) in the 31-foot sloop *Mazurek*. Almost at the same time, New Zealand-born Dame Naomi James, who had never skippered a yacht and had only about six weeks' sailing experience, was completing her eastbound circumnavigation south of the three great capes in her 53-foot yacht *Express Crusader*. Leaving the English port of Dartmouth in September 1977, James was forced to dock the *Crusader* in Cape Town and again at the Falkland Islands for repairs and so, although she was the first woman to sail the route via Cape Horn, she did not do it non-stop or unassisted. Ten years later, Kay Cottee became the first woman to achieve that, sailing the same route.

It would not be until 2006 that Dee Caffari from the United Kingdom achieved a westbound circumnavigation, single-handed and non-stop, in the 22-metre *Aviva*. In 2009, she became the first woman to sail solo non-stop around the world in both directions while competing in the Vendee Globe race.

However, they were all really following in the wake of Australian Anne Gash, who in 1975 at the age of 52 was the first woman to attempt a solo circumnavigation by sea until her 26-foot yacht *Ilimo* was extensively damaged in a collision off the coast of Ghana and had to be shipped to England. She finally returned to Australia in 1977.

On 28 October 2005, Adrian Flanagan from the United King-dom set sail aboard his 38-foot (11.5-metre) stainless-steel sloop *Barrabas* on a 30-year dream to complete perhaps the last great circumnavigation: a 'vertical' voyage westward via Cape Horn (against prevailing winds and currents) and the Russian Arctic. After 405 days of sailing and 31 000 nautical miles, with stops in Honolulu and Nome, Alaska, where the boat was slipped for the winter, and then having to be transported by ship around the ice-locked northern coast of Russia to Murmansk, Flanagan arrived back at the Royal Southern Yacht Club in England on 21 May 2006.

Since then, circumnavigation attempts seem to have just become a matter of speed and age. Oh, and the colour of the yacht.

Blackmores First Lady is now permanently housed within the Australian National Maritime Museum in Sydney and displayed as she would have looked between 25 January and 4 February 1988, just after Cottee had rounded Cape Horn and was celebrating her birthday.

PART III
LIFESTYLE

'ONE SOWETH; ANOTHER REAPETH'

James Harrison and refrigeration

Firsts

- Inventor of the first practical refrigeration and ice-making machine to produce ice in commercial quantities
- Inventor of the first commercial-quantity ice-making machines to be sold to industry
- First to attempt to ship frozen meat between Australia and England

It was late one night and editor James Harrison was working alone in his newspaper office, but he wasn't writing some news-breaking story, although that's what he'd have preferred to be doing. The problem with being the owner of a small newspaper was that you usually had to do all the different jobs yourself and this was the night someone, and that meant Harrison, had to clean the ink from the movable lead type with a solution of sulphuric ether. As he worked away, he couldn't help but notice that as the ether evaporated from the surface of the type, it left the metal extremely cold. That started him thinking about one of the great Australian problems: keeping things cool.

Keeping unpreserved food from spoiling in the Australian heat was a big issue in those un-refrigerated days, and consequently transport of fresh foodstuffs, dairy goods and meat was limited. With no artificial coolant available, there was a booming industry in cutting ice from lakes and rivers during winter in northern Europe and the United States and storing it to sell in summer when it could be used to cool food. However, there was no such industry in ice-free Australia. With no successful method available of making ice in commercial quantities, it was imported from America one shipload at a time, predominantly from Boston, and it was thus in limited supply and expensive. There was a fortune to be made for the first person who could discover a viable way of creating large amounts of ice to cool food, especially meat, in such a way that it would be preserved for both domestic use and for export. To be shipped overseas successfully, meat would need to be kept refrigerated for a potential three-month sailing voyage and then readily thawed, cooked and eaten at its destination.

James Harrison's first career choice had not been that of an engineer or even a chemist. Scottish born, the son of a salmon fisherman, Harrison was apprenticed at twelve to a printer in Glasgow and was able to take advantage of an education scheme of the time whereby the sons of artisans and traders could take night classes at Anderson's University. Here he was first introduced to chemistry and mathematics, and he continued that study at the Glasgow Mechanics' Institution. But after he completed his apprenticeship he remained working in the printing industry, moving to London when he was nineteen to work in a responsible position for Valpy's, a leading publisher of classical works, by which time he knew Greek and Latin, as well as Gaelic. Then in 1837, when he was 21, he sailed for Sydney on behalf of London booksellers and publishers Tegg & Co., which needed an experienced compositor to escort printing equipment to Sydney and set up a printing and publishing branch office there for them. Once organised, Harrison began printing the *Literary News*. He later had other printing jobs in Sydney, then in 1839 he moved to Melbourne.

Arriving in Melbourne only five years after the settlement was pioneered, Harrison quickly joined the staff of John Pascoe Fawkner's *Port Phillip Patriot* as compositor and later editor. The following year Fawkner acquired a new printing press, so the enterprising Harrison bought the old one from him and moved across the bay to the other major town in Victoria at that time, Geelong, where he started the weekly *Geelong Advertiser*. He quickly emerged as a powerful and talented journalist and popular publisher in his own right, a humanitarian with high standards and without prejudice. Soon the *Advertiser* became a daily. Inevitably, Harrison was drawn into local politics; he became a member of Geelong's first town council and then an early advocate of squatters' rights and tariff protection. He was elected to the Legislative Council in 1854 and represented the area in the Legislative Assembly from 1859 to 1860.

However, it is Harrison's interest in ice-making and refrigeration, rather than in newspapers or politics, for which he is remembered. Living and working in a major port, Harrison was well aware of the urgent need for ice to be produced artificially in commercial quantities for domestic use, and also of the potential for a meat export industry if some means could be found of freezing the meat so that it could be preserved for the long sea voyage. Widely read, with some education in chemistry, Harrison followed scientific progress towards both those goals. He would also have known that the first person to achieve them would become rich and famous.

Harrison started his refrigeration experiments with fish, rather than meat. Around 1851 he was a partner in a fishing boat venture with John Scott, a blacksmith, and they needed to keep their fish fresh. Remembering fellow Scotsman Dr William Cullen's eighteenth-century experiments that demonstrated the use of ether vapour for cooling and his own experience of the cooling effects of ether when cleaning printing type, between 1852 and 1854 Harrison began artificial-ice-making experiments using ether vapour in a shed at Rocky Point. In November 1855, he submitted a patent application for his 'Refrigerating Machine', which was granted on 1 February 1856, by which time he was busy building a full-scale version of it. Costing over £1000 with a capability to make 3000 kilograms of ice a day, it was the first successful machine of its type in the world. It used either ether or alcohol from which a refrigerant gas was compressed and then passed through a condenser, where it cooled and liquefied. That liquid then circulated through refrigeration coils and was vaporised again, cooling the surrounding system as it did so.

But Harrison's machine required higher standards of gasket and valve machining than could be found in the young colony at the time, and he quickly realised he'd need access to better engineering and manufacturing capability. He applied for and was granted British patents for his refrigeration process of 'producing cold by the evaporation of volatile liquids' in 1856, and later that year he and his family sailed to England where Harrison settled in London to resume his work. His wife, Susan, and their children then sailed for home on the *Prince of the Seas*, but sadly Susan died on board ship only a few days out from Melbourne in November. Harrison would not have heard the news until the following year.

In London, he approached the leading engineering firm of Siebe and Company, which built a small prototype machine that was on display in Bloomsbury by April 1857. Later that year he sold his first full-scale 8-horsepower refrigeration machine to an English brewery. Harrison was granted another patent for his refrigeration apparatus that produced cold 'by the evaporation of cold liquids in vacuo'. In his patent documents, he looked ahead to when small refrigeration machines could be made for domestic use and when refrigerated air could be passed from a machine through pipes in a building to cool it. His patents were so thorough and ahead of their time that they covered nearly every element of a modern refrigerator.

Harrison then built and shipped a larger machine back to Victoria in 1858 and by early the next year his Geelong plant was in full operation, producing 3 tonnes of ice a day, more than Geelong would need for some time. That same year Harrison established the Victoria Ice Works in Franklin Street, Melbourne, from where he produced 10 tonnes a day. Harrison refrigeration machines continued to be built and sold by Siebe for many years, and within the next decade they were being sold around the world for use in breweries, distilleries and hotels.

In 1861, he joined with Peter Nicol Russell to form the Sydney Ice Company, which was soon bought out by rivals Augustus Morris and Eugene Nicolle, who then opened their own ammonia-based refrigeration plant at Darlinghurst in 1863, thus removing Harrison from competition in New South Wales. Three years later, Morris and Nicolle began meeting with engineer, auctioneer and financier Thomas Mort to discuss the feasibility of shipping frozen meat from Australia to England. In 1867, Mort was granted a British patent for Nicolle's system of shipboard refrigeration and unsuccessfully attempted to raise funds to enable 203 tonnes of frozen meat to England. Two years later, Alexander Kirk in Scotland patented his successfully tested invention of a refrigeration machine that used air as a refrigerant. However, in the end neither his nor Nicolle's inventions proved suitable for shipping refrigeration.

Both Mort and Harrison were aware, though, that in 1868 the ship *City of Rio de Janeiro*, equipped with a refrigeration machine built by Frenchman Charles Tellier, had attempted to transport 300 kilograms of beef from London to Montevideo. The machine had broken down en route and the beef had to be eaten on board, but the demand would obviously continue to grow for meat to arrive at its destination in a fresh condition after being transported over long distances. Although methods such as desiccation, smoking, salting, canning, and compacting it into sausages and puddings had been used, none of these methods had addressed the issue of fresh meat transportation satisfactorily.

So Harrison had continued to keep in touch with the latest developments. He and Daniel Siebe, of Siebe & Co., had both been awarded medals for their refrigeration machine at the 1862

International Exhibition in England. They won more medals at the 1873 International Exhibition in Vienna, by which time the machines were standard equipment for field hospitals during British military campaigns in Africa. Harrison must have felt encouraged by such success, for in 1862 he got married again, to 25-year-old Emma Payne. They would have eight children.

Then, after years of development, Harrison had his big public relations break. At the London International Exhibition, held in Melbourne in 1872, diners in the refreshment rooms were astounded to discover they were eating steak that, they were told, had been cut from frozen beef refrigerated on ice by Mr James Harrison for forty days before being thawed and cooked. Everyone agreed that it was as good as any freshly slaughtered beef. Harrison was duly awarded a gold medal for demonstrating that meat kept frozen for over a month could feasibly be thawed immediately prior to eating and be perfectly edible. Harrison claimed that, using his system, 500 tonnes of meat could be deep-frozen on shore and then kept frozen during the three-month voyage to England for a cost of only £75. Rather than deal with the complexities of refrigerating an entire ship's hold with an on-board refrigeration machine, Harrison was attempting an early type of containerised shipping; in his case, frozen meat would be shipped in an insulated container tank packed with ice. Freezing the meat before shipping meant that once it was landed, it would take many hours for the temperature in the meat to rise again. It would thus remain fresh longer than meat that was loaded directly from abattoirs and shipped in coolrooms. It was an innovative idea that could prove lucrative for all concerned, especially exporters, if it worked, so not surprisingly he found a group of pastoralists happy to put up £2500 to finance a test voyage.

After considerable preparation, including test runs of his refrigeration tanks, the clipper ship *Norfolk* cleared customs and sailed for England on the morning of 23 July 1873, with Harrison and some 20 tonnes of frozen meat aboard in two insulated tanks. This was the first frozen meat shipment to leave Australia for England. Three months later, the distressing news reached Melbourne that though the ship had arrived safely, the meat had not. A defect in the construction of the tanks had caused the ice to melt more rapidly than expected; the last of the ice had melted eighteen days from London, and the meat had thawed and had to be thrown overboard. The amount of ice, and thus weight, needed in the tanks to counteract the rate of thaw seems to have been a problem of which Harrison was well aware, and so he had installed a system within the double sides and bottoms of the tanks to circulate a brine solution to retard the ice thaw. It was this circulation system that had failed, not the basic tenet of Harrison's concept. He'd had to outsource the construction of the tanks and apparently the quality control standard had been rather low due to a certain amount of drinking on the job by the workers. No blame was ever attributed to Harrison for the failure of the shipment, but public confidence in refrigerated meat was shaken.

Harrison's confidence, on the other hand, seems to have remained high. Within two months he filed a patent for his refrigerated enclosed chamber system, which was granted the following year. After a while, he resumed his interrupted career in journalism for David Syme as the London weekly *Age* columnist 'Oedipus', solver of riddles, and as the 'Scientific Gossip' columnist for the *Leader* newspaper. He had returned to journalism in 1867 as a sub-editor, feature columnist and parliamentary reporter at Syme's Melbourne *Age* and *Leader*, and from the late 1870s he would write over 1000 'Scientific Gossip' columns alone. In the meantime, his family had crossed the ocean to live with him in London, although his young son developed symptoms of tuberculosis and had to be sent back to Australia. Then, in 1891, Harrison fell ill with a bad case of pleurisy.

Within a year he and his family had returned to a small cottage at Point Henry just above the high-water mark. There he died in September 1893, survived by his wife and a number of their children. His memorial stone was erected by public subscription three years later and bears an inscription that declares Harrison a 'scientific discoverer, journalist and legislator' who 'perfected and was the first to make commercially successful the manufacture of ice by artificial process . . .' The last line reads: 'One soweth; another reapeth.'

★

The rest of the world

The Romans used terracotta pots fanned by slaves in which to cool their food, and no banquet was complete without ice and snow with which guests could cool their wine. Sultans once used camel trains to transport ice from Lebanese mountains to Cairo and, in the early days of the British Empire, Norwegian ice was shipped around the Cape of Good Hope to India.

In 1834, Jacob Perkins in the United States obtained the first patent for a refrigerating machine using ether in a vapour compression cycle. However, the ice cutting, storing and retailing industry already had a firm grip on the cooling concept there, and Perkins found little interest in his idea.

In 1850, Dr John Gorrie, director of the US Marine Hospital in Appalachicola, Florida, patented an air-conditioning system using compressed air that cooled as it drove an engine. He arranged for a large machine to be built in England by James Watt & Co., but it did not in the end prove successful. James Harrison's nearest competitor in ice making was the American Alexander Twining, who in 1853 patented his ether compressed-vapour machine, but he was able to produce only small non-commercial amounts of ice.

Frozen beef was successfully shipped by T.C. Eastman in 1875 from the United States to England in a short voyage across the cold North Atlantic using chemical freezing mixtures to maintain the temperature. After their 1868 attempt, the French tried again in 1876 using Tellier ammonia compression refrigeration equipment with which to ship meat from France to Buenos Aires and from there back to England. While some meat survived the experiment, it was barely edible. The following year, Englishman Joseph Coleman of the Bell-Coleman Mechanical Refrigeration Company successfully landed refrigerated meat in Britain from America, and a Marseilles-based shipping company successfully brought frozen meat from that port to Argentina and returned with another shipment to Le Havre. This was the first successful shipment of frozen meat across the equator. It would not be until 1879 that the SS *Strathleven*, chartered by McIlwraith, McEacharn & Co. and equipped with Bell-Coleman refrigeration equipment, successfully transported a frozen cargo of meat between Australia and England, where it arrived on 2 February 1880. Harrison had certainly been the pathfinder for that voyage.

Harrison's name has not been entirely forgotten. The James Harrison Bridge, completed in 1990, carries the Princes Highway over the Barwon River, and since 1972 the most distinguished award of the Australian Institute of Refrigeration, Airconditioning and Heating has been the James Harrison Medal. From 1864 to 2002, a model of Harrison's first industrial refrigerator was on display in the Smithsonian in the United States. When it was retired, Harrison's great-grandson Jim contacted Museum Victoria, which brought it to Australia, and it is now in the Scienceworks Museum in Melbourne pending its placement in a planned James Harrison Museum on a bank of the Barwon River at Geelong. In 2008, a James Harrison Centre was proposed for a site at Rocky Point that would contain the Smithsonian model, a Linde ammonia compressor and a Harrison steam engine, but to this day the James Harrison Museum Committee has not been able to inspire the city of Geelong to fund its construction.

AUSTRALIA'S EDISON

Henry Sutton

Firsts

- Inventor of the telephane, a forerunner of television
- First person to install a business telephone system
- First Australian to design and build the electric light bulb
- First Australian to experiment with flight

In June 1910, during a world tour Dr and Mrs Alexander Graham Bell and their friends W.F. Baldwin, a Canadian aviator, and his wife visited Australia for the first time. Although Bell was shocked by the poor standard of sanitary conditions in Brisbane, he was looking forward with great anticipation to a more pleasant encounter with the renowned Australian inventor Henry Sutton, who had done more with Bell's telephone invention than even Bell thought possible. When they did meet, he was nothing short of astonished by the achievements of a man who had largely been content to take little credit for his pioneering work across a wide range of fields.

Born in 1856 into a Ballarat family whose members became known in Australian history for their contribution to music publishing and retailing, Henry Sutton and his three brothers, Alfred, Walter and

Frederick, and two sisters, Elizabeth and Emilie, were home-schooled by their mother, Mary, and helped in the family business. Richard and Mary Sutton had been lured to Australia three years before Henry's birth by the stories of rich gold discoveries in Victoria, but finding gold had proved harder in reality than in the stories. A trained musician, Richard eventually set up a small music shop in Ballarat, importing sheet music and instruments.

Shy and more interested in science and engineering than music, Henry was a child prodigy who, after the age of eleven, educated himself. The legend persists that by the time he was fourteen, he had read every book on science in the local Ballarat Mechanics' Institute Library, where Henry kept in touch with the latest technical developments and inventions. When the institute opened a School of Design in 1870, Henry enrolled and won prizes for his design drawings, some of which were for an electric motor that could be used as a dynamo.

That same year, Sutton started work on models of an ornithopter, an early prototype heavier-than-air flying machine. Employing a principle studied by Leonardo da Vinci, it had wings that flapped like a bird rather than propellers. Powered by a wind-up clockwork mechanism, Sutton's model ornithopter could fly in a radius of 15 metres from left to right and upwards at any desired angle. It's quite possible that Sutton's model was the first of its kind, but Gustave Trouve also built one that year in France and, watched by members of the French Academy of Sciences, demonstrated that his could fly some 70 metres. This pattern was typical for much of Sutton's inventions; no one in Europe or America knew of his work taking place on the other side of the world and other people were frequently given credit for what he had already demonstrated. For example, Sutton worked for some years on incandescent globes, apparently without any idea that Edison was also working on a similar idea in the United States where he recorded his patent on 21 December 1879; Sutton wrote to R.L.J. Ellery, the Victorian Government Astronomer, about his successful experiments on 6 January 1880.

In any case, Sutton also believed at this time that scientific knowledge should be for everyone, so he often refused to patent inventions even when he had the opportunity. After years of work, his paper on flight containing designs for his ornithopter was published in the Aeronautical Society of Great Britain's *Annual Report* in 1878.

Two years earlier, Alexander Graham Bell had been granted the patent for his telephone invention. Fascinated by the possibilities of this new communication device, Sutton designed and built over twenty different types of telephone within twelve months, sixteen of which were eventually patented by others. Sutton wired up his family's music store, Sutton's, and warehouse for telephone lines; the first Melbourne telephone exchange wasn't installed until 1880. Invited to lecture in Applied Electricity and Magnetism at the School of Mines in Ballarat (now University of Ballarat) in April 1883, he also installed another telephone system there. The School of Mines is Australia's oldest technical institution and Sutton's appointment was the first in that particular field in the country. Such was his fame, even then, that he was offered responsibility for a senior class, and he continued lecturing there for four years, developing a number of ideas into inventions while he did so.

In 1881, in a paper to the Royal Society in London, Sutton described his invention of a superior electrical storage battery that offered the advantage of a controlled discharge. Known as the copper-lead type, it had a negative electrode of copper and a positive electrode of lead amalgamated with mercury in a solution of copper sulphate. Once again, Sutton didn't claim a patent but the Royal Society acknowledged his invention, which attracted a lot of international interest. Joseph Swan, who had worked with Edison on the development of carbon filaments for electric light bulbs, declared that Sutton's invention was invaluable.

Perhaps Sutton and Swan communicated, for at the end of 1881 Sutton revealed his invention of a mercurial vacuum pump that could reliably produce a greater level of vacuum than had been previously possible, something that was desperately needed by the burgeoning light-bulb industry. For the early filaments to have a useful life expectancy, all the air had to be removed from globes during their manufacture and the Sutton pump was widely put to work in this new industry, particularly at the newly formed Swan Edison Company in England.

Meanwhile, the family's music business was expanding. Sutton's father, Richard, had died unexpectedly in 1876 and so his mother had taken over management while the children all became involved in marketing and sales. In 1884, they opened a branch in Melbourne, in 1891 a new emporium on Sturt Street in Ballarat large enough to display a wide variety of music and instruments, and in 1892 another large store in Bendigo. When his mother died in 1894, Sutton moved to Melbourne to take over the large Sutton's Music House on Bourke Street. As one would suspect from his seemingly endless series of ideas, Sutton apparently didn't need a lot of sleep, frequently working into the early hours of the morning or indeed being surprised that morning had arrived so soon. Even so, he also somehow found the time to be a family man. He married Elizabeth Ellen Wyatt in Ballarat in 1881 and they had three sons. Later, after Elizabeth's death, he married Annie May Patti in Melbourne in 1902 and they had two sons.

Sutton had been interested in the concept of transmitting pictures through telegraph wires from about the age of fourteen, but it wasn't until 1885 that he formalised on paper his idea for what he called a 'telephane', an early mechanical prototype of television. Sutton's grand dream was that any big event in Melbourne, in particular the Melbourne Cup, could be seen in Ballarat through the lens of his invention, but his dream was limited by the period's technology. A telegraph line could not, of course, handle anywhere near the large packages of data needed for sharp and accurate picture transmission. Sutton's picture would have been very small and of poor quality, and it would only have been seen by one person at a time through the eyepiece, but it was way ahead of anything anyone had yet conceived of in that field.

Sutton eventually built at least one working model of the telephane; in 1887, R.L.J. Ellery, the Victorian Government Astronomer, wrote that he had seen a demonstration of it. In 1890, Sutton published an account of his telephane in the *Telegraphic Journal and Electrical Register*, later republished in *Scientific American* in 1905. He took a version of it to England while he was on a world tour during the early 1890s to meet other scientists and inventors, including Nikola Tesla, demonstrating it to the Royal Society in London and then took it across the Channel to introduce his invention to French scientists. Once again, however, Sutton never patented this pioneering work, believing it should remain accessible by the scientific community. The Scottish inventor John Logie Baird probably read those articles, for many years later he used Sutton's principles of synchronisation of transmission and reception in his own work on television.

An excellent photographer himself, Sutton continued to be intrigued with methods of photograph transmission and printing for a number of years. In 1887, he patented improvements in photo-lithography methods, and on 30 May of the following year he demonstrated before a group of engravers and printers in Ballarat his newly patented 'Sutton-type instantaneous photo-engraving process', by which a negative could be converted into an engraving plate by a heating process and be ready for the electrotyper in three to seven minutes.

Having come up with a method to make better photographic plates, in 1890 he invented a telegraph facsimile machine to transmit the plates. It didn't print out images on paper, though; it actually produced a duplicate plate ready to be used for printing at the other end. By 1890, the problem of printing photographs in a newspaper or book had essentially been solved and even today much the same method is employed. Using a special grating or screen, a photograph is broken up so that the half-tones or greys appear in the final photographic print as a series of regular black dots that are larger in dark areas and smaller in lighter areas. From a distance, the differing sizes of dots all seem to blend together into varying shades of grey. To print such a photograph with the letterpress method, the black dots would be represented by raised points of metal to which the ink would stick while white areas were cut beneath the surface of the printing plate so that they were not coated by ink. But it took time to cut the metal plate. Sutton's faster system meant that newspapers could quickly receive and print photos of topical interest from all over the world, and it gave an impetus to the search for ways to send photographs rapidly across large distances.

However, Sutton didn't always get it right. According to one of his letters to the editor of the Melbourne *Argus* in October 1893, Sutton couldn't see how cameras could be used to photograph the finish of a horse race at the track. He foresaw difficulties with light refraction, angle of view and automatic triggering mechanisms, although not with shutter speeds; he stated that he'd already seen cameras in use with speeds greater than one-thousandth of a second.

Sutton was attracted to automobiles before they even began appearing in Australia in the 1890s, and he was one of the earliest advocates of electric power for them. In practical terms, however, he was limited by the available technology, which would have involved the vehicle carrying a heavy weight of batteries. Nevertheless, he did talk up electricity as convenient power for trams and trains on routes along which a permanent power supply could be delivered. In 1897, Sutton became interested in developing air-cooled combustion engines that could run on low-grade fuel. He took out a number of patents relating to bicycles and motorised tricycles, testing one of the tricycles between Melbourne and Ballarat in September, and by the following year he had amassed around thirty patents in all. Obviously, by then Sutton had grown tired of people profiting from his earlier concept of a free ideas exchange. In 1898, he designed and built one of Australia's first cars, known as the Sutton Autocar, one of the earliest front-wheel-drive vehicles. Two prototypes were built, but local production costs proved too high for mass manufacture. At a meeting of fifty-two pioneer motor owners from around Melbourne on 9 December 1903, Sutton moved a motion that a club be formed for which he'd already written a set of objectives. Thus the Automobile Club of Victoria came into formal existence, continuing today as the Royal Automobile Club of Victoria.

From 1908 until his death in 1912, Sutton was involved with the Commonwealth Naval Forces in the development of a wireless telegraphy system known as the 'Sutton System of Australian Wireless' with a view to using his system for the Royal Australian Navy which would be established in 1911. It was considered so advanced for its time that the Ministry of Defence and the Postmaster-General's Department all agreed to delay deciding on a national wireless telegraphy system, as compared to the established system that used wires, until Sutton's had been officially tested. During the extraordinarily popular visit of the American Great White Fleet to Sydney, from 20 to 27 August 1908, Henry successfully demonstrated the range of his patented long-distance receiver for wireless telegraph messages, known then as ethergrams, receiving clear messages from at least one battleship, the fleet flagship USS *Connecticut*, while it was still some distance off the Australian coast in the Pacific Ocean. This hugely impressed the Americans.

He went on to build the first portable radio with a range of over 500 yards (450 metres). In 1909, Sutton held one of only two government-authorised experimental radio licences in Australia for an apparatus capable of a 250-mile (400-kilometre) range, the greatest range of any apparatus since licensing issue had begun in 1905 and until the first commercial station was set up in 1910. In 1911, Sutton still held Experimental Licence No. 2 for his own radio telegraphy transmitting and receiving station at his house at 9 Erskine Street in Armadale, Melbourne, where he had also built a transmission tower. It was from there in August that, during recorded testing of his new receiver, messages were picked up from the ship *Suevic* which was still over 2000 nautical miles out to sea, an unheard-of distance for signal reception at that time. In fact, Sutton could regularly receive ship-to-ship messages when the ships themselves couldn't receive messages from each other.

Nora Heysen (VFX94085), Official War Artist, photographed by George Harvey Nicholson behind the barbed wire perimeter of the Nurses' Compound, 106th Casualty Clearing Station, Finschhafen, New Guinea, 19 June 1944. AWM 073884

An early postcard depicting Pat Sullivan and his creation, Felix the Cat.

The landmark Felix sign above the Chevrolet dealership building in Los Angeles. Courtesy of Jim Childs

Peter Finch and David McCallum with a pair of national symbols while filming *Robbery Under Arms* in Australia in 1957.

Portrait of Bennelong by Samuel John Neele (1758–1824), published in 1804.
NLA 9353133

Mountain climber Freda Du Faur seated between Alexander and Peter Graham near the Hermitage. Courtesy of Alexander Turnbull Library, New Zealand F–1296-1/2-MNZ

A recent photo of the restored Wilkins family homestead. Courtesy of Regional Council of Goyder, South Australia

—and he named it
"LOCKHEED MOUNTAIN"

It stands at the bottom of the world, majestic and perennially snow-covered . . . Captain Sir George Hubert Wilkins was the first man ever to sight this Antarctic peak and he named it "Lockheed Mountain"—in honor of the ship from which he discovered it.

Captain Wilkins chose a Lockheed for his polar expeditions by air because he knew "it was the finest ship available." He flew it over the top of the world on a 2,200-mile non-stop flight from Point Barrow, Alaska, to Spitzbergen. Later he took it, as one of two Lockheeds, to the Antarctic.

Captain Wilkins' Lockheeds were flown on wheels, skis and pontoons — in temperatures which ranged from 110 degrees above zero to 54 degrees below! And today Captain Wilkins' original Lockheed, the second ever built, is still in active service!

The record of Captain Wilkins' ship conclusively proves the stamina, safety—and the speed— that are built into every Lockheed.

DETROIT AIRCRAFT
LOCKHEED
VEGA

DETROIT AIRCRAFT
FORT AND CAMPAU STREETS, DETROIT

IANIN BLDG., NEW YORK ROOSEVELT BLDG., LOS ANGELES

'CKHEED AIRCRAFT CORPORATION
ETMAN AIRCRAFT CORPORATION
AM AIRCRAFT CORPORATION
RCRAFT PARTS COMPANY, INCORPORATED
RKS AIR COLLEGE, INCORPORATED
-RKC AIRCRAFT CORPORATION

BLACKBURN AIRCRAFT CORPORATION
AIRCRAFT DEVELOPMENT CORPORATION
MARINE AIRCRAFT CORPORATION
GROSSE ILE AIRPORT, INCORPORATED
GLIDERS, INCORPORATED
DETROIT AIRCRAFT EXPORT CORPORATION

Lockheed aeroplane advertisement featuring Hubert Wilkins.

John Hoelscher (left) and Lonnie Dupre (right) at Kaffeklubben Island, North Greenland, the northern-most land in the world, in 2000. Courtesy of Lonnie Dupre

Map of Greenland showing the various expeditions made by John Hoelscher and Lonnie Dupre while completing their circumnavigation. Courtesy of John Hoelscher

Henry Sutton in 1906 with his portable wireless receiving station. Courtesy of Lorayne Branch

The Sutton Ballarat car in 2006—built by Sutton in 1900 in Ballarat and currently in storage in Tasmania. Courtesy of Chris Clemons

Portrait of Tullie Wollaston. Courtesy of Rosemary Madigan

Tullie and his wife, Emma Sarah Wollaston. Courtesy of Rosemary Madigan

Tullie Wollaston photographed with his eldest child, Wynnis, born in 1888. Courtesy of Rosemary Madigan

A 1944 oil painting of Vida Goldstein by Phyl Waterhouse (1917–89). NLA 2292721

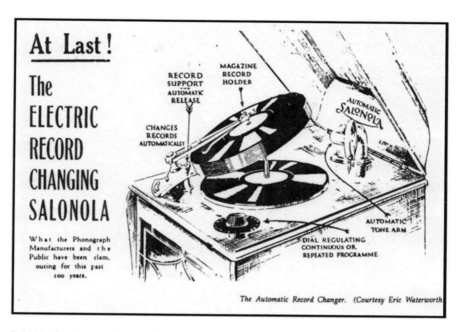

A 1927 advertisement for the Salonola player. Courtesy of Lindsay McCarthy, Sound Preservation Association

Portrait of Dr Mark C. Lidwill. Courtesy of History of Medicine Library, Royal Australasian College of Physicians

Tom Angove surrounded by the wine that he loved, 2002. Courtesy of John Angove, Angove Family Winemakers

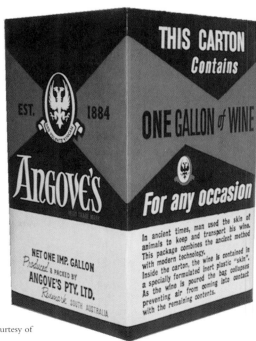

The original Angove wine cask. Courtesy of John Angove, Angove Family Winemakers

Sutton's research into wide-range reception of wireless telegraphy continued into 1912 at his private station. Visitors were able to hear radio conversations between HMS *Encounter* at anchor off Hobart and HMS *Cambrian* en route between Sydney and Hong Kong, messages from the *Orsova* some 800 nautical miles away off the east coast or radio traffic from the station on top of the Hotel Australia in Sydney. Of course, they weren't listening to voices but to the fast dots and dashes of professional Morse code telegraphers. At the time of his death in that same year, Sutton was said to be working on secret communication devices for the Australian government, and his experiments had attracted attention from the British, French, American and Japanese governments. No doubt because of that, Henry's wireless systems were eventually deemed so valuable to Australia's national security that they disappeared into that hidden realm of classified defence information; their eventual fate, at this point in time, still has not been revealed.

Sutton was a member of a string of prestigious scientific bodies, including the Institution of Electrical Engineers in England and the Royal Society of Victoria. Although he dedicated his life to improving Australian science and technology, he worked out on the edge geographically and scientifically. His pioneering inventions were developed in a country about which the rest of the world knew little. Apart from his headstone in Melbourne's Brighton General Cemetery, there is no memorial today to Henry Sutton, one of Australia's most significant inventors of the nineteenth century.

★

The rest of the world

The Italian inventor Guglielmo Marconi is often referred to as the father of long-distance-radio transmission and duly shared the 1909 Nobel Prize in Physics in recognition of his contributions to the development of wireless telegraphy. After failing to gain support for his work in Italy, Marconi went to England, where he made the first public transmission of wireless signals on 27 July 1896. He was supported by William Henry Preece, who had developed a wireless telegraphy system in 1892. In March of the following year, Marconi sent the first wireless communication over open sea and in 1899, aboard the liner *St Paul*, he broadcast her arrival while 66 nautical miles off the English coast. In 1902, the first radio transmission crossed the Atlantic.

THE OPAL MAN

Tullie C. Wollaston, the first to take Australian opals to the world

Firsts

- The first person to purchase, market and sell Australian opals internationally as a gem-quality stone
- The discoverer and first cultivator of the claret or raywood ash tree (*Fraxinus oxycarpa*)

Tullie Cornthwaite Wollaston was born Henry Herbert Wollaston on 17 May 1863 at Lake Hamilton Station on the Eyre Peninsula in South Australia, where his father, George, was the manager with his wife, Mary. During the next twelve months, his parents changed their minds about his name and he was christened Tullie Cornthwaite after his grandfather's nephew, the theologian, artist, master of six languages, archaeologist, and botanical collector and cultivator Reverend Tullie Cornthwaite (1807–78).

Tullie Wollaston's grandparents, John and Mary, had migrated from England to Western Australia, where with his five sons John built a church at Port Leschenault where he ministered. He eventually became Archdeacon of Western Australia. His sons, George, Henry and William, moved to South Australia where George became manager of Poonindie Aboriginal Mission. In 1860, he became manager of Lake Hamilton Station near Port Lincoln, where Tullie and his brother Edward spent their childhood.

Tullie had been fascinated by crystals and gemstones ever since childhood, so his later involvement in opals is probably not surprising. As a young man, he gained employment in the government Survey Office in Adelaide where he devoted a lot of his time to mineralogy and arboriculture. By 1885, he evidently felt relatively settled and married Emma Sarah Manthorp. Wollaston built 'Sunningfield' in Glenelg, a large mansion standing within an exotic garden of palms, roses, trees and aviaries. Here he and Emma raised six daughters and three sons. After investing in rubies that were discovered around Mount Pleasant in South Australia in 1887, and in Tasmanian sapphires, Tullie resigned from his government job and was working as a private surveyor when he became involved with opals.

The word 'opal' is variously said to derive from the Sanskrit *upala*, meaning 'precious stone' or the Latin *opalus* or the Greek *opallios*, referring to an alteration or change in colour. The first European opal mining began in about 400 BC in Slovakian open-pit mines in the area of present Dubnik in the Carpathian Mountains and for centuries these stones were what people knew as opals. These milk-white to pale-lavender European opals, though, were quite unlike their more brilliantly hued counterparts in Australia and South America where the Aztecs revered opals and buried their noble dead with carved opal masks and head-pieces.

In 1888, Wollaston learned from fellow surveyor and experienced bushman Herbert Buttfield that opal had been discovered by Joe Bridle at Stoney Creek in the Kyabra Hills area of south-west Queensland, north-west of Quilpie and south of Windorah. At that time, it's doubtful that Wollaston had even seen an Australian opal, but nevertheless Tullie somehow managed to convince a group of people to invest in the possibility that he could sell these new opals overseas as precious gemstones. Obviously with only a sketchy idea of the type of countryside he was about to experience, Wollaston left behind his young wife and six-week-old baby and set out in what would prove to be one of the hottest summers on record to travel overland from Adelaide north-east across South Australia to Queensland.

Wollaston and Buttfield left Adelaide by train on 21 November 1888 in 44-degree Centigrade heat. Two days later, they arrived at Farina, South Australia, where they purchased camels and added a young indigenous man to their party. On 27 November, the party left Lyndhurst in scorching conditions and travelled north-east between waterholes and station homesteads across desolate gibber plains and sandhills, through choking dust storms and over baked claypans littered with the decaying carcasses of dead cattle and sheep. 'The air is tainted for miles,' Wollaston wrote in his journal, 'and the whole country is a roasting gehenna.'

A month later, the camels could no longer be ridden as their feet had become too tender and the men had to walk, travelling at night to avoid the intense heat. Finally, the party reached Cooper's (now Cooper) Creek near the Queensland border. Also known as the Barcoo River, it was where the explorers Robert O'Hara Burke and William John Wills had met their deaths in 1861, near what became the tiny settlement of Innamincka, which is where Wollaston's party arrived to find it was pouring with rain. Now, instead of dust and flies, they had to compete with mud and mosquitoes. If only they'd waited a few months; in April a fortnightly stagecoach mail route was established from Farina to Innamincka.

Crossing the border into Queensland, they arrived at Tanbar a week later and then moved on to Stoney Creek, near Eromanga. There they were given directions to Bridle's camp that involved following the horse tracks of one of his mates who was returning to the camp with supplies. However, unknown to Wollaston and Buttfield, the man in question had spent some time in the pub before attempting to make his way back to the camp and got lost. Consequently, the men wandered in circles through the bush for nearly two days without water before finally staggering into the camp on 10 January 1889, with Buttfield ill and exhausted. They had covered more than 1100 kilometres in seven torrid weeks to find a man in the middle of nowhere.

For two weeks, Wollaston explored the surrounding area, a very different landscape from the flat limestone countryside to which he was accustomed. He prospected, pegged claims and made his first opal purchases from Charlie Whitehead at nearby Breakfast Creek, buying sixty-one pieces for £27 and 10 shillings. He then travelled to Windorah to apply for the mining leases on his claims, nearly dying from drinking bad water along the way. From there he returned to Adelaide by coach and train, only to learn that Buttfield had died from thirst and exhaustion only a kilometre from water while surveying the Breakfast Creek claims.

Within a few days, Wollaston was aboard the SS *Sydney* en route to London with his wife and baby and a bag of rough opals, arriving in July 1889. But gem dealers and jewellers wanted nothing to do with the new Australian opal. For three months he battled their scepticism, along with supply problems and bad management at the Kyabra Hills mines, until he finally found the jewellers Hasluck Brothers in Hatton Garden, who were willing to take a chance on this new gemstone. Before he returned to Australia, they had a cutter working there and had sold the first parcels of cut opals to be sent to America.

Back in Adelaide later that year, Wollaston found those in his syndicate unwilling to speculate with their money. A new manager had closed most of the mines and they were unwilling to reopen them. A dejected Wollaston considered turning to farming, but he had a deep love for his opals and a wish to visit Buttfield's grave. He organised a new syndicate with Adelaide solicitor David Morton Tweedle, and once again departed for the opal fields to buy more stone. There he heard of a new find of sandstone opals by William Johnson near Euronghella and purchased sixty pieces of pure red-grained 'firsts' as large as walnuts for £1000. Wollaston would say later that all the opals he had ever seen up until then paled into insignificance beside this type.

Understandably, they called the mine 'The Little Wonder'. It became an immense producer, employing at its height of operation some fifty men.

Meanwhile, in 1889 three kangaroo hunters had accidentally discovered the opal field at White Cliffs, about 100 kilometres north-west of Wilcannia in north-west New South Wales. The opals were large and of high quality. Eventually the field would also yield opalised fossils and bunches of crystal known as opal pseudomorphs, or 'pineapples'. In 1890, Charlie Turner, one of those who discovered the field, presented some White Cliffs opals to Wollaston, who was quickly on the road, buying up the first parcel of White Cliffs opals for £140 and sailing with it for England as soon as possible.

Once again, he did business with Hasluck Brothers. Within a year they were employing six cutters just for Australian opals and selling the stones as fast as they could produce them. Once they saw how popular opal was becoming, the large wholesale dealers who had once turned Wollaston down now clamoured for rough stones and so, before he sailed back to Australia, Wollaston saw the trade in his country's opal fulfil his predictions for its success.

But with success came competition. By the time Wollaston had returned to White Cliffs, other buyers were as thick on the ground as the miners. Fortunately, one of the miners he met on this trip was the big, quiet, slow-smiling and impressively bearded Edmund Francis Murphy, who became his buying agent and eventually the manager of White Cliffs Opal Miners Ltd. Wollaston subsequently sold White Cliffs opals to European and American buyers in London faster than the cutters and polishers could turn them out. In 1897, the richest pocket of opals found at White Cliffs was discovered only 2 metres below the surface, and in 1901 miners found the 1100-carat Mackenzie's Opal there. According to Australian writer Ion Idriess, between 1891 and 1903 White Cliffs officially produced around £1.5 million worth of opals; no one has any idea of what the worth of unrecorded finds might have been. In 1910, the largest known solid opal ever discovered was found there, known as the White Cliffs Number Two Opal and weighing in at 5½ pounds (2.5 kilograms) and 12 474 carats.

Ten years previously, a type of opal never seen before had been discovered at Nobby Hill, later known as Lightning Ridge, in New South Wales. While the body-ground of the usual opal is pale to milky white, that of this new opal was jet black. Percy Marks, opal miner, dealer, and renowned cutter and jeweller, is credited with coining the name 'black opal' for this new gemstone. Initially these stones were rejected in Sydney by sceptical dealers when miners attempted to sell them and so, led by the experienced Charlie Nettleton, they put together a 3.6-kilogram package of stones and rode to White Cliffs, some 700 kilometres distant, to present them to Murphy. Having never seen black opals before, Murphy had no idea how to value them. He gave Nettleton a down-payment and then waited until 1903 when he could show the stones to Wollaston, who bought them immediately. It took him three years and another period of living in London in 1906 to get more than one dealer to buy them for any more than £1 an ounce, and it wasn't until 1910 that black opals found a steady market in England and America.

One of the miners on the Lightning Ridge field was Ion Idriess, who would become one of the most prolific and entertaining writers of Australian history. In fact, it was because one of his fellow miners nagged him so much that Idriess sent off his first article to the *Sydney Mail*—the start of his career. He would later write of his opal-mining experiences in his book *Lightning Ridge*, in which he recounts his triumph at successfully negotiating a price with Murphy of £72 for a package of stones, the most he and his mates ever made.

Wollaston had briefly been sidetracked by an unsuccessful pearling venture at Broome when white-base seam opal was discovered at Stuart's Range, 750 kilometres north-west of Adelaide, at a place now known as Coober Pedy (or Coberpedy) in South Australia. Again, Wollaston was on hand in early 1915 to buy up the first parcel from this new field from Jim O'Neill for £10 000. By October 1916, he was in the United States successfully selling the Coober Pedy opals, and in 1919 he sold over £50 000 worth of the light opals in Paris.

Despite his undoubted dedication to opals, the slim, dapper, religious and talented Wollaston did have other interests. He wrote several books, including *The Spirit of the Child* (1914), *Our Wattles* (1916) and the semi-autobiographical *Opal: The gem of the Never-Never* (1924), and like his grandfather's nephew was also fascinated by plants. In 1898 he had begun buying land in the Adelaide Hills, where he eventually owned over 120 hectares, and by 1904 this included 11 hectares along Cox's Creek that would eventually become part of the 28 hectares known as Raywood at Bridgewater. Within three years, Wollaston and his family had established a garden there. Containing trees, shrubs, rock-garden plants and terraces of roses and other flowers from all over the world, despite the altitude of over 500 metres, it was already attracting international attention. Wollaston loved children, and their tradition of holding children's picnics was carried on at Raywood to raise money for children's charities. On his many overseas trips, he collected and exchanged seeds with fellow gardeners at various botanic gardens and nurseries, and even went on two seed-collecting voyages to Pitcairn Island.

He was the first to discover and grow the claret ash tree from an odd-coloured seedling he found within a group he bought from a nursery in 1910. When the foliage took on a purple tint in autumn, Wollaston knew he had a new type. At first generally known as the Raywood claret ash, it was officially recognised in 1928 by the Royal Botanical Gardens at Kew with the scientific name *Fraxinus augustifolia* subsp. *oxycarpa Raywood*, often simply known these days as *Fraxinus augustifolia 'Raywood'*. Some time around 1925, Wollaston established the Ray Nursery adjoining Raywood, due to the many requests from visitors for seedlings or cuttings from his garden. Although the nursery closed on that site in 1945, Wollaston's grandson Quentin continued the family tradition with his Raywood Nursery at Cape Jervis, on the Fleurieu Peninsula in South Australia.

After Wollaston's death from cancer in 1931, the family had problems selling a property with an internationally acclaimed garden but with no substantial residence on it. Raywood was eventually bought by Sir Alexander Downer, father of the former foreign minister of that name, who constructed a large Georgian mansion designed by Kenneth Milne there in 1935 on a site that Wollaston originally had designated for a future home, and renamed the property Arbury Park. The Downer family added to and formalised Wollaston's garden, including such features as a lily pond, water meadow and deer park. However, in the early 1960s, the South Australian government decided with typical government insensitivity to drive the Adelaide freeway through the property. After proposing various alternative routes to no avail, a sadly defeated Downer sold Arbury Park to the government in 1964. The freeway was duly slashed through the property 100 metres from the house, cutting a swathe through a magnificent stand of white gums. In 1965, the mansion and 9 hectares, renamed Raywood in honour of Wollaston, became a conference facility for the Education Department. The rest of the property was subdivided and sold.

The Raywood garden and residence were entered on the National Estate Register in 1980. However, when the property was recommended for the State Register, only the mansion house was finally entered in 1989. Now unencumbered by a high-maintenance botanical garden, it was quickly sold to private owners the following year. Fortunately, despite changing hands several times, the two-storey, seven-bedroom house with its fifteen main rooms, guest wing and three-bedroom caretaker's apartment still stands, and is once again known as Arbury Park.

Late in life, Wollaston offered his huge collection of opals and geological specimens to the South Australian government. When a public servant suggested that a bribe would be needed to secure the sale as a complete collection, a furious Wollaston withdrew his offer and made overtures to the federal government instead. He need not have bothered; as it would today, the short-sighted Australian government turned down the kind of offer made only once in a lifetime, and an irreplaceable asset was broken up and sold piecemeal at auction.

★

The rest of the world

When Louis S.B. Leakey found opal artefacts in a cave near Nakuru, Kenya, he was able to date mankind's involvement with opals from as early as 4000 BC. Romans referred to opals as *ceraunium*, meaning thunderstone, harking back to the legend that they fell from heaven with lightning trapped within them during thunderstorms.

In 1889, gem-quality opals were found inside 'thunder eggs' at Peters Butte, Morrow County, Oregon, later known as Opal Butte. A thunder egg is a nodule formed within a rhyolite lava flow. Unlike a geode, which has a hollow centre, a thunder egg has a solid centre composed of agate, jasper or opal, and while usually about the size of a cricket ball, the largest one discovered was over a tonne. The name comes from the legend that when the thunder spirits are angry at each other, they throw these spherical rocks.

In 1890, gem opal within basalt was discovered in the area of what is now known as Gem City, Idaho, although most of the mining was actually carried out in Washington state. In 1911, in north-western Nevada, opal was discovered in the Virgin Valley, Humboldt County, in what became the Rainbow Ridge Opal Mine, the world's first patented precious opal prospect.

SITTING WOMEN

Vida Goldstein, Nellie Martel, Mary Ann Moore-Bentley and Selina Anderson

First

- The first women to stand for election to a national governing body

Australia was the first nation in the world to grant women both the right to vote in a national election and the right to stand for election to its national parliament. Rather ironically, those rights were granted by an all-male governing body, albeit against strong opposition. However, there was then a longer wait in this country between women gaining the right to stand for the national parliament and them actually being elected to it than anywhere else in the world that had granted those rights.

The Commonwealth Franchise Act of 1902 entitled all white Australian citizens over the age of 21, whether male or female, married or single, to vote in federal elections. Unlike in New Zealand, that enfranchisement did not extend to the country's indigenous women and men, who were not given those rights until 1962. The act also granted Australian women and men the right to stand for election to parliament if they were eligible to vote in federal elections. However, except in South Australia and Western Australia, only Australian men were eligible to vote before 1902, and so until the franchise act only men had been eligible to stand for election to state parliaments.

However, it is possible that due to a loophole in the law women may have voted in the Victorian general election of 1864, in which case they would have been the first in the world to do so. This brief chance for equality came about when the Electoral Act of 1863 enfranchised all ratepayers listed on municipal rolls for local elections, unintentionally overlooking the possibility that there could be female ratepayers listed. So some women may actually have cast votes in that 1864 election, but they were not given another chance; the error was quickly amended early in 1865 so that the right to vote once again applied solely to male ratepayers.

Technically, writer, educator, and social and political reformer Catherine Helen Spence (1825–1910) was the first federal female political candidate, although not for parliament. The first woman known to have stood for election in any Australian political contest, Spence ran for election to the National Australasian (Federal) Convention in 1897, which would be responsible for the framing of the new constitution. Only those with enough votes to rank them within the first ten of a field of thirty-three were selected; Spence ranked twenty-second with 7500 votes. Whether she could legally have taken her seat even if she had actually won it would have proved an interesting debate.

As a result of the act's provisions, the 1903 federal election was the first in which women were entitled to stand for the new national parliament. Despite all that had been said by Australian women about enfranchisement, though, only four women were nominated for election: Vida Goldstein in Victoria, and Nellie Martel and Mary Ann Moore-Bentley in New South Wales, who stood for election to the Senate; and Selina Anderson, who alone stood for election to the House of Representatives in the seat of Dalley in New South Wales. None was elected. Only four years later, nineteen women in Finland were successful in their election to the national government after being given the right to vote and stand for election in their Parliament Act of 1906. To make matters worse, not only were the Australians unsuccessful but they lost their contests in areas where there were more women than men on the rolls and where more women than men voted. Nevertheless, these were the first four women in the world to stand for election to a national governing body and they did it in the face of opposition and prejudice from the media and from the general public of both genders. These are their stories.

★

Vida Goldstein not only ran as a Senate candidate in Victoria in 1903 but also ran in 1910 and 1917, and she was a House of Representatives candidate in 1913 and 1914. Born in the Victorian coastal town of Portland in 1869, Vida moved as a child with her family to Melbourne. There her father, who believed that charitable care for the poor and needy should be organised rather than consist of random handouts, became a founding member of the Charity Organisation Society of Melbourne and remained associated with social welfare work throughout his life. Vida's mother was also a social reformer as well as an ardent suffragist and supporter of the temperance movement, so Vida and her three sisters were all encouraged to be economically and intellectually independent women.

In about 1890, Vida helped her mother collect signatures for the Women's Suffrage Petition, and from then on worked tirelessly for social welfare and female enfranchisement causes. She attended Victorian parliamentary sessions, read widely, became an impressive and talented public speaker and, after the death of Annette Bear-Crawford in 1899, became leader of the women's rights movement in Victoria. Vida was not only influential in female suffrage in Australia, but was heard in the United States at the International Woman Suffrage Conference and at the International Council of Women Conference in 1902, after Australia had granted federal suffrage.

Goldstein's bid for the Senate seat in 1903, like those of her fellow women candidates, was the subject of prejudice. After all, that same year saw the Legislative Assembly in her home state of Victoria reject the Women's Suffrage Bill for the seventh time; women would not be granted suffrage there until 1908. Opposed by the *Daily Telegraph* in Sydney and *The Age* and *The Argus* in Melbourne, and by the Labor Party, which published a pamphlet warning electors not to vote for her, Goldstein was also the victim of a nasty smear campaign just prior to the election, which spread rumours that she had alternative views on marriage, supported easy divorce, did not attend church and would not legally be allowed to take her seat if she won it. None of this, of course, was true. Although she didn't win a Senate seat, Goldstein polled well for those times with nearly 15 500 votes, but she ranked only fifteenth out of the eighteen candidates.

Undaunted, she then embarked on a campaign to educate women voters through the Women's Political Association, national lecture tours and in her papers, *The Australian Woman's Sphere* and *Woman Voter*. Often heard to say that she would persist in politics until she became prime minister, she stood unsuccessfully for election four more times, always as an independent, and as a pacifist during World War I, and in the face of a predominantly negative media attitude to independent and politically conscious women. She opposed the White Australia policy and supported conciliation and arbitration and equal pay for women in a workplace where it was not unusual for poor women and young girls to be working a 72-hour week for a third of award wages. She also supported equal property rights for women, and in 1906 she had the satisfaction of seeing her long-advocated Children's Court Act passed, the terms of which she had helped draft. Five years later, she visited England on a speaking tour and drew huge crowds; 10 000 people came to hear her in the Royal Albert Hall alone. In 1919, she represented Australian women at the Women's Peace Conference in Zurich.

Goldstein was a reforming, inspirational and visionary trailblazer. By the time she died in 1949, virtually unnoticed at the age of 80, much of what she had advocated had come to pass. In 1984, when federal election boundaries were changed, the seat of Goldstein was established in Victoria in her honour. Goldstein had finally made it into politics.

★

Well known later in life for her luxuriant auburn hair, her taste in elaborate wide-brimmed feathered and plumed hats, and her many rings and bracelets, Nellie Alma Martel was born Ellen Charleston in Cornwall in 1855 and emigrated to Australia when she was 30. There she married Charles Martel, a Sydney photographer and property developer. Nellie took up elocution as a profession and started a successful school. Her brother, David Morley Charleston, had been associated with the labour movement in England and was elected to the South Australian upper house in 1891. That same year, Nellie was one of the first members of the Womanhood Suffrage League (WSL) of New South Wales and was soon serving on the league's council. However, along with some other women, she became disenchanted with the centralised decision-making process of the WSL and left it to help found and become president of the more working-class New South Wales Women's Progressive Association, formed by the Irish Catholic suffragist sisters Kate and Annie Golding, as well as president of the Women's Liberal and Reform Association of New South Wales.

The passionate and politically committed Martel was the subject of prejudice by women as well as men in her bid for the Senate. It may have been no accident that she was successfully sued for libel by fellow women's rights activist Annie Golding only a few weeks prior to the election. Martel polled slightly over eighteen thousand votes, ranking her eleventh in the New South Wales field of twelve.

The following year, she returned to England with her husband and quickly became a prominent public speaker for women's rights there, sometimes addressing twelve meetings a month. In 1905, she led some 400 women, including Emmeline Pankhurst, the suffragette leader, in protest outside the House of Commons when the Suffrage Bill did not succeed, and she consequently became associated with the founding of Pankhurst's London Committee of the Women's Social and Political Union (WSPU). She later worked for the union as an organiser. Nellie's unflinching gaze and attitude, along with her gift for powerful oratory, could sometimes earn her some equally determined opposition. In 1906, the year she published her pamphlet, *The Women's Vote in Australia*, she was arrested at a large women's protest in the lobby of the House of Commons and sentenced to two months in prison; two years later, she was on a speaking tour through the West Country with Pankhurst when a gang of young men pelted them with lumps of clay and rotten eggs, then punched and beat them. Nevertheless, a month later Nellie was once again giving speeches around the country, including to an audience of 7000 at the Royal Albert Hall. She helped organise, and spoke at, the great Hyde Park rally on 21 June 1908, in which half a million people took part. But by 1909 she was in her early fifties and becoming uncomfortable with the increasing militancy of the WSPU and concerned that a small group of wealthy women had monopolised a controlling influence in it. Perhaps she decided to retire then, for Nellie Martel slipped quietly out of sight until her death aged 85 at home in Notting Hill, London, in 1940.

★

The tall and slender Mrs Henry H. Ling, better known as Mary Ann Moore-Bentley, who also stood for the Senate in 1903, was an early Australian science-fiction writer. Her best-known work was *A Woman of Mars, or Australia's Enfranchised Woman*, the story of a Martian girl named Vesta who is sent to Earth to organise the emancipation of women because Martians, as we all know, regard women's rights as the foundation on which a progressive social state can be founded. Her novel covers some fairly radical ideas about the status of women in society for the time, including issues concerning overpopulation.

Born in 1865 on a small farm near Braidwood in New South Wales, Mary had three years' half-time bush schooling after which she was predominantly home-schooled by her mother as her large family moved several times. They finally settled on the dairy farm 'Coconella', at Durran Durra near Braidwood in New South Wales. After she had established a dressmaking business in Homebush, Sydney, she married postal clerk Henry Ling in 1889, but they separated and then eventually divorced in 1906, hence her return to her family name. Having developed an early interest in books and reading, the independently minded Mary was a compulsive writer of poems, fiction and non-fiction. *A Woman of Mars*, published by Edwards Dunlop in Sydney in 1901, was followed by *Sketched from Life* in 1903.

A woman of forthright opinions and a great believer in Australian democracy, Moore-Bentley joined the Sydney Single Tax League and then the newly formed Women's Social and Political League but failed to gain their support when she stood for the Senate because they didn't agree that the time had arrived for women to be senators. Nevertheless, she ran on a platform of free trade and a sole tax on land values to finance federal revenue, and sold her books at rallies to raise money for her campaign. Unfortunately, in the final count she was well down in the field, polling just over eighteen thousand votes and ranking tenth in the New South Wales field of twelve.

For a few years she continued as a public speaker, advocating the abolition of state parliaments and proposing a state bank. By 1906, she had retired to write in the peace and quiet of a small cottage in Bangor near Menai, Sydney, and in 1917 her *Psychological Interpretation of the Gospel*, which is still in print, was published in America. Her memoir about her rural childhood, *Journey to Durran Durra 1852–1885*, was written around 1935 but not published until 1983, and then only privately. Sadly, she spent the last ten years of her life in a mental facility at Stockton, Newcastle, until her death in 1953.

★

In the election of 16 December 1903, the young and eloquent Selina Sarah Elizabeth Anderson was the first female candidate for the House of Representatives. Born Selina Charters in 1878 near Hill End in New South Wales, she later worked as an artist and photographic retoucher. An active member of the Shop Assistants Union of New South Wales and president of the Pyrmont branch of the Women's Political Labor League, she contested the seat of Dalley in New South Wales as a protectionist candidate after thinking the matter over for some time and being assured of strong support. 'I feel,' she said on announcing her bid, 'I am called upon to do something to better the conditions of womankind.' She declared that if a woman could do a job as well as a man then she should have equal pay. Although Dalley had slightly more female voters than men, Selina came second with 3036 votes against William Henry Wilkes, with 12 814. She later claimed that there had been interference with votes at some polling booths. That wasn't just sour grapes; newspapers around the country commented that possibly thousands of Australians had been disenfranchised in this election because of electoral office bungling.

In June of the following year, Anderson claimed she originally had intended to run for the Senate, but had been forced to contest a lower house seat because she had been aware of rumours about her reputation that had been spread around Hill End by Henry Beech, a local shopkeeper. In a Sydney Supreme Court slander suit for £1000 damages that Anderson brought against Beech, possibly prompted by an over-protective father, she explained that this change came about because she had been widely known in rural Senate electorates to which the rumours may have spread, whereas in the Dalley electorate she was a stranger and so there was a better chance of votes not being influenced by the rumours. Anderson didn't have a chance with her suit. Not only was the matter heard before a Chief Justice (Sir Frederick Darley) who suggested this case that 'had no doubt afforded considerable amusement' should never have gone to court in the first place, but Beech was defended by the New South

Wales Attorney-General James Conley Gannon. The jury took all of ten minutes to decide in his favour.

Nevertheless, Selina plunged right back into politics. She became a member of the organising committee of the Labour Council of New South Wales and helped establish the Cardboard Boxmakers Union, mostly made up of female members. By 1906, she was one of seven women on the state executive of the Australian Labor Party, and as secretary of the Anti-Chinese and Asian League she was involved even then with issues concerning competition between immigrants and Australians for jobs, with sex trafficking of underage Chinese girls and with illegal importation of drugs.

As an organiser for the Sydney Labour Council, Selina became an advocate for the conditions of women working in laundries (literally sweated labour). She attended the 1906 Political Labor League of New South Wales Annual Conference at the Sydney Trades Hall as an official representative of laundry employees, where she also brought to the delegates' attention the awful conditions faced by female workers in hospitals. She was, incidentally, an advocate for female doctors. That same year she announced her intention to run for the House of Representatives again, this time for the seat of East Sydney against the Leader of the Opposition, G.H. Reid, but in the end she did not nominate.

In 1908, she married Christopher Siggins in Wellington, New Zealand, and lived mainly in Dunedin until returning to Australia in 1918, when Selina Siggins and Jeanne Young were the first two women to stand for election to the South Australian parliament. This time she polled only 2 per cent of the vote. Four years later, she was the first woman to be endorsed by the new Country Party for the House of Representatives seat of Calare in New South Wales (and the only one until 1949), but once again she did not fare well. She eventually became a racehorse trainer and owner, living near the Canterbury racecourse in Sydney until her death in 1964.

★

Despite these early attempts to give women a political voice, to Australia's shame the first woman was not actually elected to any Australian parliament until women's and children's rights pioneer Edith Cowan won a seat in the Western Australian Legislative Assembly on 12 March 1921. More than twenty years would pass before Dame Enid Lyons, the widow of former prime minister Joseph Lyons and mother of twelve children, became the first woman to be elected to federal parliament when she won her seat in the House of Representatives on 21 August 1943, despite her own party having endorsed two men to contest the seat against her. Incidentally, the House of Representatives remained so male-oriented that it didn't have female *Hansard* reporters until 1969. In the same election, Dame Dorothy Tangney became the first Australian woman elected to the Senate.

More than forty years would go by before Janine Haines became the first woman in Australia to lead a political party, when in 1986 she was elected leader of the Australian Democrats. The Democrats, more than any other Australian political party, have had a long history of female leaders, including Janet Powell, Cheryl Kernot, Meg Lees, Natasha Stott Despoja and Lyn Allison. Four years later, Dr Carmen Lawrence made history by becoming the first Australian state leader when she became premier of Western Australia. Finally, of course, Australia has joined a number of other countries by having a female prime minister—only fifty years after Sri Lanka (Ceylon) led the way.

Despite these gains, by 2010 Australia ranked only thirty-third on the Inter-Parliamentary Union's international index of Women in National Parliaments, with a 27 per cent female membership of the House of Representatives. This contrasts with countries such as Rwanda (56 per cent female membership of the lower house) and Sweden (45 per cent). As is the case with many women's issues in this country, Australia is no longer the leader in women's emancipation it once claimed to be.

★

The rest of the world

Although in 1893 New Zealand was the first self-governing nation to grant all adult women the right to vote, including both Maori and *pakeha* (white) women, it did not grant women the right to be candidates for national election until 1919, and the first woman was not elected to parliament there until 1933.

Finland, then a part of the Russian Empire with autonomous powers, was actually the next country after Australia to grant universal and equal suffrage, on 1 October 1906, when Finnish women became the first in Europe to be entitled to stand as candidates in general elections. At the first elections for their new unicameral (federal) parliament in March 1907, Finland became the first country in the world to elect women to its national governing body when nineteen elected female MPs took their places in parliament.

In the United States, New Jersey was allowing woman with a property qualification to vote by 1790 but this lasted only until 1807 when a law was passed to exclude them. In 1869, the first territorial legislature of the Wyoming Territory granted women suffrage and in 1890 they were admitted to the Union as the first state that allowed women the vote. In 1896, Welsh-born Mormon doctor Martha Hughes Cannon, a Utah Democrat and fourth wife of a prominent Salt Lake City official, became the first woman elected as a state senator in the United States, but it was not until 1916 that Jeannette Pickering Rankin, a Republican pacifist from Montana, was the first woman to be elected to the US Congress. Nevertheless, American women had to wait another four years to be granted suffrage at a federal level when Congress ratified the Nineteenth Amendment in 1920.

Louise McKinney was the first woman elected in the British Empire when she won a seat in the Alberta legislature in Canada in 1917, and Mary Ellen Smith was the first woman Cabinet minister in the

British Empire, in British Columbia in 1921. Agnes MacPhail was the first woman to be elected to the Canadian national government when she won a seat in the House of Commons on 6 December 1921, after women won the right to vote in federal elections in 1918 and to sit federally in 1921.

The first woman elected to parliament in the United Kingdom was Countess Constance Markiewicz, who stood as an Irish MP for the Sinn Fein Party in the House of Commons in 1918 while still in Holloway Prison for her part in the Easter Rising of 1916. Having won the seat, in line with Sinn Fein policy, the Countess chose not to take it.

The first British woman to actually sit as a member of parliament in the House of Commons was the very beautiful, very rich, non-suffragette, American-born Viscountess Nancy Witcher Langhorne Astor, the wife of Viscount Waldorf Astor. For many years, Waldorf Astor had enjoyed a promising career in the House of Commons, but when he succeeded to his father's peerage he automatically became a member of the House of Lords, vacating his seat of Plymouth Sutton. Lady Astor contested it and was elected in 1919, mostly on the basis of her charitable work during World War I, the women's vote and her bottomless campaign fund. Remarkably, despite her often controversial remarks and political views that were anti-communist, anti-Semitic, anti-Catholic and pro-appeasement with Germany prior to World War II, Astor's political career endured until her reluctant retirement in 1945. Her political durability was no doubt due, at least in part, to a reputation for cruelty and callousness combined with a biting wit. 'I married beneath me,' she once quipped, 'all women do.' However, she met her verbal equal in Winston Churchill, to whom she once remarked: 'If you were my husband, I'd poison your tea.' Winston volleyed back: 'Madam, if you were my wife I would drink it.' Perhaps she is best summed up by her reply to those who complained about her attitude: 'I'm a Virginian. We shoot to kill.'

GO TO WORK AND DO IT

Eric Waterworth and the automatic record-changer

First

- Inventor of the first stepped-spindle automatic record-changer for discs

When Tasmanian teenager Eric Waterworth was about fifteen, his father came back from a visit to Melbourne with a gramophone that quickly became the focus of family entertainment. Now, once you wound up a 1920s gramophone, put the 78 rpm record on the turntable and lowered the needle, the turntable would just keep on revolving until the mechanism ran down; it didn't stop when the record had finished playing. So, the new gramophone quickly became the centre of arguments between Eric and his two younger brothers over whose turn it was to get up, stop the player and put on another record. After one argument too many, Eric set to work to design a record player that would play records continuously.

Eric Newham Waterworth was born into an innovative Tasmanian family in 1905. His father, John Newham Waterworth, had emigrated with his family from England to Tasmania, where he worked as a tailor before moving to Brisbane to become a Baptist lay preacher, hypnotist and 'magnetic healer'. It was there that he met schoolteacher Edith Alice Hawker, and immediately after their marriage in 1903 they moved to Sydney and John began studying optometry. Once he had qualified, they moved back to Tasmania where Eric was born. John eventually developed with R.M. Ross the firm of Waterworth & Ross, Opticians, in Elizabeth Street, Hobart, into a thriving business. John was responsible for drafting and steering through the Tasmanian parliament in 1913 Tasmania's Opticians Act, the first act to legally recognise and regulate the practice of optometry in Australia, despite strong resistance from the Australian Medical Association. Eric's mother, Edith, who became a welfare worker after marriage, was an energetic campaigner for women's rights and a member of the Women's Criminal Law Reform Association. She influenced organisations such as the Women's Health Association and the Child Welfare Association in the areas of health, welfare and justice for women and children. She stood unsuccessfully for the Tasmanian parliament three times, as did her husband, and received an OBE in 1935. She attended major international women's conferences, and was delegated by Prime Minister Joseph Lyons to represent Australian women at the 1936 League of Nations convention in Geneva. She was a woman, Eric once observed, 'of very forceful opinions'.

As he grew up, Eric was never in any doubt about what he wanted to do with his life. He'd always had a love of machinery and he learned as much as he could about tools and construction. He even set up his own small workshop, in which he built a billycart with steering and brakes that worked the same as a car, developing a strong belief that if you wanted to do something, then you just went to work and did it. If you didn't have the tools, you built them; if you didn't have the materials, you went and found them. When he left school, he tried the family optometry business but found he was really more interested in making a living out of engineering and design. His thoughts turned once again to the family gramophone that only played one record until someone physically changed it.

Eric was about seventeen when he began to tinker with the concept of a gramophone that would change records automatically, and it took some three years of experimentation before he had a working prototype. In October 1925, Eric demonstrated at his father's offices in Elizabeth Street his revolutionary automatic record-changer to an audience of well-known Hobart politicians and businessmen, including Joe Lyons, (then premier), the mayor, Alderman Francis David Valentine, former Tasmanian Agent-General Sir Alfred Ashbolt and Sir Henry Jones of IXL fame. The stepped-spindle record changer could take six 10-inch (25-centimetre) or 12-inch (30.5-centimetre) records at a time. After each record had played through, the needle arm would lift and swing out of the way, the next record would drop down and the arm would swing back and lower the needle to begin playing the record again. It could play any or all of the records through as many times as the listener wished. In fact, as Mr Waterworth explained, the listener could actually sit by the fire for an entire thirty minutes, listening to their choice of music without having to touch the gramophone if the motor and the needles held out that long. This was at a time when the average 78 rpm record lasted only about four minutes, so this invention was quite significant in terms of music enjoyment for serious listeners. The 33⅓ rpm record wouldn't be put on the market by RCA Victor until 1931 and music listeners would have to wait even longer, until 1948, for Columbia to release the long-play (LP) record that would run for about twenty minutes per side.

Eric and his father eventually took Eric's record-changer prototype to Sydney where they came to an agreement with Home Recreations Ltd to incorporate the technology into its gramophone model, the Salonola. Eric remained there for a year, directing Alpha Engineering Company Ltd in its manufacture of the tools with which the parts of the Salonola would be made. However, although the Salonola was successfully demonstrated at the 1927 Sydney Royal Easter Show, Home Recreations went into liquidation soon afterwards and, despite all that hard work, the product was never actually released into the market.

The following year, the Waterworths set out for London, where they eventually sold the patents outright to a new company, the Symphony Gramophone and Radio Company Ltd. Symphony Gramophone's products, all made in their own factory, included a five-valve portable receiver, a battery-powered radiogram with a wind-up turntable and a deluxe mains-powered radiogram with high-quality loudspeakers housed in a cabinet. As it turned out, Eric was lucky to have successfully sold his invention when he did; the following year the Depression practically eliminated the gramophone industry worldwide and, unfortunately, any chance of his invention actually being incorporated into current models disappeared with it. After a few years, the patents lapsed and immediately, without acknowledging Waterworth, the British company Garrard produced the first mass-marketed gramophone with a stepped-spindle record-changer in 1932.

Although Eric had been offered a job in England by Symphony Gramophone, he didn't take it up and he returned to his home country in 1931. Having made enough money from his patents to free him from regular work for a while, he helped his father restore an electronic-action pipe organ that he'd bought some years previously, originally built by J.E. Reeve of Nunhead in England in about 1923, which had been lying around the house in pieces. It was eventually installed in the Methodist (now Uniting) Church in Princes Street, Sandy Bay. As a by-product of this restoration, Eric gained so much experience and interest in speakers and electronics that he was invited to install the sound equipment in Hobart's first 'talkie' movie theatre, the Avalon.

His money wasn't going to last forever, though, and sooner or later Eric had to go back to a steady job, which in his case was managing a razor-blade factory for three years. Of course, he hadn't suddenly developed an urge to be Tasmania's King Gillette; he was really interested in designing and building improved machine tools to make them, and it was during this period that he also became involved with making scientific equipment for the professor of physics at the

University of Tasmania, A.L. McAulay, and for Dr Ernest Kurth, Head of the Chemistry Department.

At the outbreak of World War II, the Australian Army Ordnance Department discovered that although it was able to manufacture a 25-pounder artillery piece, it was not able to obtain the gunsight for it. Every university physics department promptly received a telegram asking for advice. Upon reading his telegram, Professor McAulay realised he had at his fingertips two men uniquely qualified to polish lenses: Eric Waterworth and his brother Philip, who was already a partner in the family firm.

With the approval of the Ordnance Department, McAulay and the Waterworths set to work, realising they faced a daunting task. Starting from scratch, they would have to develop the ability to manufacture different types of optical instruments and components. Within two weeks, Eric had produced their first machine and he went on to invent two very significant types of tools: kinematic jigs that could be adjusted to hold different sizes of prisms so they could be finely ground, and a diamond saw at a time when there was none in Australia. McAulay proved talented at solving the problems of optical design, while the Waterworth brothers then used his calculations to design and make the machinery. Within twelve months they were producing prisms and had begun to employ a workforce of mostly women and students. By 1943, some 200 people now working in what was called the Optical Munitions Annexe, situated in a factory building constructed next to the physics department, were able to fill an order for 10 000 prisms from the Frankford Arsenal in the United States. The arsenal later told Eric that the annexe's prisms were better than their own. When the government decided it would sooner pay a private firm than a department of the university, Eric Waterworth officially became the manager of what was now called the Waterworth Hobart Annexe.

In 1942, after a ship carrying 400 camera lenses for the RAAF had been sunk, the annexe was given the job of making new lenses. McAulay developed a method of designing and making camera lenses within such a short time that the process remained classified until after the war. Once they had their system under way, the annexe under Waterworth could produce three sizes of telephoto lenses in six weeks. During this time, Waterworth designed a combined range-finder and gunsight for tanks and a type of telescope sight for naval guns that would enable the muzzle velocity to be measured so the range of the guns could be estimated. For the first time, the navy was able to carry out muzzle velocity tests on a ship at sea. Waterworth then adapted his sight for army guns. By the end of the war, the annexe was turning out prisms not only for field gunsights but for army and naval range-finders and for submarines, and director prisms for anti-aircraft predictors.

After the war, the federal government decided it would no longer continue to fund the annexe, so Waterworth bought the entire operation, including the buildings. With a smaller workforce of about fifty, the business continued as a successful private profit-sharing company for civilian optical projects, such as manufacturing, coating and repairing lenses for cinema projectors, cameras and the printing industry. Eventually Waterworth was approached by the Tasmanian Education Department's visual aids section to design and manufacture a foolproof, unbreakable slide projector for use in schools, which could be operated by either students or staff. The Waterworth filmstrip projector became one of the company's most successful products, sold widely around Australia to schools and the general public. These projectors, which could still be found in the cupboard of the occasional state school until comparatively recently, were in time superseded by carousel projectors and then by computer slide shows.

Then the brothers became involved in something completely different. Philip Waterworth's father-in-law happened to be Dr William McIntyre, gynaecologist at the Launceston Queen Victoria Hospital. During the 1940s, McIntyre was seeking an alternative 'hands-off' method of artificial respiration for babies rather than traditional practices such as dipping in ice water, slapping them, or swinging them like a pendulum while holding them either by the shoulders (known as the Schultze technique) or ankles. Dr McIntyre's idea was to design a portable infant-sized version of the iron lung machine, but one inside which you could place a baby—in other words, the first version of what we now call a humidicrib. His initial design in 1944 actually involved an Electrolux vacuum cleaner as the basic operating device. Lacking the technological expertise or equipment to design and manufacture a full working prototype, he approached Philip, who invited Eric to join the team, and together they designed and built the Waterworth Infant Respirator in 1950.

Waterworth finally retired from managing his factory in 1965 and sold it. He continued doing design work, however, and helped his son, Dr Mike Waterworth, develop a laser firelighter for forestry department workers carrying out burn-offs. It would enable them to light a fire from a safe distance, using an optical system including a range-finder to concentrate a laser beam onto a spot the size of a twenty-cent piece from well over a kilometre away. In 1988, the University of Tasmania awarded Eric Waterworth an Honorary Master of Science degree.

Eric Waterworth built only three working prototypes of his automatic record-changer, one of which was sold to Home Recreations Ltd for use as a model of their proposed changes to the Salonola gramophone. Waterworth and his father took another of the prototype versions to England and this was sold to the Symphony Gramophone and Radio Company. The disassembled parts of the third version were stored at the Waterworth home where they remained forgotten for approximately sixty years. Discovered by Waterworth's family after his death, the parts were offered to the members of the Sound Preservation Association of Tasmania who reassembled this last remaining prototype to working condition. It is now on display at the Sound Preservation Association's resource centre in the Hobart suburb of Bellerive.

★

The rest of the world

Although there was a 1913 Autophone in the United States that held twelve wax cylinders in a kind of Ferris-wheel arrangement, the first disc record-changer that was actually successfully manufactured was the twin turntable Automatic Change Gramophone made in 1927 by the British company His Master's Voice (HMV). This gramophone used an assembly-line change mechanism. Records were placed in a stack on a shelf at the left side of the gramophone from which a vacuum arm picked up the top record from the stack and placed it on the first turntable to be played. After the side finished, the record was flipped over onto a second turntable, and the same arm played the second side.

The first successful American record-changer was the Victor Talking Machine Company's Automatic Orthophonic, also made in 1927. On this machine, a record stack was held vertically on a hook on the end of a support at the left side of the turntable, from where each record was lifted off onto the turntable.

For many years after 1932, Garrard remained the only company manufacturing stepped-spindle record-changers, and a number of its models looked suspiciously like Eric Waterworth's original design.

CHATEAU DE CARDBOARD

Thomas W.C. Angove and the portable wine cask

Firsts

- Inventor and developer of the first resealable portable wine cask: a polyethylene bag filled with wine contained within a cardboard box
- Pioneer of the use of stainless-steel tanks for wine storage in Australia

The next time you and your friends are sitting out on the patio one sunny afternoon sampling a few wines from a modern cardboard cask or two, whether you know it as goon, boxy or chateau de cardboard, spare a thought for, and perhaps lift your glasses in a toast to, Thomas W.C. Angove. Without his invention, which has been so thoroughly assimilated into modern Australian life, you would still be carting wine home in heavy and breakable glass bottles or flagons into which air would flow once opened, beginning the inevitable process of ruining the wine.

For the South Australian winery Angove Family Winemakers, air had become something of a sales problem by the 1960s. Having been instrumental in persuading Australians to drink more wine, Angove was aware that one of the major factors hindering the sale of red wine in bulk was that once the bottles or flagons were opened, air flowed in and the wine would go off within a relatively short time. The Angove vineyards had initially been established by Cornishman Dr William Thomas Angove, an accomplished general practitioner and surgeon, who had arrived from Suffolk with his wife, Emma Carlyon, and young family in 1886 to establish a medical practice in South Australia. As the district medical officer, Angove was a busy man who needed some relaxation, and so as a hobby he began experimenting with growing vines and with winemaking and distillation at Tea Tree Gully in the Adelaide foothills. This would be the forerunner of one of the largest vineyards in the southern hemisphere: the magnificent Nanya Vineyard at Renmark in the Murray Valley of South Australia.

With the success of early vintages from Tea Tree Gully, the vineyard expanded and a winery and cellars were constructed from local stone. Soon the Burgundy-style dry red was supplemented by the production of dry whites, as well as fortified wines, which in the nineteenth century were believed to have medicinal benefits. In 1910, Dr Angove's eldest son, Thomas 'Skipper' Angove, branched out from Tea Tree Gully and set up the distillery and processing plant at Renmark, becoming the head of the business two years later. Despite the disruption of two world wars, his operation there grew steadily and, as well as developing a fine reputation for table and fortified wines, Angove quickly won respect for their distillation of high-quality brandy. The winery's St Agnes label, named after an area in Cornwall, became a hallmark for quality brands in Australian and overseas markets. The Renmark facility eventually developed into a major winemaking and distilling enterprise, with a storage capacity of more than 15 million litres of wine and spirits.

Born in 1917 in Renmark, Thomas William Carlyon Angove, Dr Angove's grandson, followed in his father's footsteps, studying agriculture and oenology before becoming a director of the company in 1941. In 1947, Angove became managing director and steered the company into a new era. He expanded the crushing and processing facilities and supervised the planting of the 480-hectare Nanya vineyard, one of Australia's largest. Then, in the early 1960s, Angove perceived that there was actually quite a traditional answer to the problem of wine deterioration after a bottle had been opened.

For centuries, wine had been drunk in Europe from soft bladders, usually that of a goat. As the wine level fell, the bladder collapsed, keeping out air and maintaining the freshness of the wine. Thomas Angove brought this concept into the modern era, substituting for the goat's bladder a soft, flexible polyethylene bag that was filled with a gallon (4.5 litres) of wine—six standard bottles or two flagons at that time—and then put into a cardboard box. Unlike the modern cask, though, his original version didn't have a tap. The drinker simply opened the flaps on top of the box, pulled up the neck of the bag, snipped off a corner of the neck and then decanted the wine. When they were done pouring, they folded over the neck of the bag and slipped a rubber band or large paper clip over it, folded the box flaps back over and stored the box in the refrigerator. The cubical cardboard container not only made wine drinking more economical for both the casual drinker and the party host, but its shape allowed the cask to be stacked and stored conveniently with an economy of space, and the box protected the bag of wine from rough handling—important factors for the Angove company, which was exporting wine to England.

The concept took two years to develop, including experimental shipment of the casks back and forth between Australia and England, before Thomas Angove applied for and was granted Australian patents for his invention, termed an 'improved container and pack for liquids', on 20 April 1965. His son John Angove, who was then about fifteen, recalls: 'I remember Dad coming home with this sort of prototype of a plastic bag inside a cardboard box and I remember thinking to myself, and I probably said to Dad, "That's crazy, nobody will buy wine in a plastic bag stuck inside a cardboard box," but in his usual manner he persisted. He thought he was onto a good thing and history certainly indicates that he was.' In November 1965, 1-gallon packs of table white, table red, port, sweet sherry and muscat were launched on an unsuspecting drinking public, whereupon the ubiquitous cardboard cask seized the Australian imagination by its dry throat and changed the image of wine from something one drank on special occasions to an everyday drink.

Improvements to Angove's original concept came quickly. Only two years later, Penfolds winery produced its cask as a bag inside a steel can fitted with a tap, but the cask tended to leak because the bag would rub against the metal and puncture, and the tap design was poor. Penfolds dropped the idea, but David Wynn of Wynn Winegrowers Pty Ltd, who was already producing low-cost wine in glass flagons, thought he could improve on it. In a conversation with liquor retailer Dan Murphy, Wynn heard about the efficient plastic Airesflow tap developed by Geelong engineer Charles Malpas for oil drums. He promptly bought the rights in 1970 and included it in a cask design in which the user had to insert their own tap into a clear plastic bag in a cardboard box. However, plastic manufacturers at the time struggled with storage and sealing issues. Despite experimenting with various types of lamination, the bag remained permeable to oxygen, which still allowed the wine to deteriorate, rather defeating the purpose of the invention. There were also ongoing quality problems with persistent pin-hole leaks in the bags. Eventually, Wynn developed the innovation of applying a metallic coating and fusing the tap to the bag so it could be pulled through the box for use. He was so successful that the company went public on the stock exchange that year and within two years had been bought out by Castlemaine Tooheys. The cardboard wine cask had become the cask we know today, where the bag is retained within the sealed box and tapped much like a traditional wine cask.

Other wine companies quickly jumped on the barrel-wagon; for example, most Australian television watchers of the 1970s would probably remember the television commercial jingle about Dr Lindeman making us smile. According to wine writer Drew Lambert, in 1973 on average each Australian drank 9.8 litres per annum; after ten years' exposure to wine casks, that amount had escalated to 19.3 litres. By 1988, the Orlando Winery alone was producing 12 million casks a year, and liquor stores displayed such well-known brand names as Berri Estate, Coolabah, Kaiser Stuhl, Stanley and Yalumba.

However, due to the damage that the Penfolds and Wynn design issues had on the reputation of casks, Angove had opted out of the market in 1971. He re-entered it thirteen years later, once the design had improved, with the Paddle Wheel 5-litre wine box. The name celebrated an aspect of early Angove history, when the product was taken downstream on the Murray River from Renmark to Murray Bridge by paddle steamer and then transported by rail to the capital cities. Although that proved successful, the Angove company is now again moving away from the cask market, believing that the market share of cask wine has dwindled in recent years along with its image. In 2005, bottled wine outsold cask wine for the first time since 1981. Two main factors explain the change. Quite good wine can now be bought in bottles at cheap prices due to a market glut. As well, the traditional issue of storing and reusing opened wine has been reduced with the introduction of screw-top bottles. Basically, in Angove's opinion, the day of the cask has come and gone. Angove is evidently not the only winemaker to feel that way. Fosters Group (Lindemans, Kaiser Stuhl) and Hardy (now Constellation Wines Australia and probably best known for the Berri Estate and Stanley brands) have both recently reviewed their cask wine production.

On the other hand, some winemakers feel that there is still a significant market out there for good old 'Chateau de Cardboard', now more politely known as 'box wine', and that while sales may be slightly down they still remain substantial. In 2010, for example, cask wine made up 39 per cent of all domestic wine sales in Australia, down from around 66 per cent at the height of cask wine's popularity in the late 1980s. Sales of cask wine declined less than sales of bottled wine and the recent market share of cask wine has remained constant. Wineries are also currently reducing cask sizes from 4 or 5 litres to 1.5 and 2 litres, and offering the same specific labelled varieties as in bottles, not just a generic name. Some wine brands now even come in 1-litre Tetra packs like fruit juice or milk. After all, the cask will always have that market edge of convenience, environmental friendliness and lower pricing due to the lower level of alcohol tax levied on cask wine in Australia. Screw-top or cork, an opened bottle of wine still has a comparatively short lifespan, whereas that cask in the fridge will last much longer.

Having remained chairman of the board of directors until 1998, Thomas Angove died on 31 March 2010, aged 92. He had also pioneered the use of stainless-steel tanks in Australia for storing wine in bulk and, it was said, he knew more than anyone else in Australia about distilling brandy. He was awarded the Queen Elizabeth Silver Jubilee Medal in 1977 and an Order of Australia in 1994 for his services to the wine industry. Thomas Angove was a generous man whose contribution to the wine industry reflects a broad vision not only of the industry itself but of the world and of life.

*

The rest of the world

Thomas Angove may have been the first to apply the bag-in-a-box concept to wine casks, but the Scholle packaging company in America was also applying the same idea to the storage of liquid chemicals, and it is now one of the main manufacturers of packaging for boxed wine (as cardboard casks are known there). Unlike in Australia, boxed wine in the United States is rapidly increasing its share of the domestic wine market. Having come late to the cardboard wine-tasting, some American vineyards are now ceasing bottling and are instead promoting the advantages of boxed wine as environmentally friendly packaging consisting of, for example, unbleached and chlorine-free cardboard made from recycled paper and printed with soy-based ink. Companies are also experimenting with innovative packaging design, such as octagonal or cylindrical 3-litre casks.

Both red and white wine have been sold in Germany in 5- and 10-litre casks since about 1984, but Italy released its first boxed wine only in 2008. Although the French began selling wine in 1986 in 250-millilitre ring-pull cans, in 2009 the Australian company Barokes won its case with the European Patent Office to have the European patent confirmed for its Vinsafe Wine in a Can product. Having been granted the Australian patent in 2003, Barokes has now been granted patents in some forty-one countries and is now recognised as the world leader in delivering quality wine in a can.

Now, Australia is a land of big icons, so of course there is a Big Wine Cask. Standing at the entrance to the Stanley Winery in Buronga, New South Wales, this cask is 8 metres high, 11 metres long and 7 metres wide. If it was a real cask, it would hold 400 000 litres of Australian riesling!

THE MARLIN AND THE PACEMAKER

Dr Mark C. Lidwill and his external cardiac pacemaker

Firsts

- Designer and user of the first external cardiac pacemaker to restart and regulate heartbeat
- Designer and user of the Lidwill anaesthetic machine
- Boated the first black marlin to be recorded as caught anywhere with rod and reel

The concept of stimulating a heart by some form of electricity is not new by any means. During the late 1700s, a number of experiments were carried out using galvanic currents, as electricity was then called, and in fact the Royal Humane Society was founded in London in 1774 primarily as a fraternity devoted to resuscitating the seemingly dead. The first recorded case of human resuscitation was in London in 1788 when a three-year-old child who had fallen out of a window and was to all appearances dead was resuscitated by a doctor using a current generated from a Leyden jar, a device that stores static electricity between two electrodes.

Various experiments and resuscitations continued through the early part of the next century. In the 1820 edition of his book *The Medical*

Guide, London surgeon Richard Reece describes a 're-animation chair' that combined artificial respiration by means of a bellows and oesophageal tube with galvanic (electric) shocks administered by an electrode touched to the body. However, it was John Alexander McWilliam, a brilliant young Scottish physiologist, who in 1889 reported in the *British Medical Journal* that application of an electrical impulse via a needle electrode attached to a metronome could restore regular ventricular contractions. He had found that he could restore normal heart rhythm by applying periodic timed electric shocks, as opposed to once-only or intermittent shocks, to restart a heart. But his pioneering research went unrecognised and ignored for decades after his death.

It was an Australian specialist in anaesthetics, Dr Mark Cowley Lidwill, known to his friends as 'Bunny', who made the next major step forward. He was born in 1878 in Cheltenham, England, into a wealthy Anglo-Irish family with estates in England and County Tipperary, Ireland. He studied at Westminster School in London before much of the family's assets were lost in the bank crash of 1893. Seeking to make a new start, the Lidwill family moved to Melbourne in 1894. A brilliant student, Mark graduated from University of Melbourne, gaining a Bachelor of Medicine (Honours) in 1902, a Bachelor of Surgery in 1903 and a Doctorate of Medicine only two years later in 1905. That same year, Dr Lidwill moved to Sydney and in 1906 he married Constance Sydney-Jones, the youngest daughter of noted surgeon, co-founder of Royal Prince Alfred Hospital and Chancellor of the University of Sydney, Sir Philip Sydney-Jones.

After spending their honeymoon canoeing down the Hastings River in one of Dr Lidwill's patent collapsible canoes, the couple soon moved into their own striking two-storey residence known as Lorne, in Beecroft, then a quiet semi-rural village-suburb on the outskirts of Sydney. Lorne was designed by his architect brother-in-law George Sydney-Jones to include Dr Lidwill's surgery and, with its flat roof and cuboid lines, it stood out from other houses in the area. The

Lidwills eventually had two daughters, Sylvia and Kathleen. Dr Lidwill apparently liked a game of golf for relaxation and so was instrumental in creating a golf links and golf club in Beecroft, of which he was the first president in 1906.

In 1913 Dr Lidwill was appointed to Royal Prince Alfred Hospital, Sydney, as honorary assistant physician and as its first tutor in anaesthetics. In that same year, he became the first lecturer in anaesthetics at the University of Sydney Faculty of Medicine. During World War I, he served as a captain in the Royal Australian Army Medical Corps and carried out valuable evaluation of the various types of ether in use at the time. After the war, the Lidwills moved to Strathfield and Dr Lidwell set up a practice in Macquarie Street where he had the first electrocardiograph in Sydney. The size of an upright piano, it required the patient to have both hands and one foot in jars of saline while readings were being recorded.

In 1921 he patented his Lidwill anaesthetic machine, which allowed surgeons continuous access to the patient during operations of the face and pharynx while ether was being administered, instead of the traditional alternating application of the mask with surgical procedure. Produced and sold by Elliot Brothers in Sydney, this portable machine, weighing only 7 kilograms and able to be packed into one case or two small handbags, remained in use throughout Australia for over thirty years.

As both a physician and anaesthetist, Dr Lidwill was interested in the problems associated with the role of the neuro-muscular system in cardiac arrest. He observed that the heart muscle could still act long after the nerves had ceased to stimulate it, and so he theorised that with artificial stimulation the heart could be kept working. In 1909 and 1910, he had already proved that adrenalin could be used as a heart stimulant, but its success was unreliable. So, with the assistance of physicist Major Edgar H. Booth at the University of Sydney and Dr Briggs of the Crown Street Women's Hospital in Sydney, he began work on designing a device by which electrical stimulation could be applied directly to the heart muscle. After much experimentation, by 1926 Dr Lidwill had constructed the first external portable cardiac defibrillator/pacemaker, a portable apparatus that plugged into a wall socket. According to Dr Lidwill's report to the Australasian Medical Congress in 1929, one pole of the device 'was applied to a pad on the skin, say the left arm, and saturated with strong salt solution. The other pole, which consists of a needle insulated except at its point, is plunged into the ventricle.' The apparatus was then switched on to administer impulses. The operator, presumably an anaesthetist, could vary the voltage and the rate of impulses from about 80 to 120 pulses per minute.

Dr Lidwill foresaw that this instrument could enable the restarting of the heart in emergency situations where someone may have gone into cardiac arrest under general anaesthesia during surgery or as a result of drowning, gas poisoning, diphtheria or heart disease; it could also be used on infants at childbirth. Because the needle could be left in the heart, the impulses could be governed and regulated until the heart had not only started but had settled into its own rhythm. Even though he recognised that his device might not succeed every time, he thought it better to save one life in every fifty, or even one hundred, than to have no chance of doing so at all.

Between 1926 and 1928, Dr Lidwill used his defibrillator/pace-maker to attempt revivals of several stillborn infants at Crown Street Women's Hospital. Finally, one baby's heart continued to beat of its own accord after the delivery of 16-volt impulses to the right ventricle at regular intervals for ten minutes. In September 1929 when Dr Lidwill spoke at the third Australasian Medical Congress, he was able to report that the child was still living and quite healthy. That unknown Australian baby was the first human being to undergo successful pacing of the heart and while no further details of that person were recorded, they were hopefully able to live a full life because of Dr Lidwill's first artificial pacemaker.

The first that the medical fraternity outside the women's hospital knew of Dr Lidwill's remarkable achievement was when he delivered a report about his work and demonstrated his device to the Australasian Medical Congress in 1929. But he never took out a patent for his invention. In any case, by then Dr Briggs had left the women's hospital and as he and Dr Lidwill were the only people who knew how the apparatus worked, the pacemaker was no longer used. No photograph, model or diagram of the instrument is known to exist and, after the congress, Dr Lidwill chose to remain anonymous for many years to avoid controversy. After all, successful use of his invention could resurrect the dead and artificially extend life. In those more conservative times, when such artificial interference with the brain or heart was regarded as defying God's will, this was asking for a public outcry. Probably for quite similar reasons, nor was there any strong demand to obtain units of the apparatus from members of a medical profession that largely regarded cardiac arrest as an irreversible condition, despite the invention's proven ability to save lives. Even with the injection of stimulants directly into the heart, a successful restarting in those days was a rare phenomenon indeed. Electrostimulation had long been associated with medical quackery, a view probably reinforced in the popular mind by the 1931 release of a film version of Mary Shelley's *Frankenstein*. Consequently, Dr Lidwill's report had a negligible impact on Australian medical science. He never went ahead with further development, apparently leaving the records of his invention with his lawyer to be destroyed on his death.

However, Dr Lidwill never seemed to allow ignorance about this potentially great gift to his country to embitter the rest of his life. In 1930, he was appointed the first honorary Director of Anaesthetics when the board of the Royal Prince Alfred Hospital created its first Department of Anaesthetics, and he held that position along with a lectureship at the University of Sydney for the next three years. He then remained honorary physician until his retirement from the active staff of the hospital in 1938; that same year he was accepted as a Foundation Fellow of the Royal Australasian College of Physicians. The following year, when war was declared, he came out of retirement to work for the Allied Works Council as the medical superintendent of the Captain Cook Graving Dock at Garden Island, Sydney, where he was responsible for the medical care of over 400 divers, and developed additional safety equipment for them. After World War II, he took over the role of medical superintendent at the Dame Eadith Walker Convalescent Hospital (Yaralla), a rehabilitation centre for military and civilian patients in Concord, Sydney. He became the second Honorary Fellow of the Faculty of Anaesthetists, Royal Australasian College of Surgeons, in 1954.

Dr Lidwill was also a gifted flautist who played on occasion with both the Melbourne and Sydney symphony orchestras. The Mark C. Lidwill Travelling Fellowship Award was created in his honour by the North American Society of Pacing and Electrophysiology, and at the Victor Chang Cardiac Research Institute in Sydney there is a Mark Cowley Lidwill Research Program in Cardiac Electrophysiology. He died in Nowra in 1968, aged 90. He was remembered for his friendliness, constant smile and witty conversation.

★

Back when Dr Lidwill was a young man, he was the first to do some things entirely unrelated to medicine that would gain him fame in very different circles. In order to enjoy some relaxation away from the heavy demands of his practice, Lidwill was a boating enthusiast and angler. Having patented a collapsible canoe as well as designing his own large cruiser, *Vialeen*, he explored and mapped a number of coastal streams within the Hawkesbury River system, just north of Sydney. A member of the New South Wales Anglers' Casting Club, he was fishing off Port Stephens, New South Wales, in early February 1913 when he boated a 70-pound (32 kilogram) fish after a twelve-minute fight using a rod fitted with a reel that he'd designed himself. At first glance it appeared to be an impressive swordfish, so it was put on ice and loaded aboard the SS *Karuah* coastal paddle steamer for shipment to the Australian Museum in Sydney. There, it was skeletonised and at first displayed as a swordfish (or spearfish). It wasn't until 1998, when the Newcastle and Port Stephens Game Fishing Club historian Peter Silcock conducted research into the capture, that the fish skeleton finally was identified with the assistance of Ichthyology Collection Manager Mark McGrouther as that of a *Makaira indica*, or black marlin. It was the first black marlin to be caught with rod and reel not only in Australian waters but anywhere in the world. The skeleton can still be seen in the museum's Skeleton Gallery.

★

The rest of the world

Although it had negligible influence in his home country, on the other side of the world Dr Lidwill's report to the Australasian Congress would influence a major step forward in the development of the cardiac pacemaker. It was clear by now that there were two closely related but separate challenges with heart stimulation: defibrillation, or starting a stopped heart and ultimately being able to artificially stop and start a heart during surgery; and correcting the pulse rate of a heart that had not stopped but was functioning irregularly.

During his study at Harvard Medical School, Albert Salisbury Hyman became interested in the second challenge, and his research after he set up practice in New York resulted in his 1930 patent of an electrical defibrillator/pacemaker. Powered by a spring-wound, hand-cranked motor that delivered six minutes of uniform electric current at a time, the small, portable, 7-kilogram machine could be easily carried by a doctor. He then developed an instrument for controlling the repetitive electro-stimulation of the heart that he named an 'artificial pacemaker', the term that is still used to this day. However, although six Hyman pacemakers were built by the German company Siemens AG, they were never proved successful in testing and there is no evidence that his pacemaker was ever used in medical circumstances. In 1932, he published his seminal paper on his work that referred to the successful development and use of a similar apparatus by an Australian named 'Gould', yet although throughout the years Hyman's work was repeatedly acknowledged, no one ever said anything further about the mysterious Mr Gould. The reason, of course, is that Gould never existed; an examination of Hyman's references clearly reveals that he was actually referring to the work of Dr Mark Lidwill.

It would be nearly twenty years before two Canadian researchers, Wilfred Bigelow and John Callaghan, and an electrical engineer, John Hopps, would make a further step forward. In 1950, they created another version of an external pacemaker, demonstrating with it that they could restore the heartbeat after it had stopped from hypothermia.

In 1957–58, Earl E. Bakken, co-founder of the Medtronic company in Minnesota, worked with Dr C. Walton Lillehei to develop the first wearable, transistorised, battery-powered external portable pacemaker, about the size of a paperback book. In his autobiography, *One Man's Full Life*, Bakken credits Dr Lidwill with his ground-breaking discovery.

Now, for those fishing enthusiasts among the readers, we need to put Dr Lidwill's black marlin into perspective. The beginning of big-game angling is generally regarded to be the 1 June 1898 landing of a 183-pound (83-kilogram) bluefin tuna on rod and reel by Dr Charles Frederick Holder off Catalina Island, California, which led to the formation of the pioneer angling organisation the Tuna Club. The first-ever marlin caught with rod and reel was a 125-pound (56.7-kilogram) striped marlin, off Catalina Island, by Edward Llewellyn on 28 August 1903. After Dr Lidwill's catch, it would be twenty years before another black marlin was caught in Australian waters with rod and reel, and that 262-pound (119-kilogram) fish was boated by Roy Smith in February 1933 off Montague Island, New South Wales.

SEARCHING FOR HER HOLY GRAIL

Dr Fiona Wood and her quest for scarless healing

Firsts

- The invention of 'spray-on skin' to aid the healing of burns victims

At the beginning of October 1992, a young high-school teacher was rushed into the Royal Perth Hospital (RPH) Burns Unit with severe burns to 90 per cent of his body. Dr Fiona Wood had only just begun her new role as head of that unit, and she had never come across a patient this severely injured. She spent hours in surgery performing operation after operation, even seeking advice from overseas on procedure, realising as time went on how significant this case was becoming to her personally and professionally. By the time that patient finally left the hospital nine months later, Dr Wood was thinking that there must be an easier and quicker way to assist such complicated healing procedures.

Fiona Wood was born in 1958 in a small coal-mining village in Yorkshire, England, near the Frickley Colliery. Her father was a miner, her mother a sports-oriented youth worker who became a physical education teacher at Ackworth, a Quaker boarding school, and eventually the coordinator of the Duke of Edinburgh Awards for northern England. Fiona attended the same Quaker school, the Latin motto of which translates as, 'Not for oneself, but for others.' As an athletically competitive schoolgirl nicknamed the 'Frickley Flyer', she dreamed of a career as an Olympic sprinter but eventually had to admit to herself that she wasn't going to be fast enough. Instead of becoming discouraged and overwhelmed by what she couldn't do, she asked herself what she *could* do, discovering in time that she was just as hungry to learn as she had been to run. She became one of those students who kept asking, 'Why?'

Inspired by parents who could see there was something special in each person, Fiona decided she wanted to make a difference in her lifetime and so she left Yorkshire when she was seventeen to accept the challenge of study at St Thomas's Hospital Medical School in London, where she was one of only twelve women in her year. On her first day in medical school there was an anatomy dissection. By the end of the session, despite a number of others 'feeling faint', Fiona was still standing. Fascinated by anatomy, she knew that a surgeon was responsible for putting it all back together. She knew that was what she wanted to be. As she gained experience in a variety of surgical areas, Fiona realised that bringing together the three stages of treatment within the burns field—keeping the patient alive post-injury, performing surgical interventions and then rehabilitation to heal the whole person—provided the ultimate challenge for her. Here was where she felt she could make that difference, where there was room for innovation and creativity with opportunity for research and further work in related developing fields such as microsurgery and tissue expansion. But it would take a lot of hard work while she was training; her roster meant sometimes working twelve days and seven nights straight, and there was no point complaining as there would be somebody else right behind her to take her job.

After finally graduating in 1981, Dr Wood continued to work intermittently at St Thomas's as a junior registrar while carrying out research into blood and nerve supply to the skin and muscle layers. It was during this period that she first became involved in neurophysiology research on tissue-expanded skin used in scar repair. Instead of scar minimisation, Dr Wood decided that she wanted to try to eradicate scarring altogether by effectively controlling infection and removing tissue damaged beyond its ability to repair and regenerate. The quicker the wound could be closed, the less likelihood there would be of scarring.

After marrying Western Australian-born surgeon Tony Kierath, Dr Wood moved with him to Perth with their first two children in 1987. There she completed her training in plastic surgery and became a consultant, having four more children along the way. Needless to say, she became an expert in time management as her surgical and research careers developed alongside her role as mother.

After that epiphany at the RPH Burns Unit in 1992, Dr Wood began to collaborate after hours at night with scientist Marie Stoner, who already had experience in skin-tissue engineering and in commercialising medical technology. The two were trying to improve on the American cultured skin treatment methods then being used, in which sheets of skin were developed in cultures from donor cells and then placed over the burn victim's wounds where, all going well, they eventually grew back over the wound. Of necessity, however, it was a very slow process and thus open to complications from infection and rejection. Dr Wood wanted to change the dynamics of the healing process, to speed it up to reduce those complications and thus also reduce scarring as much as possible. Skin constantly regenerates, so she was simply harvesting that regenerating capacity and replanting it in an area where that capacity had been overwhelmed.

One night after some frustrating research dead-ends, Dr Wood joked that they should just be able to spray on the tissue, and from that came her innovation: the spray-on skin technology that in 1995 they named CellSpray®. Where there is insufficient skin left on the body to use as donor sites that could be used for grafting, a small sample of healthy skin cells is taken to be fed and grown in a lab. The expanded cells are then harvested and sprayed onto the patient's burns to cover many times the area of skin than would otherwise be possible by attempting to lay skin sheets over burns. After being sprayed on, the live skin cells then quickly multiply to cover the damaged area, encouraging healing with the aim of reducing scarring and infection and promoting stronger new skin growth to augment traditional methods. With the new covering generated from the patient's own cells, there is also minimal chance of rejection.

Discovering through their research that scarring can be greatly reduced if replacement skin is provided within ten days, Dr Wood and Stoner formed the Clinical Cell Culture (C3) company, now known as Avita Medical, which offers a 24-hour service to ensure cultures are always available to clinics. To achieve this aim, they developed ReCell, spray-on skin cells, a kit used at the bedside to harvest a patient's own skin cells for immediate use. The company also enables Dr Wood and Stoner to generate funding for future research. Ongoing research is undertaken in both the McComb Foundation, established in 1999 by Dr Wood and Stoner and directed by Dr Wood, and the Burn Injury Research Unit at the University of Western Australia, linked with the clinical research of the Burns Service of Western Australia.

In October 2002, Dr Wood's work gained media attention when a number of those injured in the terrorist bombings at Kuta in Bali arrived at the RPH Burns Unit. Of the sixty-one patients that had been received at Royal Darwin Hospital within a few days of the disaster, most had been evacuated to burns centres around Australia. Over half of them went to the RPH Burns Unit; some 15 per cent of the unit's annual workload arrived in one day. Dr Wood led a disaster-trained medical team in treating people suffering from burns to between 2 and 92 per cent of their body surface area, along with deadly infections, lung and ear injuries from the blast's pressure wave, and delayed shock.

The team used the spray-on skin as part of routine care, along with traditional techniques. For five days, the multidisciplinary team of over sixty clinicians worked in shifts to successfully stabilise patients. The last of those patients finally left hospital after forty-four days in a coma, followed by four weeks undergoing surgery and then extensive rehabilitation to burns over 64 per cent of his body.

However—as is often the case with new procedures—as well as receiving much praise from both her own patients and the media, Dr Wood also attracted controversy from other burns surgeons because the spray-on skin treatment had not yet been subjected to clinical trials. Some burns specialists declared that there was little evidence the treatment actually reduced mortality, and that patients from such disasters should not have been subjected to experimental procedures. As late as 2005, the burns unit at the Alfred Hospital in Victoria denied there was sufficient scientific evidence to justify use of Dr Wood's treatment. Her reply to naysayers was that, rather than taking time to prove her treatment didn't work, they should be using the time to develop something that worked better.

Dr Wood's holy grail is 'scarless woundless healing', and so she and Stoner have continued to further develop the spray-on skin treatment. In March 2007, following the crash landing of Garuda Indonesia Flight 200, Dr Wood travelled to Yogyakarta, Indonesia, to assist in the emergency medical response for burn victims there, and in April 2009, she and her team worked to help the twenty-three asylum seekers who were hospitalised after their boat exploded at Ashmore Reef. They now use the ReCell kit, which has been the subject of trials in Europe with current ongoing trials in the United States and China, almost exclusively. Their technology, which includes the ReCell kit, was recently approved for use by the European Union. In July 2009, Avita was given a US$2 million grant by the US Armed Forces Institute of Regenerative Medicine to fund a 100-patient, multicentre clinical trial that should accelerate the approval process for ReCell with the US Food and Drug Administration. Royalties from commercial licensing are ploughed back into the work of the McComb Foundation, which continues to facilitate networking between hospitals and such organisations as universities, for example, to bring together clinical expertise and research experience to help improve the journey to recovery. Dr Wood regards it as her foundation for tomorrow.

As a consequence of her revolutionary and caring work, Dr Wood was recognised as a Member of the Order of Australia in 2003. She has topped the *Reader's Digest* Most Trusted Australians list for five successive years from 2005 to 2009 and was named 2005 Australian of the Year. Western Australia's only female plastic surgeon, she is currently a Winthrop Professor at the University of Western Australia School of Surgery, director of the Burns Service of Western Australia and director of the burns units at both RPH and Princess Margaret Hospital for Children in Western Australia, as well as performing many other services.

This passionate and determined doctor, who has described herself as a 'rabid optimist', does not believe that today's medical wound treatment is good enough; she believes that we can always do better. 'The concept of whether our best is good enough is not really a question we should be asking,' she elaborates. 'What we should be asking is, how can we make our best better?' Having made the personal choice to work at the extreme rebuild end of plastic surgery, Dr Wood knows that if she ever has the time and inclination to look back, it would be to know that she has made a serious contribution to her field. But for now she always looks forward, seeing that in years to come skin won't be grafted to heal wounds; it will be regenerated from cell-based therapies. Perhaps one day, the suffering involved in healing from such severe injuries will be minimised. 'What should drive us all,' she says, 'is to look at that suffering every day and know we can impact on that.' Over her desk she has a photo of the face of a young man who was scarred as a boy of four. She's been trying to work out how to remove that scarring—she hasn't yet, but she hopes that one day she will.

★

The rest of the world

Reconstructive surgery was being carried out in India as early as 800 BC, and by the ancient Egyptians, the Greeks and later by the Romans. Aulus Cornelius Celsus wrote descriptions of early reconstructive surgery involving skin grafts.

However, it was really not until anaesthesia techniques were developed that the problems of pain and infection could be lessened and reconstructive surgery could be further developed during the nineteenth century by the work of such surgeons as John Mettauer in America, and James Israel and Jacques Joseph in Germany.

The New Zealand surgeon Sir Harold Gillies is usually regarded as the father of modern reconstructive facial surgery. Working in England and France during World War I with wounded and disfigured soldiers, he became particularly successful in a field into which few had dared to venture. During World War II, his cousin Archibald McIndoe carried on his work with treatment for RAF crew who had suffered from severe burns in crashed aircraft. His experimental and often radical treatments led to the formation by his patients of the Guinea Pig Club.

PART IV
SPORT

RUNNING BLACK

Bobby McDonald and Charlie Samuels, Aboriginal sprinters

Firsts

- Bobby McDonald was the first person to be recorded using a crouch start in an official running race
- Charlie Samuels became the fastest man on a running track in the world, and he was the first Australian Aboriginal athlete to hold the Championship of Australia

Australian Aboriginal athlete Bobby McDonald became a legend when one clear, cold night in 1887 he surprised the usual crowd of spectators gathered at Sydney's Carrington Athletic Ground track at Moore Park by starting his race from a semi-kneeling or 'crouch' position, instead of standing. Many years later he recalled that night in a letter published in the July 1913 edition of the Australian sporting journal *Referee*:

> I first got the idea of the sitting style of start (as I always called it) to dodge the strong winds which made me feel cold and miserable while waiting for the starter to send us away. One day while sitting down, almost, the starter sent us away, and I found I could get off the mark much quicker sitting than ever I could standing, and

afterwards I always used the sitting or crouch start. I never saw anyone using what is known as the crouch start before I did.

McDonald had, in fact, been using his start since the age of fourteen, long before 1887. In one early race, the starter had looked down at him and asked if he was going to get up off his knees.

Handsome and lightly built, McDonald was an excellent sprinter, or 'pedestrian' as professional runners were known at that time. By the 1870s, pedestrianism had become popular in both Australia and England where large sums of money changed hands in prize money and in bets. The races that carried the most promise of fame and fortune were the 'gift' races of which the 130-yard (120-metre) Stawell Gift, held annually in Victoria since 1878, still remains the oldest and richest sprint race in Australia with a first prize of $40 000. Because legislation in most Australian states by the late nineteenth century largely prevented the Aboriginal people from earning wages in the form of actual cash in hand, many of them became involved in sports competition of one kind or another in order to earn money of their own and so achieve some form of financial independence and respect. The problem was that because Aboriginal athletes were frequently superior in endurance and speed to the local white Australians and visiting Englishmen, both money and respect could be given grudgingly and taken away readily. In 1903, after a number of previous attempts at exclusion, the Queensland Amateur Athletics Association declared all Aboriginal athletes to be permanent professionals. As such, they were automatically ineligible for membership of the association, making it extremely difficult for them to enter major races.

McDonald was born in 1859 and eventually settled at the Cummeragunja mission settlement near Moama and the Barmah Forest on the New South Wales side of the Murray River, then the last major home of the Yorta Yorta people after their decimation as a result of white settlement. After starting out running in casual races on stations where shearers would race against each other, he began to compete in handicaps in towns. One of the runner Tom Malone's brothers saw him run at Orange and invited him to Sydney so they could train together, and McDonald went on to win several gift races in the late nineteenth and early twentieth centuries, including the Maryborough Gift in 1901. That year, McDonald moved back to Cummeragunja where he married and became a father of three children. He died there from pneumonia on 3 August 1919.

By the early 1930s Cummeragunja had produced some fourteen gift race winners, including the 1929 World Professional Sprint champion, Lynch Cooper.

At the time of McDonald's radical crouch at the start line, a runner traditionally stood up while waiting for the starter's gun, adopting a stance commonly known as the dab, or the Sheffield, for which the athlete stood at the line with one arm and the corresponding leg forward with the other arm held behind them horizontally at shoulder height. When the starter's gun sounded, the runner made a pecking or poking stroke beyond the line with his lead foot, swung the opposite arm sharply forward and was off. Because it was a standing start with no blocks, a runner using this method gained very little thrust from their start and consequently took a few paces to gather speed. McDonald's crouch start, on the other hand, gave him the advantage of much quicker acceleration and it was evidently an advantage he'd realised early.

Advocated in Australia as part of sprint training by 1905, use of the crouch start had rapidly spread internationally. American champion Lon Myers claimed to have brought it there from Australia where he'd seen it used in 1886. Thomas L. Nicholas of Monmouth was in 1888 the first British sprinter known to have used the crouch start. By the early 1890s it had gained a strong foothold among American colleges and athletic clubs, despite still being described in 1904 as a novelty not suitable for all runners. However, others also laid claim to originating the start. In 1913, Michael Murphy, an American professional sprinter and famous athletic coach of the nineteenth and early twentieth centuries, claimed in his book *How to Become a Sprinter* that he had used the crouch start in 1880, but this has never been verified and was doubted by his peers even during his lifetime. According to the *New York Times* of 22 December 1912, Murphy taught the crouch start to sprint champion Charles Sherrill in 1887, who on 12 May 1888 was the first athlete seen to use it in America at a race on Long Island, New York. Although in turn claiming to have invented it, Sherrill didn't particularly like the crouch start and eventually reverted to the traditional standing start. However, in the 1916 edition of his book *How to Become an Athlete*, James E. Sullivan, former secretary of the Amateur Athletic Union in America, argued that 'the "crouch" which should be called the "Kangaroo" or "Australian" start, is the perfect and up-to-date method of starting'. He went on to verify that it had indeed been Bobby McDonald who had first used the crouch start, having 'got the idea from watching the Kangaroo, and for years it had been known as the "Kangaroo start".'

★

Without doubt, the king of nineteenth-century indigenous Australian athletes was Charlie Samuels. Born in 1863 on Sir Joshua Bell's Jimbour Station near Dalby in Queensland, Charlie Samuels (or Combo, as he was known on the station) was a boundary rider and horse-breaker before he started substituting in races on the Darling Downs for his quarter-mile-champion brother George Combo, regarded as the premier Queensland sprinter, whose wife didn't want him to leave his local area. Of medium height and build, Samuels had remarkably long legs that gave him a fleet-footed, skimming stride estimated at an average of 7 to 8 feet (2.1–2.4 metres). However, at one event at the Carrington Grounds his stride at the finish was actually measured at 9 foot 3 inches (2.8 metres). Said to be a quiet, intelligent gentleman, Samuels trained for his fast times on that well-known fitness diet of a box of cigars, a pipe with plenty of tobacco and some sherry. He liked running purely for the pleasure of it, and so he was said to have some issues with technical matters such as handicapping, and pacing himself.

Nevertheless, he started serious athletic competition in Sydney in 1885 when he beat Australian champion Jim McGarrigal at Dalby over 130 yards after giving him a 4-yard (3.6-metre) start. The following year he ran 136 yards (124 metres) in 13.2 seconds in the Botany Handicap, claimed at the time to be an Australian record, and was credited with 300 yards (274 metres) in 30 seconds. That time had been equalled only by the Englishman Harold Hutchens, who was then generally believed to be, not the least by himself, the fastest man on Earth and the greatest amateur or professional nineteenth-century sprinter. Then 29, Hutchens had been running since 1875. So, in late 1886, Hutchens was brought out from England ostensibly to race Tom Malone and William Clarke, the current white Australian running champions, but it's quite possible that the real purpose, and where the big money lay, was to actually race Samuels.

On 17 January 1887, the two fastest known men on foot met at Carrington for their first race of 150 yards (137 metres), billed as the 'Great Race for the Championship of the World' and the 'Greatest Pedestrian Contest ever witnessed in Australia'. Hutchens was the popular favourite for the race and started well, but Samuels passed him before the finish line in a time just under fifteen seconds. Then on 4 February the men raced against each other again at Carrington for much higher stakes in another 150-yard race. Samuels had drawn away by the time they'd covered half the distance, but this time Hutchens nearly caught up to him and was only 2 feet (60 centimetres) behind as they crossed the line in just over fifteen seconds. Strangely, having won a previous race against the Irishman 'Peerless' Tom Malone in a time of 14.3 seconds, a world record at the time, Hutchens had just been beaten by Samuels who had taken nearly a second longer to run the same distance. By 5 February, when he appeared at the 'First Grand Electric Light Handicap of 150 Yards' at Carrington, Samuels was already being billed as Champion of the World.

Then on 2 March, before a crowd of 4000, for a stake of £200 and the championship, the two met for a final 150-yard race at Carrington. Although he again overtook Hutchens at about the halfway mark, this time Samuels couldn't sustain the pace and fell back to let Hutchens win for the first time by about a metre in 14.5 seconds. While Australian publications hailed Samuels as the clear winner of the series, Hutchens was never going to admit he'd run second to a 'colonial', and an indigenous one at that. Claiming that he was in poor condition and had 'thrown' those first races deliberately to build up the bets for his win in the last race, Hutchens called the series an 'exhibition' instead of a contest and thus denied Samuels the official title of fastest man in the world. However Hutchens chose to prevaricate, though, the clocks hadn't lied and he'd been beaten. Charlie Samuels had for a few weeks been the fastest man in the world.

The following year, there were unconfirmed reports that Samuels ran 100 yards (91.4 metres) in 9.1 seconds at Botany, Sydney, a time which would have put him in second place to the disqualified Ben Johnson in the 100 metres at the 1988 Seoul Olympics. In December 1888, he ran a record 124 yards (113.4 metres) in 12.5 seconds at the Sir Joseph Banks Grounds in Sydney. He also beat Tom Malone, an immigrant to Australia in 1882 so he could run for the big prize money offered here, who at that time held the records for 120, 130, 150, 175 and 440 yards. By 1894, the *Referee* was claiming for Samuels the Championship of Australia, writing that: 'Samuels has, in a long course of consistent and brilliant running, established his claim, not only to be the Australian champion, but also to have been one of the best exponents of sprint running the world has ever seen.'

However, managers took advantage of him; he reportedly won £90 000 for his backers in 1897 against Ted Lazarus but was paid only the prize money, a fraction of that amount. He fell on hard times, drinking and collecting a list of police charges; then he made a comeback, but slid back into drinking. Finally, an alcoholic suffering from hallucinations, he was arrested in Sydney and sent to the Callan Park Lunatic Asylum in late 1896. He found his way out again, though, and returned to Jimbour as a stockman. He appeared for the last time in public in May 1901, on the occasion of the visit of King George V and Queen Mary to Brisbane, standing on an Aboriginal arch.

Samuels and his wife, Maggie, and their two children were eventually removed to the Aboriginal settlement at Barambah, 'on the Minister's order', where Samuels died on 13 October 1912, aged only 49. At the time of his death, he still held the Australian record of 12.5 seconds for 124 yards, which he had set in 1888.

★

The rest of the world

The first known indigenous Australian runner was Manuello in Victoria, who in February 1851 beat Tom McLeod, at that time regarded as the fastest man in Australia over 100 yards (91 metres). He also beat Freddie Furnell, the New South Wales champion over 100 and 150 yards.

Victorian runner Bobby Kinnear, born and raised on the Antwerp Mission near Dimboola, was in 1883 the first indigenous runner to win the prestigious Stawell Easter Gift, the oldest Gift in the world, covering the 130 yards (119 metres) in 12.5 seconds. He was followed by Tom Dancey in 1910 and Lynch Cooper in 1928. Bundjalung man Joshua Ross became only the fourth Aboriginal athlete ever to win the event in 2004 and only the third person to win a second title when he won the following year.

The most famous male Australian Aboriginal athlete to compete in Australia was Sir Douglas Nicholls, in his time the fastest Gift sprinter in the country. A well-known Victorian footballer with Northcote and then Fitzroy, a boxer in Jim Sharman's troupe, civil rights activist and religious leader, Nicholls was in 1957 the first Aborigine to be awarded an MBE, in 1962 the first to become Father of the Year, the first to qualify as a Justice of the Peace, and in 1972 the first Aboriginal person to be knighted by the Queen. Appointed as Governor of South Australia in 1976, he was the first and has remained the only Aborigine to hold vice-regal office in Australian history. He was known within his own culture as *Bapu-mamus*, father of the people.

While Percy Hobson was the first Aboriginal athlete to win a gold medal for Australia at the Commonwealth Games, awarded for the high jump in 1962, Cathy Freeman was the first Aboriginal woman to win a track gold medal for Australia at the Commonwealth Games, in the 4 x 100 metre relay in Auckland in 1990. She went on to become one of Australia's greatest ever athletes, triumphing in her famous 400-metre victory at the Sydney Olympic Games in 2000. She was announced Young Australian of the Year in 1990 and Australian of the Year in 1998—the first person to receive both awards.

THE PERFECT WOMAN

Annette Kellerman, swimmer and movie star

Firsts

- First woman to attempt to swim across the English Channel
- First woman in Australia recorded as swimming a 10-mile (16-kilometre) distance
- First female celebrity to publicly wear a one-piece swimming costume
- First female Hollywood star to appear nude in a major motion picture
- First woman to write swimming and fitness manuals

'Talk about Annette Kellerman,' wrote Jack London in his 1913 novel, *The Valley of the Moon*, and for many years a lot of people around the world did just that. One day during the summer of 1908, a young Australian woman wrapped in a Navajo rug was led up onto a platform at the front of a Harvard lecture theatre by Professor Dudley Sargent. With a dramatic flourish he whipped off the rug, leaving her standing shivering before more than two hundred students dressed only in her notorious one-piece bathing suit. 'I want you to carry this figure in your minds,' he declared. 'In all your work keep it as an ideal of what a woman's figure should be . . . I will say without qualification that Miss Kellerman embodies all the physical attributes that most of us demand in the Perfect Woman.'

Yet as a child Annette Kellerman had been far from perfect. Born in July 1886, in Darlinghurst, Sydney, she was not able to stand upright by the age of two. With badly bowed legs, she was diagnosed with rickets and had to wear heavy iron half-body braces during her childhood in Marrickville until she was nearly seven. Wearing long dresses to hide them, she was very conscious of the difference between herself and younger sister Marcelle, older brother Maurice and younger brother Fred. Her parents were both musicians who were partners in the well-known Le Conservatoire de Musique in Paris—her mother, Alice Charbonnet, was an impressively talented pianist who had taught a young Nellie Mitchell (later Melba), and Frederick was an accomplished violinist. They had founded the Sydney Orchestral Society and were involved in the beginnings of the Sydney Philharmonic, and their soirées attracted important local and visiting international musical personalities. Annette, on the other hand, would sooner find a quiet corner where she could escape into reading fairytales.

Doctors recommended swimming to strengthen her legs. Kellerman at first hated it because the exercise was extremely painful, but by the time she was seven she was beating everyone else in the pool and often neglecting school to go swimming. She swam mostly at Cavill's Baths at Lavender Bay, really just a section of coastline fenced off with shark-proof netting. Frederick Cavill had attempted the English Channel and his sons would later become famous as pioneers of the Australian crawl. One of them, Percy, was Annette's swimming teacher. While in other countries swimming was a sport for men who predominantly used breaststroke, a much higher percentage of women and children swam in Australia, and tended at this time to use the trudgeon, an early form of a crawl but with a very different kick. While she was at Cavill's, Annette met Reginald 'Snowy' Baker, who was already one of the best divers in the country, and he taught her a lot about the sport, although she proved to be a natural. Once in and under the water, she underwent her fairytale transformation from crippled girl to mermaid princess.

Soon Annette was not only swimming, but practising ballet and walking 16 kilometres a day. She also promised herself she would never drink alcohol, smoke or eat red meat, a vow she maintained for the rest of her life. Now on the road to being healthy, she would stay that way and always be in control of her body. At fifteen, she established a new speed record for swimming the mile (1600 metres) and her father took up her training, realising that his talented daughter could help out her family, whose music school had been devastated by the 1890s economic depression. The family moved to Melbourne and she began training in the Yarra River, setting a record of 40 minutes and 30 seconds for a distance of 3.6 kilometres along the river in 1904. In 1880, the huge Exhibition Building had been constructed to house the Melbourne International Exhibition, and now it housed the aquarium, which included a large glass tank some 6 metres long, 3 metres wide and 1.8 metres deep, full of fish. Annette was soon giving exhibitions in it, becoming famous as the aquarium mermaid able to hold her breath under water for long periods. She was about to leave the country to demonstrate her skills at the St Louis Exhibition in 1904 when she was injured in a diving accident at the Bijou Theatre, so after she had recovered Annette did some shows at Broken Hill instead.

In February 1905, she returned to the Yarra River, swimming the 5 miles (8 kilometres) from the Swan Street Bridge to Princes Bridge in 1 hour and 48 minutes, cheered on by spectators lining the river banks and by her father following behind in a boat. While this was certainly an Australian record for a female swimmer, Kellerman had not equalled the time for the same distance established in 1875 by the fourteen-year-old English swimmer Agnes Beckwith, who swam from London Bridge to Greenwich along the Thames River in 1 hour and 7 minutes.

Then in April, once again followed by her father, official timekeepers and hundreds of spectators, Kellerman swam the longest known distance by any Australian female swimmer at that time: the 10¼ miles (16.5 kilometres) along the Yarra from the Johnston Street Bridge to Princes Bridge in 4 hours and 25 minutes. For almost half that distance, she had to battle the incoming tide, a stiff headwind and very choppy water. Although the forgotten Miss Beckwith had swum the same distance in 1876 down the Thames from Chelsea to Greenwich in a little over half the time, 2 hours and 46 minutes, the Australian press touted Kellerman's effort as a world record.

As undoubtedly the fastest woman in water in her own country, it made sense that by May she was on her way to England. However, when Kellerman and her father arrived in London they found themselves to be small fish in a bigger pond, and at first no one was interested in them. So, at the end of June, Kellerman decided to swim from Putney down the Thames River, through the City of London to Blackwall in the Docks area. It was a distance of 13¼ miles (21.32 kilometres) along what was then practically an open sewer, and she did it in just under four hours. She got the attention of the British public and media. The *Daily Mirror* christened her the 'Australian mermaid', and the editor suggested she should attempt to become the first woman to swim across the English Channel to France. Kellerman settled in to do some serious training by making an attempt on the women's distance record, set by none other than Agnes Beckwith, who had returned to the Thames in 1878 to cover 20 miles (32 kilometres) in 6 hours and 25 minutes. In July 1905, the nineteen-year-old Kellerman convincingly broke Beckwith's record by becoming the first woman to swim the 20 miles along the Kentish coast of England from Dover to Ramsgate, a feat previously accomplished by only three men, covering the distance in 4 hours and 20 minutes.

At the end of July, Kellerman made her bid to become the first woman to swim the Channel from Dover to Calais, a distance of about 57 kilometres, along with two male swimmers, but was defeated by fog and rough seas. Thirty years previously, Captain Matthew Webb had been the first—and so far only—person to achieve the crossing, completing it in 21 hours and 45 minutes. Still, Kellerman was the first woman to attempt the feat at all, and by the time she'd been pulled from the water she was a long way in front of the other two. On 23 August she made another attempt, swimming with competitors including Montague Holbein, but once again rough seas forced them all to retire. Kellerman announced that she would try again the following year.

In the meantime, she competed in a 12-kilometre race along the Seine in Paris in September. True to her promise, by June 1906 she was back in training for a third cross-Channel attempt, along with five other swimmers, once again including Holbein. She won a 37-kilometre race against the Austro-Hungarian champion Baroness Isacescu along the Danube to Vienna, and then competed in another race along the Seine. At the beginning of August, she battled her Channel nemesis for the last time, once again defeated by high seas. She conceded at the time that while having motivation for endurance, she didn't have the brute strength to compete with the weather conditions. One can't help but speculate how she might have fared a few years later in her career, after more training and experience. However, she continued to break records while in England, including her own women's record for the mile (1600 metres), and was reputed to have invented the first version of her famous swimming costume there when invited to perform for the Duke and Duchess of Connaught. When told she couldn't appear before His Highness in her customary men's costume with her legs bare, Annette sewed a long pair of black stockings onto it.

With her fame spreading rapidly, Kellerman was lured to White City in Chicago in October 1907 to thrill crowds with her aquatic showpieces, quickly becoming the highest-paid vaudeville star in the country. Her father thought it high time she had a manager, and appointed Jimmie Sullivan. He and Kellerman became close friends, especially after her father died, and he stayed by her side when she moved on to appear in Wonderland's Water Palace at the popular summer resort of Revere Beach, Boston, where she organised what may have been one of the twentieth century's great publicity stunts. In the summer of 1908, wearing her usual one-piece neck-to-toe bathing suit, she was reputedly 'arrested' at Revere Beach in Boston for indecent exposure. We only really know about this event because Kellerman began to tell the story many years later; actual reports of the incident at the time are conspicuous by their absence. Kellerman says that when she was brought before a judge, she referred to the 1904 *General Slocum* excursion steamer disaster on New York's East River in which over 1000 people died, mostly women and children who couldn't swim or whose heavy clothing pulled them under. She was just being practical, Kellerman declared, because there was little difference between the women's swimming costumes that were legal at the time and having chains around their legs. The judge saw the point, according to Kellerman, and dropped the charges on the condition that would be the suit she wore.

Only a few days later, on 30 July 1908, Kellerman was the first person to attempt the 21-kilometre swim from Revere Beach to the Boston Light and back. Only three men had attempted the Boston Light swim previously, and they had taken the shorter route from the Charlestown Bridge. Only one had finished. It was the ensuing newspaper coverage of this event that attracted the attention of Harvard University's Professor Dudley Sargent, who had been researching the female body for many years. He declared that at 163-centimetre tall, with a 66-centimetre waist and 84-centimetre chest, Kellerman was the first in 10 000 women to so closely match the measurements of the classical statue of the Venus de Milo.

Kellerman married Jimmie Sullivan—a non-swimmer—in 1912, forming a partnership that would last sixty years. Her fame led to offers to appear on stage in aquatic vaudeville shows for managers such as Edward F. Albee, who had a 21-metre-deep diving tank built for her that held 95 000 litres for shows in Boston and New York, but it was more economical and feasible to appear at fairs, resorts and hippodrome theatres that already had pools or tanks, or where they could easily be installed. There she could give swimming and diving exhibitions that by 1910 had developed into elaborate showpieces earning her $2000 a week.

However, claiming she was tired of appearing like a trained seal in tanks, Kellerman made a diversion into movies in 1909, and she was soon packing out theatres with her appearances in *Siren of the Sea* (1911), *The Mermaid* (1911), in which she was the first female film actor to wear a swimmable mermaid costume, and *Neptune's Daughter* (1914). Costing only $35 000 to make, *Neptune's Daughter* grossed over a million dollars and during it Kellerman was said to have set a women's high-dive record of 92 feet (28 metres). Two years later in 1916, she was the star of the world's first million-dollar movie, Fox Pictures' *A Daughter of the Gods*, filmed in Jamaica over eight months using twenty thousand people and 150 personally trained 'mermaids'. Kellerman shed her clothes for a waterfall scene in which she was covered Godiva-like only by artfully arranged long hair, becoming the first Hollywood star to appear nude in a mainstream studio-released film. She also dived into a pool containing live crocodiles, making a very fast exit. In her 1917 film *Queen of the Sea*, sticking to her principle of never using a double, she made a high dive into Bar Harbor in Maine from a cable strung 18 metres in the air between two towers. Unfortunately, of the dozen films in which she appeared, only the New Zealand-made *Venus of the South Seas* (1924) and *Siren of the Sea* are known to have survived in complete form. Only 25 minutes of footage from *Neptune's Daughter* is known to exist, along with the short film *Jephtah's Daughter* (1909).

While busy making movies, Kellerman had been lured back onto the stage at regular intervals. In 1914, she was badly lacerated during a performance when a 36 000-litre glass tank burst at the aquarium in Hamilton, Bermuda. Then, in 1916, she appeared in *The Big Show* at New York's Hippodrome Theatre, which was equipped with a 60- by 30-metre stage that opened to reveal a huge swimming tank beneath.

In a segment known as 'The Enchanted Waterfall', Kellerman appeared as the queen of over two hundred female water sprites who played about and then dived into the pool, remaining magically out of sight. The audience didn't know that there were tunnels under the floor at either end of the tank enabling the women to surface backstage. Kellerman would then provide the high point of the segment by high-diving into the pool from the top of the waterfall. People couldn't see enough of the show; it ran for 426 performances, and consequently she returned the following season in a show called *Cheer Up*, in which she cavorted as 'Siren of the Seas' with 'nymphs' in a lagoon under a starry sky.

Superbly fit and a shrewd businesswoman who was said at one time to be the highest paid woman in America, Annette embarked on the health and fitness lecture circuit and penned the first diet and fitness book, *Physical Beauty: How to keep it* (1919), as well as *How to Swim* (1918) and *Fairy Tales of the South Seas* (1926). Reported to have insured her figure for US$250 000 (or around $2.6 million in today's currency), Kellerman designed and marketed her own successful one-piece swimsuit range for women, which quickly became known simply as 'the Kellerman'. Actor Tallulah Bankhead once recalled that her sister gained a tinge of notoriety in 1918 as one of the first girls to be seen in Washington DC in a Kellerman suit; it was green and earned her the nickname 'Froggie'. The popularity of the sleek, close-fitting Kellerman suit among young, liberated women caused mixed reactions. Whereas in some cities the suit was banned at mixed-gender public pools or, as in 1919 in Dayton, Ohio, banned from being worn in a public street, in some places, such as Newark, New Jersey, the old-style bathing suits were officially rejected at public swimming establishments in favour of the Kellerman outfit. Without doubt, Annette Kellerman single-handedly changed social attitudes towards women and the water—yet it was often women's organisations that led the critical charge against the suits being worn, whereas men, for some mysterious reason, didn't seem to have a problem with them.

Kellerman formally announced her retirement from the stage in 1925 in order to devote her time to developing swimming training therapy for physically challenged children at a specially built facility north of Hollywood. For a number of years, she also toured throughout the United States and Europe, lecturing on physical fitness and diet in not only English but French and German, often dressed in her black tights to demonstrate her famous figure, mingling with the rich and famous such as Coco Chanel and Grace Kelly. She even advised President Roosevelt on exercises for his polio-damaged legs. In 1939, she and her husband moved to Newry Island on the Great Barrier Reef. When war broke out, she produced water shows for charity causes and set up the Red Cross Theatrical Unit, writing, directing and appearing in shows up and down the east coast and in New Guinea for Australian and American servicemen. Back in Hollywood, Greer Garson was so impressed with her efforts that she sent Kellerman a memento from the film set of *Mrs Miniver* that could be sold to raise money for the Red Cross.

Then the peace of her semi-retired life was interrupted when she signed a contract with MGM in early 1951 for the rights to make a movie based on her career. Originally entitled 'One Piece Suit', the film later became *Million Dollar Mermaid* starring Esther Williams, who had been pushing the studio for years to do it. Signed on as technical adviser, Kellerman went to the United States in the middle of the year and lived in Los Angeles during shooting. Then she went on a United States promotional tour, while the media marvelled that she had retained much the same figure and weight she had in 1908. Kellerman replied that you could grow old gracefully with proper nutrition and exercise.

After she and her husband returned from the United States, they lived quietly on the Gold Coast where Kellerman swam every day. In 1974, she was inducted into the International Swimming Hall of Fame in Fort Lauderdale, Florida. She died the following year, and her ashes were scattered out over the Great Barrier Reef, reuniting her with the water she loved and to which she had dedicated her life.

★

The rest of the world

Nineteenth-century teenage swimming phenomenon Agnes Beck-with is largely forgotten today, but in many ways her career curiously paralleled that of Annette Kellerman. Beckwith was also ill as a child, was trained by her father and began swimming at a young age. She swam similar distances to Kellerman and also had a career of exhibition performances in England and America, during one of which she set the world record of 30 hours for treading water while immersed in the whale tank at the Royal Aquarium in Westminster; she occasionally read the newspaper or sang to pass the time. With a similar reputation for revealing her beauty in daring swimming costumes, by the mid-1880s Beckwith was advertised as the 'Greatest Lady Swimmer in the World'. In later life, she also became a swimming teacher who advocated swimming as part of a healthy exercise regime.

It was not until September 1911 that W.T. Burgess made the second crossing of the English Channel—on his fourteenth attempt, in just under 24 hours. He still didn't beat Webb's 1875 time of 21 hours, though, so Kellerman shouldn't have felt too bad, especially as it wasn't until 6 August 1926 that the first woman, Gertrude Ederle from the United States, completed the distance (on her second attempt). Swimming from France to England, Ederle set a record of 14 hours and 31 minutes that wasn't beaten until Florence Chadwick's 13 hours and 20 minutes in 1950. Swimming the Channel is now so popular that prospective swimmers have to go on a waiting list to secure the requisite escort boat.

Although Annette Kellerman's mile record for women had been broken by English women swimmers by 1912, the first woman to take it under 30 minutes was another Australian, Fanny Durack, who in February 1914 swam the distance in a pool in 26 minutes and 8 seconds and who proceeded to hold every women's world record at that time for distances up to the mile.

In 1994, Marrickville Council in Sydney named its aquatic centre in Enmore Park the Annette Kellerman Aquatic Centre after the Marrickville Mermaid.

THE CRESSY, THE LISMORE AND THE RED SEAL

Alfred Alexander and his tennis racquets

Firsts

- Inventor of the first laminated wood tennis racquet
- The first company in Australia to wholly manufacture tennis racquets

Australians have always been great tennis players and enthusiastic tennis watchers, so it seems rather fitting that in 1922 Alfred Alexander and his younger brother Douglas invented the first laminated wood racquet. Then in 1925 they invented a company, the Alexander Patent Racket Company in Launceston, to manufacture and sell it.

To understand the importance of their innovation, we need to have a quick review of how tennis racquets came to be. Tennis probably began as a form of handball; one version of the origin of the word 'racquet' is that it's derived from *rahat*, the Arabic word for the palm of the hand. By the eleventh and twelfth centuries, French monks were playing a crude form of this handball game against monastery walls or over a rope strung across a courtyard. However, by the fourteenth century players were using a racquet (or racket) with strings made of gut fastened to a wood frame, and within two hundred years these were being used widely. Early racquet designs usually had long handles and small oval heads, more like modern squash racquets. Much like squash, too, the game was played indoors using walls and angled surfaces for rebound, but the ball, which was more like a baseball of cork or hair wrapped in wool, felt or leather, was also hit across a net. This is the game played by Henry VIII that came to be called 'real' or 'royal' tennis.

What we see today as modern tennis was really born in 1874 when Major Walter C. Wingfield registered his patent in London for the equipment and rules of outdoor tennis, or lawn tennis. That same year, Mary Outerbridge learned the game from a British officer in Bermuda and so introduced both game and equipment to America when she returned home to Staten Island. Wingfield, by the way, didn't actually call his game 'tennis'; his name was 'sphairistike', the Greek word for ball game or playing ball. The net height was around 2.1 metres and his court was shaped more like an hourglass, but the racquet-head size remained much the same until the 1970s—the end of the wooden racquet era. Early racquet-head shapes were rounder, usually wider and more flattened at the top than later designs. They were heavier than modern racquets (368–453 grams), had smaller heads overall (400 square centimetres), were about 68 centimetres long and were neither as flexible nor as powerful. They were usually made of a solid strip of wood bent to shape and secured to the handle.

Then along came Alfred Alexander, a young tennis player and woodwork teacher in Tasmania, who had been born in 1885 to Alfred Alexander from Hobart and Susan Elizabeth Davey from Launceston. While he was training as a trade teacher in 1918 at the Teacher's Training College in Hobart, Alfred Jr found that he had some time on his hands in the late afternoon and took up playing tennis. However, he didn't own a racquet and when he discovered how much a good one would cost, the creative but poor student decided he could make one himself. Shortly after that, he was offered a position at the Launceston Technical College where he continued with his racquet experiments in the cellar with the help of his brother, Douglas. Such industriousness greatly intrigued the principal, Walter Miller, who happened to meet a local tennis goods business entrepreneur, Stephen Bromby Hopwood, in the street one day and mentioned Alexander's racquets to him. Hopwood duly dropped by to have a look at what was going on and, very impressed, encouraged the Alexander brothers to continue their work.

Alfred had observed that the one-piece wooden frames then being used for tennis racquets tended to warp quickly because the steaming and bending process used to shape the single lengths of wood weakened the wood fibres, which were then further strained by tightening of the gut strings and the impact of the racquet hitting the ball. Wanting to make a racquet that wouldn't warp, Alfred and Douglas experimented with methods of wood laminating to produce a stronger handle and frame combination, and eventually they perfected their dry-bent timber laminating process whereby the racquet frame was formed from thin strips of glued wood that were pressed together. Using a similar technique to that used in the construction of wooden propeller blades, Alfred and Douglas used long-grained strips and cross-grained strips in alternate layers, extending them down to form part of the handle that could then be made thinner and flared out where it joined the rim, adding to the strength of the racquet.

In 1921, they applied for a patent for their unique dry-bent, cross-grain, alternating-layer laminating process, which was granted in 1922. Within five years, they also took out patents in America, England and New Zealand to further protect their interests.

They started out making single racquets in the college cellar and then from a workshop at their home. When these new racquets eventually featured in winning matches during the finals of the Tasmanian tennis championships, players praised their exquisite balance and soon enquiries were coming in for them from abroad as well as locally. By 1923, Alfred had formed a business partnership in Launceston with Hopwood—the Tasmanian Tennis Racket Company, which two years later became the Alexander Patent Racket Company. They established their successful factory in Wentworth Street, in the Launceston suburb of Newstead, becoming the first company in Australia established to manufacture only tennis racquets. They proudly stated that no steam was used during their manufacturing process in which four pieces of English white ash, each 5 feet 2 inches (158 centimetres) long and cut from imported logs, were dry bent and glued together under a high pressure of 9 tonnes to form the racquet frame. Their process enabled Alexander racquets to have a standard shape with perfectly identical rims, something that had not been possible with the one-piece wood frame, and then there was the added feature of their keystone wedge that strengthened the throat of the racquet. Rather than being balanced when the racquet was nearly finished, Alexander's racquets were balanced before the rim was bent, ensuring that they were not so heavy in either the handle or the head that the player would tire quickly.

Beginning with an output of around seventy racquets a week, by 1927 the factory had already expanded and its forty employees were working a 44-hour week, turning out around five hundred racquets a week. In the face of rapidly burgeoning demand, the factory and the workforce were again expanded and by the end of the decade a 100-strong Alexander workforce was making eight hundred racquets a week with overseas markets in New Zealand and South Africa. The factory was undoubtedly riding the wave of tennis's rising popularity as a sport in Australia. In Brisbane, as a typical example, the Suburban Tennis Association alone had three thousand members and every Saturday fielded 320 six-member teams playing on predominantly hard courts. Even people on outback Queensland stations would think nothing of travelling 100 kilometres to play.

The Alexander company created a number of racquet designs. The Alexander Lismore, promoted from about 1926, was one of the earliest racquets, along with the Cressy Perfect. In the 1930s, the company introduced the Hot Shot, followed by the Blue Moon, with its elaborately decorated wooden handle, the Pembroke and the Super

Flight. Other models included the Dover, Murray, Understudy, Hunter, Masterpiece, Mersey and Red Seal. However, it was the Cressy that remained a flagship brand name from the start to the end, the name originating from the small town outside Launceston which was the birthplace of one of Tasmania's great champion players. The Cressy's longevity as a brand—some thirty-seven years—may well mark the longest continual marketing of a racquet brand, right up there with the Dunlop Maxply.

Distributed worldwide, Alexander racquets were chosen by champion players. 'Gentleman' Jack Crawford, an Australian who was the number-one world player in 1933, won at Wimbledon that year with a Cressy Wizard that had a flattened rather than rounded top, a design that dated from the earlier 'royal' tennis game. The story goes that Wimbledon champion Sir Norman Brookes showed this early racquet design to Alexander's marketing/sales manager, W.J. Sheehan, after using one in a game with him at his holiday house. Brookes and Crawford, who was also there, liked the way it played and so Sheehan, who was obviously a man who could take a hint, went back to the factory where they fashioned a new style of flat-top racquet that was christened the Wizard, derived from Norman Brookes's own Wimbledon nickname. This new flat-top design became associated with Crawford's Wimbledon win and inspired the racquet industry in Australia, with many manufacturers, as well as Alexander, producing both oval and flat-top models.

By 1935, the Alexander company had to build even more additional factory space for almost 190 employees. By then, as a means of successfully combating the Depression, Alexander's had diversified into manufacturing a wider range of sporting goods such as cricket bats, hockey sticks, and squash and badminton racquets. The company sponsored tennis tournaments and training sessions, and maintained its own purpose-built tennis court facility behind the factory where Crawford frequently tested the product. A man who took pride in his company's community spirit, Alexander employed local sporting stars to keep them in the state, as well as national figures such as Don Turnbull, a South Australian Davis Cup player, who was the company's representative in Adelaide.

However, the stresses of life seem to have taken an early toll on Alfred Alexander's health. Foremost, of course, he was the popular and respected manager of his increasingly successful organisation. An excellent carpenter and cabinet-maker in his own right, he would do the rounds of the timber stacks every day and personally turn the wood to ensure it was drying evenly. He'd also been injured when his car had somersaulted three times one night on the road just outside of Westbury. With a large circle of friends, Alexander was also at various times a JP for Northern Tasmania, a Mason, the vice-president of the Northern Tasmanian Lawn Association and the president of his local Australian Labor Party branch. He was without doubt a very busy man.

No wonder his doctor advised Alexander to get away from it all with his wife, Elvie, and take a relaxing sea voyage north, and so they set sail with Stephen Hopwood along the east coast on board the *Ormiston*. Unfortunately, Alexander developed symptoms of bronchial pneumonia after leaving Brisbane, and so the trio disembarked at Cairns. But his condition quickly deteriorated and, despite being hospitalised, he died on 15 June 1937, aged only 52. After burying Alexander in Cairns, Elvie was left to return with Hopwood a few days later on the *Manoora* to the family home in Launceston and their five children: Kenneth, Davey, Robert, Barry and Joan.

W.J. Sheehan took over as manager of the company and under his leadership the company focused on improving product presentation. Racquets appeared with more elaborate paint and decal treatments complemented by decorative shoulder wrappings. Overwhelming market success indicated a level of customer approval of the new designs that forced other manufacturers to also improve, to the point where entirely new departments of skilled line painters, spray painters and decal application were created. As a promotional gimmick, Alexander even produced a hand mirror that was a miniature replica of the Cressy racquet.

After experimenting with a number of Australian timbers to provide raw materials for its factory, the Alexander company eventually attempted to develop a local timber industry by forming Ash Plantations Limited, one of the directors of which was William Alexander Walker, a Tasmanian nurseryman and producer of the Lalla Red Delicious apple. In 1933, they bought land at Hollybank in the Underwood area, intending to plant some 109000 English ash trees on it. However, because of problems with planting and growing the trees, the Alexander company returned to importing its ash wood from England.

By the late 1950s, the Alexander factory was in financial trouble due to cheap imports and new technology. In 1961, the company went into liquidation and was sold to Spalding in Victoria. By now Spalding, Dunlop and Slazenger dominated the mainland retail scene and were acquiring most of the high-profile players to endorse their products. The last Alexander racquets were produced in 1961, although the Cressy name was revived for one season in 1966 under the Spalding brand.

Within the space of his lifetime, Alfred Alexander had revolution-ised tennis racquet design and manufacture. From a basement workshop, his factory had developed into one of the largest sporting goods manufacturers of its time in the world.

★

The rest of the world

Wooden racquets quickly became antiques after the American company Wilson Sporting Goods introduced its T2000 steel racquet in 1967, which Jimmy Connors used well into the following decade, ensuring its popularity. Oversized aluminium-framed racquet designs followed with string areas more than 50 per cent larger than the old wooden racquets.

These were quickly succeeded in the early 1980s by racquet frames of carbon fibre bonded by plastic resins that became known as 'graphite'. This is still the material mostly used, although new materials have been tried with it, such as ceramic, fibreglass, boron, titanium and Kevlar. Typical head sizes now range between 85 and 110 inches (280–16 centimetres) wide and about 28 inches (71 centimetres) long; racquets weigh around 10 or 11 ounces (284–312 grams) with some as light as 8 ounces (227 grams).

The Alexander Racket Company buildings, with their saw-tooth roof and high windows, still stand in Newstead, occupied as a sport and recreation facility by the Launceston Police Citizens Youth Club since 1968. The factory was added to the Tasmanian Heritage Register in 2009. The old plantation area remains today as the Hollybank Forest Reserve.

THE GUV'NOR

Sir John (Jack) Brabham and his BT19 Formula One car

Firsts

- First person to win a Formula One World Championship race in a car of his own construction and bearing his own name
- First person to win a Formula One World Championship in a car of his own construction and bearing his own name
- First person to be knighted for services to motor sport

To Australian racing-car driver Jack Brabham's horror, the car ahead of him driven by Dave Macdonald suddenly flicked broadside, lost control, slammed into the concrete wall on the inside of the track and exploded in a fireball before ricocheting back onto the track in front of him. As Brabham braked hard, Eddie Sachs's car shot past him, smashed into Macdonald's and exploded as well. This was the second lap of the 1964 Indianapolis 500, and the track in front of Brabham was a wall of orange flame with little room to manoeuvre. Reacting quickly, he veered left towards the outside wall as the car slowed under brakes, dodged the burning wrecks and accelerated through the flames out the other side, miraculously emerging unscathed, whereas MacDonald and Sachs were both killed.

Brabham eventually had to retire from that race due to damage to the car. He wouldn't race in an Indy again for a number of years, but two years later in another race he would achieve a very different result. In 1966, at the French Grand Prix at Reims-Gueux, driving a Brabham BT19 with a 3-litre Repco engine and a chassis designed by Ron Tauranac, Jack Brabham became the first driver to win a Formula One Grand Prix in a car that he had developed bearing his own name. After also winning the British, Dutch and German Grand Prix in the same car, he also became the first driver to win the Formula One World Championship in his own personally developed and named car. Not only that, but he was the first driver other than Juan Manuel Fangio to become a Formula One triple World Champion.

Born in 1926 in the Sydney suburb of Hurstville, Brabham was taught by his father to drive at the age of twelve and began driving one of the three trucks used for his father's green-grocery business on weekends. Always interested in anything that moved, from steam engines to aeroplanes, Brabham had had enough of school by the time he was fifteen and briefly worked in an engineering shop before training as a motorbike mechanic in the garage that looked after his father's vehicles. After World War II broke out, Australians became very adept at improvising and turning out their own motor vehicle parts because they could no longer just be bought over the counter, and Brabham was no exception. Given a 350cc Velocette motorbike as a sixteenth birthday present, Brabham quickly learned how to take it apart and reassemble it, and then figured he could do that for profit. Before long, he had established his own business repairing and selling motorbikes.

In 1944, when he turned eighteen, Brabham was called up and joined the RAAF, but his dreams of flying were shattered when he was told they had enough pilots at that time. Instead, he was trained as a flight mechanic and spent the rest of the war at Williamtown, maintaining Bristol Beaufighters. After the war, he set up his own business as a one-man motor repair and engineering workshop. Persuaded to become involved in midget car racing by his American friend Johnny Schonberg, he flatly refused to join drivers he thought were lunatics on the track but, intrigued by the technicalities of these miniature race cars that hurtled around 400-metre oval cinder tracks, he agreed to help build one. Five months and £400 later, Brabham had built his first car, including the 1350cc engine.

At that time, midget car racing was very popular in most Australian capital cities, as it was in the United States. Promoters would bring in American drivers to give an edge to competition, and it wasn't unusual to have crowds of 40 000 attend major events. But it was also very dangerous; these were small, powerful cars only just under control on dirt tracks that flung dirt and rocks into the driver's face, and with cars on the verge of being out of control most of the time, nasty accidents were commonplace. Schonberg's wife eventually prevailed on him to retire from driving, and so Brabham not only found himself unexpectedly driving in Schonberg's place but discovered he had a knack for it. In his first season he won the New South Wales Championship at the Sydney Showgrounds, and he was leading the South Australian Championship one night in Adelaide when the engine blew up and caught fire. He thought it might be time to consider other options, one of which was driving his father's truck interstate. But the deal to buy a new rig fell through, and Brabham drifted back into road racing. If that truck had been bought, then Grand Prix racing might have had a very different history.

Brabham had begun driving his midget car in competitive hill climbs. At one of these, he met Ron and Austin Tauranac, two young engineers with whom he teamed up to build and drive a midget in the 1951 Hawkesbury Hill Climb. Years later, Ron would become a pivotal member of Brabham's racing team. Brabham went on to win the 1951 Australian Hill Climb Championship. Having abided by the rules, he was the winner whether the Light Car Club of Australia liked it or not—and, needless to say, they didn't like it.

Road racing was looking like a better option, so Brabham acquired a Mark IV Cooper chassis which he fitted with a 500cc engine. Finding that combination too quiet, he eventually moved up to a Mark V Cooper chassis fitted with an 1100cc JAP alloy engine. By now he was in contact with the Cooper Car Company in England, with which he would have a profitable association for many years. It was really no surprise that his next car was the Cooper Bristol, which came to be known as the Redex Special after his sponsor, the Redex fuel additive company. The sponsor's name featured prominently on the car, something that the newly formed Confederation of Motor Sport frowned upon. It forced Brabham to take the words off the car and he lost his sponsorship.

Fed up, Brabham left the country to race in New Zealand, competing in the first New Zealand Grand Prix in 1954, then returning to Australia to drive a Holden in the Redex Trial around Australia. Just out of Marble Bar, Brabham tore off the entire front end on a large rock. Using an oxy torch borrowed from a nearby mine, Brabham and his co-driver rebuilt the front axle, steering, radiator and engine sub-frame on the side of the road until they could reach Meekatharra and make further repairs. The car was rebuilt at General Motors in Perth. They reached Sydney two weeks after the trial had finished.

Competing in the second New Zealand Grand Prix in January 1955, Brabham was persuaded by Dean Delamont, competitions manager for the Royal Automobile Club in the United Kingdom, and Dunlop competition manager Dick Jeffrey, to travel to Europe for a season of racing there. Basing himself in the United Kingdom, Brabham initially raced his own Cooper-Alta from New Zealand, but he was unhappy with the engine and, after meeting with the Coopers, father and son, he built himself a rare rear-engine, 2-litre Bristol 'Bobtail' Cooper Formula One car. This was the car he used for his World Championship debut in the 1955 British Grand Prix at Aintree. Then he shipped it home and won the 1955 Australian Grand Prix at Port Wakefield, South Australia.

After buying a Maserati 250F in 1956 that turned out to be a lemon, Brabham returned to Cooper to drive the Formula Two season. At the beginning of 1959, Brabham was able to drive the new, small, aerodynamic 2.5-litre rear-engine Cooper-Climax to win the Monaco Grand Prix and then the British Grand Prix at Aintree. He became the first British driver in a British car to win a World Championship that year, despite being thrown from his wrecked car onto the track during the Portuguese Grand Prix in Lisbon and having to push his car over the line in the US Grand Prix at Sebring in Florida after running out of fuel in the last lap. He won the championship conclusively in 1960, having built a new low-line, rear-engine Cooper T53, winning five consecutive Grand Prix races. It was a tough season; two drivers were killed that year during the Belgian Grand Prix on the extremely fast road circuit where Brabham reached speeds of 314 kilometres per hour. But the big thrill for Brabham was being able to win the British Grand Prix in a British car that he always considered to be the best Cooper built.

Brabham made his first official entry in the Indy 500 in 1961 in a modified version of his Formula One Coventry Climax, with a stiffened suspension and a 2750cc engine converted to run on methanol. It was small, lightweight, rear-engined and painted British racing green. Indy drivers are notoriously superstitious and, second only to never having women near racing cars (which didn't happen until 1971), racing in a green car was bad luck. Brabham's was not only the first rear-engined car, but the first green one. He and the car came in for some mockery, but he ran as high as third before finishing ninth.

However, by the early 1960s Cooper technology was being left behind. Since the days of driving in hill climbs, Brabham had kept in contact with Ron Tauranac, suggesting he come to England and design cars with him. When he finally did make the move in 1960, they made the ideal team: Jack was the experienced driver who knew exactly what he wanted and could make it if necessary, while Tauranac was the man at the drawing board. Their cars were always a combination of input from both men and so the type numbers were always preceded by the letters BT—Brabham and Tauranac. By then, Brabham had formed his own UK company, Jack Brabham Motors, as well as establishing a good relationship with the Australian parts company Repco. He'd always wanted to build and drive his own car, so Brabham and Tauranac set out working at night to do it. During the day, they were producing upgrade kits for Sunbeam Rapiers and Triumph Heralds, known as Formula Junior cars. Reluctantly Brabham had to tell Charles and John Cooper that he wouldn't be driving for them anymore, and in partnership he and Tauranac set up the Motor Racing Developments company (MRD), followed by Brabham Racing Developments (BRD) when they realised 'mrd' didn't come over well in French.

By July 1962, BRD's first Formula One car was finished, and Brabham still thinks it was one of the best-looking cars they ever built. The BT3 had a Coventry Climax V8 mounted at the rear in a stiff tubular chassis, and a strengthened cockpit and bulkhead. The water pipes predominantly ran outside the cockpit to reduce the appallingly high cockpit temperatures Brabham had endured in the Coopers. The exhaust had twin tailpipes made in Australia by Brabham's friend Len Lukey and were known as Lukey Mufflers. However, in an arrangement drivers today would probably find a little hair-raising, the fuel tanks were fitted behind the seat and on both sides of it, and were joined under the driver's legs with another smaller tank over his knees.

For the next year, BRD continued building, racing and learning, making twenty of the BT6 chassis for Formula Junior cars during 1963. Each time they built a new car, they incorporated new ideas and their designs progressed across the range of racing cars: Formula One, Two and Three as well as Formula Intercontinental and Indianapolis. By 1964, they were even building a 2-litre sports car known as the BT8; twelve of them eventually were built between 1964 and 1966. When the American driver Dan Gurney joined them, the Brabham Racing Organisation team was formed, winning the French Grand Prix in 1964.

A new 3-litre formula category would be created for Formula One in 1966, and Brabham knew that he would have to look for a new engine. Brabham spotted an opportunity and persuaded Repco to develop a new 3-litre Formula One eight-cylinder engine, based on Oldsmobile's aluminium alloy 215 engine block. It would not be immensely powerful, but it would be light and reliable. Repco sent Phil Irving over to the United Kingdom to work with Brabham on development. When the engine was ready, it was everything Brabham had hoped for, but Repco would only loan them the completed engines for three years and at the end of 1968 declined to go on with the project.

However, in 1966 the Brabham Formula One car, the BT19, with its V8 Repco 3-litre engine, would prove an unbeatable combination for Brabham and his team mate Denis 'Denny' Hulme. When he won the French Grand Prix at Reims when Lorenzo Bandini's throttle cable broke in the lead car, Brabham became the the first driver ever to win a Grand Prix race in a car bearing his own name. Later, by the time he was forced to retire from the Italian Grand Prix after only seven laps, he had already amassed 39 points, winning the French, British, Dutch and German Grand Prix one after the other. Brabham was also the first person to win the World Championship for Drivers, as well as the Constructors' (Manufacturers') Championship, driving a personally designed and built car.

The Brabham team was just as successful in Formula 2 that year, driving a Honda; a Brabham car won every start except one and Brabham won ten of fourteen races as driver. Then came the news that he was to be awarded an OBE. He would have to appear at Buckingham Palace in top hat and tails to collect it personally from the Queen. After some initial resistance to the idea of dressing up, he finally went and was impressively invested with the award. But when he came to start his car after the ceremony, the starter was jammed and so he ended up deep in the engine bay in his formal attire, spanners in hand, until he could get the car started. Invited back to the palace for dinner with the

Queen and Prince Philip a few months later, the Queen joked with him about taking an engine apart in her forecourt.

The following year, the Brabham team continued winning when Denny Hulme won the World Championship, giving Repco-Brabham its second Constructors' Championship. In July, Brabham beat Graham Hill and Jim Clark in Lotus cars and Jackie Stewart in a BRM in the French Grand Prix at Le Mans. This was followed by Repco-Brabham wins in the German Grand Prix in August with team mate Hulme first and Brabham second; and in the first Canadian Formula One Grand Prix later that month, Brabham came first and Hulme second.

In 1969, Brabham suffered serious ankle injuries in a mid-season testing accident, but he raced for one more year in Formula One, finishing the 1970 season in a tie for fifth place with Jackie Stewart. Then, after twenty-three years of professional racing, he officially retired. Thousands of people attended the Brands Hatch, United Kingdom, farewell meeting held in his honour. For Brabham, though, retirement was just a word and he has continued to make the occasional racing appearance. Ironically, it wasn't until the Goodwood Revival in 2000, long after his so-called retirement date, that he was in a race accident bad enough to put him in hospital overnight—he was knocked unconscious and cracked some ribs when his car spun backwards into a bank.

As a symbol of the respect in which he has been held, few drivers have had so many nicknames. Racing writer Denis Jenkinson christened him the 'Nut Brown Australian' from his tanned features gained after so many years in open cockpits. The Cooper Car Company mechanics called him 'The Guv'nor', the French press often referred to him as 'Le Grand Champion', and he earned the name 'Black Jack' Brabham from his dirt-racing days. Then there were the official titles: Australian of the Year in 1966, Officer of the Order of the British Empire in 1966, Knight Bachelor in 1978, and in January 2008, he was named an Officer of the Order of Australia for his services to motor sport.

He once commented that he was going to die without an enemy in the world: 'I aim to outlive the bastards,' he said. So far, he has.

★

The rest of the world

In designing and building his own racing car, Jack Brabham was following a tradition that goes back to the early days of automobiles and some famous names. In 1905, Swiss mechanic Louis-Joseph Chevrolet set a speed record of 109 kilometres per hour to win a race in the United States only four years after he had emigrated there from France and then Canada. Having learned automobile design while working for Buick, he began work on his own engine before partnering with William Durant in 1911 to form the Chevrolet Motor Car Company in Detroit, Michigan. However, the two men couldn't agree on the design of the new car and so in 1915 Chevrolet sold his interest in the company to Durant who in the following year brought the Chevrolet Motor Car Company into General Motors. Louis Chevrolet then went into the racing business, partnering with Howard Blood to design the Cornelian car in which he raced in the 1915 Indianapolis 500. Louis also went into partnership with his brother Gaston to form the Frontenac Motor Corporation, and went on to compete in the Indy four times. In 1920, Gaston Chevrolet drove one of their cars to an Indy 500 victory.

The American racing driver Ralph de Palma had an association with Packard for many years, working with their chief engineer Jesse Vincent to design and build race cars from 1917 through to the mid-1920s. De Palma successfully raced their Packard 299 with its reworked 300-cubic-inch aero engine on American board tracks during 1917 and 1918. In January and February of 1919 De Palma set every land speed record in America with their Packard 905 in which he achieved a speed of nearly 150 miles per hour for the measured mile, faster than the air speed record at that time.

In more modern times, racing driver Carroll Shelby, who won the 24-hour Le Mans race in 1959 co-driving an Aston Martin DBR1/300, began work in 1961 designing a sports car based on a chassis built by AC Cars in England and powered by a 260-cubic-inch Ford V8. The following year his company, Shelby-American, began production of the Cobra. In 1963, driving a Cobra at Bridgehampton, Dan Gurney became the first American driver to win an FIA race in an American car. In 1964, the first Shelby Mustang GT350 race and street cars were built, followed by such cars as the 427 Cobra Roadster, the GT500, the CSX 3015, and the GT40 which won at Le Mans 1-2-3 in 1966, the first time an American team had won there. In the 1980s he worked with Dodge on the production of Shelby Chargers, the Omni GLH and the Viper, and in late 1995 his company produced the CSX4000 series 427 Cobra Roadsters. Once again associated with Ford, Shelby-American is still producing new models of the GT and the Cobra.

THE TRACK AHEAD

Geoff Healey and the RaceCam

First

- Inventor of the first over-the-shoulder, driver's-eye-view race camera for television

The television audience watching the Hardie Ferodo 1000 race in 1979 could hardly believe their eyes. Able to look over driver Alan Moffatt's shoulder for the first time, expecting to see sharp focus at high speed concentrated in a tight two-handed grip on the steering wheel, what they saw was a man who looked as though he was on a Sunday drive casually steering with one hand as his car hurtled headlong down Conrod Straight among other cars at the Mount Panorama circuit at Bathurst. That revealing personal insight into a champion driver's technique was due to a camera that we nowadays take completely for granted: the RaceCam in-car point-of-view system.

Geoff Healey, then chief engineer at Channel 7 Sydney (or ATN-7), was driving his son to school one day during the late 1970s when his son picked up a camcorder that had been lying on the back seat and began filming the drive to school, holding the camera on top of the dashboard and shooting through the windshield. Watching the tape a few days later, Geoff and his son observed how fast the road unrolled towards them because of the wide-angle lens. Healey suddenly had that epiphany that can sometimes occur when you see something happening in a different context, in this case a camera being used in a completely different place. Wouldn't it be great, he thought, if they could use this for the Hardie-Ferodo 1000 race. They could secure a remote-controlled camera to the roll-bar behind the driver so it would look over his shoulder and basically show the track to the viewer from the driver's point of view. No longer would the television viewer be a passive watcher of cars going around a track; now they would feel as though they were actually in the driver's seat.

The concept of placing a camera inside or on top of a vehicle certainly wasn't new. It had been around in movie-making for decades, but involved either placing a cameraman with a bulky camera inside the car secured in such a way that they wouldn't be thrown around, or constructing a frame on top or to one side of the vehicle to hold a camera and operator. Neither of those methods really worked for car racing. At Bathurst there had been recent experiments with putting a camera and operator in the back of the car for short periods; in 1973, Screen Sound Australia mounted a 16 mm camera into a Holden HQ and obtained some excellent footage. But it was still a novelty gimmick, and television sporting events as a whole up until that time were objective; the viewer sat back and watched from a distance, with little if any sense of close-up personal involvement.

All that changed in 1979 on the Mount Panorama track at Bathurst as RaceCam was born, after Channel 7 had invested three years and hundreds of thousands of dollars developing the system. Geoff Healey and his team placed a single camera on a movable mount, giving the camera a 180-degree view in Peter Williamson's Toyota Celica for Channel 7's coverage of the race. For the first time, viewers could experience something of the sensation of how fast the car was actually zipping down Conrod Straight, leaning into the corners and climbing the hill. Not only that, they could actually hear Williamson giving his colourful bend-by-bend commentary through a headset under his helmet. The camera sat in a specially fitted shock-absorbing mount that cushioned it from severe vibration that could otherwise shake it apart, allowing the picture to remain steady. The camera and mount also had to be rugged enough to withstand high-speed crashes or roll-overs without flying apart and injuring the driver, while at the same time not being so heavy that they would penalise the speed of the vehicle. The camera also had to be heat-resistant, as the Bathurst event is a six-hour long-distance race during which vehicle interiors can reach abnormally high temperatures.

By the next year, RaceCam had developed from a one-camera to a two-camera system that could pan, tilt and zoom, linked by remote control. The cameras were mounted on remote-controlled pan-and-tilt heads, allowing them to pan outside to show other drivers' passing manoeuvres, zoom in on gauges on the instrument panel, photograph the driver at the controls, or look straight through the windscreen at the track unrolling at high speed in front of the car. By 1984, the camera had become small enough to be fitted inside the headlight mount of a BMW and, although there had been initial resistance because of weight issues, drivers were clamouring to have them fitted. Fourteen years later, twelve RaceCams were fitted to six cars as well as the pace car, and the Channel 7 team could monitor on-board engine performances.

There was more to it than just the cameras, of course. Pictures and voice commentary were transmitted using microwave to a helicopter overhead, which then bounced the signal to the outside broadcast station on the ground. As microwave signals travel in line of sight—that is, the transmitter has to be theoretically visible to the receiver—the helicopter was a necessary addition, especially on the Bathurst track with its hills and curves where the cars could be out of sight of the base station but visible from the helicopter overhead. Through digital data carried on a UHF channel, a trackside camera operator could see what the RaceCam saw while at the same time controlling its point of view with a joystick. Meanwhile, back in the outside broadcast station, the director mixed those signals with what was coming in from helicopters, planes or perhaps even an airship (ideal camera platforms because they are so steady in flight) to assemble the pictures sent to the satellite and eventually to the television screen.

When Channel 7 returned to international coverage of the Bathurst 1000 in 2007, after a hiatus of a few years, the station brought with it improvements that lifted the original RaceCam technology into the digital age. A new graphics system allied with on-screen information not only took viewers inside the car with the driver but could also take them within the engine components to show them the location of a mechanical problem. Some eighty in-car cameras were used during the entire race series, forty-nine positioned in ten V8 Supercars for the major race, each camera made predominantly from carbon fibre to be as light as possible and mounted to withstand severe crashes and high cab temperatures for six hours. They are now linked with ground-based digital technology that replaces the previous helicopter-linked version, enabling producers to have continuous access to the in-car cameras with at least three available at any time. Flycams that can travel at 160 kilometres per hour and swivel 360 degrees were also added to cover Pit Straight and part of the track on Mount Panorama. Located around the 6.2 kilometres of track, 36 kilometres of cable now link thirty-two on-track cameras as well as a helicopter-based camera platform. The total number of cameras at the Mount Panorama circuit for races across the weekend that year amounted to 116, the largest-scale broadcast undertaken by Australian television at that time. Compare that to the three cameras in place for the 1963 coverage, all in Pit Straight.

Geoff Healey could well have saved motor racing as a spectator sport. People who were becoming tired of just watching cars going round and round from a distance could now experience the thrills first hand. Looking back on it three decades later, it is evident that Healey in fact changed the entire relationship between the spectator and the sport. The very next thing was that Channel Nine picked up the technology with 'stump-cam' for cricket, allowing viewers to see almost exactly what the batsman saw of the oncoming ball. Then microwave transmitters were added so that the driver's comments could be heard and they could have two-way conversations with race commentators and their own pit managers. When they added sound to the cricket pitch, however, sometimes the program manager wasn't sure that the viewers should be hearing exactly what the Chappell brothers were saying at the time until editing technology caught up.

Healey won a Sports Emmy Award in 1983 for innovative technical achievement from the US National Academy of Television Arts and Sciences, making ATN-7 the first Australian company to receive such an award. As head of technical operations and engineering for the Sydney Olympic Broadcasting Organisation, host broadcaster of the 2000 Olympic Games, Healey designed the technical facilities for the coverage of the 2004 Summer Olympic Games in Greece. In 2002 he was made a Fellow of the Society of Motion Picture and Television Engineers in Australia.

As cameras become more miniaturised, perhaps the next step will be 'athlete cam', allowing the viewer to experience the 100-metre-sprint from the runner's perspective, or that of a boxer, or even footballers or Rugby League players. On the other hand, perhaps there are some experiences best watched from a distance.

★

The rest of the world

American audiences were introduced to RaceCam after CBS sports commentator Ken Squier saw it in action at Bathurst in 1980 and brought a tape back to show to network heads. After obtaining the exclusive American rights, CBS installed it for the 1981 Daytona 500 secured to the roll-cages of cars driven by Terry Labonte and Richard Childress. It wasn't an auspicious beginning: there was no audio link, Labonte blew his engine and had to retire, and electrical interference in Childress's car kept breaking up the picture. By now, Healey and his team were claiming it was the smallest television camera unit in the world, about 30.5 centimetres high by 25.4 centimetres long and weighing only 1.3 kilograms.

Rival network ABC then acquired the rights to the technology in 1983 for RaceCam to be fitted to cars for the Indianapolis 500. Rear-mounted cameras for looking behind were added in 1988, nose-mounted in 1994, and roof mounts three years later. The first winning car fitted with a RaceCam didn't cross the line until Rick Mears saw the chequered flag first in 1991. Cale Yarborough was the first to drive a RaceCam-fitted car across the finish line at the Daytona 500 in 1984. Since then, 'bumpercam' and 'roofcam' have been developed to enhance the experience.

RaceCam technology was adapted for yachts in the 1985 America's Cup, raced off the coast of Fremantle, Western Australia. Since then, it has been modified for other sports such as motorcycle racing, basketball ('slamcam'), snow skiing and many other sports.

THE £10 BET

Michael O'Brien and the sporting streak

First

- The first person to streak naked across a major sports arena while a game was in progress

Although various students had been running naked around American college campuses for some time, apparently no one had either gathered enough courage or been paid enough money to dash across a major sporting arena—until 20 April 1974. On that very cold Saturday, between 45 000 and 53 000 Rugby fans were packed into Twickenham Stadium in Greater London, the home of the English Rugby Union team, for a match between England and France. Among the spectators was Princess Alexandra, grand-daughter of King George V, and a 26-year-old long-haired, bearded Australian accountant, Michael O'Brien, who was working for an English stockbroking firm. As the match neared half-time, a few Fosters had been consumed among O'Brien and his friends and £10 was wagered that he would not be able to run naked across the field and touch the boundary fence on the other side. His friends warned the person laying the bet not to waste money; O'Brien would do it.

This story isn't just about Michael O'Brien, though. It's really about a convergence of coincidence between two people after which their lives would never be the same again. O'Brien's naked run would probably have been consigned to a couple of lines in the history of curious events if it hadn't been caught in the lens of Ian Bradshaw's camera. It was the photo of O'Brien's naked figure being escorted from the grounds by uniformed bobbies while his groin was covered by policeman Bruce Perry's helmet that immortalised the event. At that time, Bradshaw and his colleague Ed Lacey were working as sports freelancers for the *Sunday Mirror*, using long lenses to cover the width of the field from a distance. While Lacey was in the stands, Bradshaw was sitting behind a goalpost as the first half ended. Suddenly, as the players left the field, O'Brien jumped the half-metre wall onto the field and started his run for the other side—stark naked.

Having accepted the bet, O'Brien had been too focused on working out the logistics of the run with his friends to consider how he felt about actually doing it. They planned the run for the half-time whistle so the players would be off the field and O'Brien would have a clear run across the halfway line. Occupying a seat near the quarter line, O'Brien would have to strip and send his clothes around to the other side of the field, then wait for the whistle, climb over the fence, run along the sideline to the halfway line and then sprint for the other side to touch the fence. The bobbies would have lots of time to see him coming, so it would make for a great chase and fairly equal odds. With luck, he'd make it to the other side of the field to touch the fence there and then, in the days before international television coverage of sporting events, be able to dress quickly and disappear into the crowd before anyone knew who he was.

History had other plans for him. O'Brien made it across the full width of the field in front of the laughing crowd and crossed the touchline, but then the constabulary caught up with him. However, when he explained that his friends had bet him he couldn't touch the fence, the bemused policemen took him over and let him touch it. As they led him off the field, Constable Bruce Perry took off his helmet and covered O'Brien's groin with it because, as he later admitted, Perry felt embarrassed. According to Perry, as he was reciting the arrest caution the streaker turned his head and said loudly, 'Give us a kiss.' At that instant, Bradshaw pressed his shutter button.

It was Ian Bradshaw's lucky day. The rest of the press pack was at the other end of the field with the players. Carrying a spare manual Nikon camera with a 200 mm fixed lens, Bradshaw found himself right in front of the group leading O'Brien away. As they came towards him, the helmet covering O'Brien's groin bobbed up and down, sometimes slipping away from his crotch completely, so Bradshaw snapped off eight frames trying to capture an instant of full coverage. Then he raced back to the newspaper office.

Once the police had O'Brien off the ground and he'd dressed again, he was taken to the local police station where they filled in the appropriate forms. In what could only be a reflection of those more peaceful times, Perry and the other police constables then took O'Brien back to Twickenham where he resumed his seat in time to see the second half of the game. The wager was duly paid, but the money went towards the magistrate's fine on the following Monday—which was £10.

A clean-shaven and much more conservative O'Brien would say many years later, in a 2006 interview for the Channel 7 television program *Where are They Now*, that he would never advise anyone to do it and that he regretted having been the pioneer of a craze that continues to the present day. Bruce Perry, now a council licensing officer, showed up on the same show to present O'Brien with his helmet, which had been auctioned for charity in 2000.

Bradshaw's photo of O'Brien covered by Perry's judiciously placed helmet became an iconic image of the decade. The *Sunday Mirror* published it as a rare front-page wraparound and it was then picked up by publications in some thirty-five countries, earning a series of awards such as *Life*'s Picture of the Year, the British Press Photographer of the

Year, the World Press Photo Award and *People* magazine's Photo of the Decade. The Rugby Club in London was said to have erected a statue by Walter Keethner based on the photo, and the image appeared on cards, billboards, T-shirts and even in advertisements. In 1991, Holeproof in Australia had O'Brien asking Perry for directions to the '20 per cent off' Holeproof underwear sale, while British Telecom used it in 1995 to advertise adding a new digit to phone numbers. Even Canon used it to advertise its cameras, despite Bradshaw having used a Nikon.

The photo, now titled 'The Twickenham Streaker', has come to mean many things to many people. Some see the streaker as an anti-establishment symbol of freedom, others see a homoerotic exchange between a policeman and a streaker on the verge of kissing, while another group sees religious connotations in the Christ-like appearance and pose of a naked man with outstretched arms seized and surrounded by uniformed and helmeted guards. At the time, Bradshaw was not aware of any of this. He didn't have time to visualise the composition of the photo before he took it. So focused was he on making sure the helmet was in the right place at the right time that he didn't even notice Mr Grundy, the official running behind the group holding the overcoat. Now living in the United States where he has an education photography business, Bradshaw comments that, even though in a way it was the easiest picture he's ever taken, 'When all has been said about the luck element, it comes down to the same situation as any news event. If it happens in front of you and you are a professional photographer, you should not miss it. It is, after all, what you are paid for.' But in fact it's the very serendipitous nature of that photograph that allows the observer to appreciate this captured instant in time in which an intoxicated accountant becomes more than the sum of his naked parts.

'Streaking' at first referred to intentionally running naked in public or through a public space, but now it includes the use of a multitude of transport modes, such as rollerblading, motorbikes and even parachuting. The word originally derived from 'stretch' and, before people began to take their clothes off while doing it, 'to streak' simply indicated you were moving very fast. Apart from Lady Godiva, who was on horseback anyway, protesting while standing around naked has been a fairly regular practice since the Middle Ages. There is a story that a group of students, including future US president John Adams's son Charles, ran naked around Harvard Yard, the centre of Harvard University, in the late 1700s, and that in 1799 an unknown man accepted a wager of ten guineas to run naked from Cornhill to Cheapside in London, but the first actual recorded streak was run by college student George Crump through Lexington, Virginia, in 1804. Still involving college students, the practice would have to wait another 170 years to really take off, culminating in the record for the largest simultaneous group streak being established on the University of Georgia campus when 1543 naked students ran across Sanford Stadium bridge in the Great Streak on 7 March 1974, while several thousand more clothed students gathered to urge them on.

The most famous female streaker in Australia is probably Helen D'Amico, who at the time of her appearance was a seventeen-year-old stripper. Reputedly at the request of her employer, she dashed onto the Melbourne Cricket Ground in front of 100 000 spectators and millions of television viewers wearing only a Blues scarf during the 1982 VFL Grand Final between Carlton and Richmond, and tried to cuddle Carlton footballer Bruce Doull. An entire year later, and eight months pregnant, she was finally arrested for the deed, led away in handcuffs and fined a thousand dollars.

In these more modern and less carefree times of mobile phone cameras, internet social networking and conservative nanny states, streaking at major public venues in Australia can now invoke major penalties and life bans from the grounds (the MCG included), apparently prompted by a series of seven streaking incidents during a one-day cricket match in January 1996. Whereas previously streaking usually had only invoked an indecency fine of around $150, now 'pitch invasion' can lead to fines of $5000 and streaks at major sports events are less frequent. For his streak at the 2004 Houston Super Bowl, Englishman Mark Roberts was banned from further entry to the United States and charged with criminal trespass; he paid a $1000 fine to avoid jail. Still, however much they try, police, venue authorities and sports officials have never been able to totally eradicate it. Somewhere out in the crowd, there's always another bet being made.

★

The rest of the world

The first female public streaker to be recorded in newspapers is generally recognised as Laura Barton, eighteen, a Carleton College (in Minnesota) freshman, who streaked the curtain call of the school play *Measure for Measure* on 2 February 1974 (think serious snow). The bouncy, short-haired Ms Barton dashed across the stage with the house lights up in front of several hundred people, wearing only a ski mask, white tennis shoes and of course socks that were red, white and blue. The leading man was so shocked that he promptly dropped the girl he was carrying on his shoulders. Barton was helped to escape by other female friends and, according to her, was afterwards congratulated by the dean on an excellent streak. She did, however, lose her boyfriend and catch a cold. 'I wouldn't have streaked the play if it hadn't been a comedy,' she observed a month later.

The first streaker of any gender to be photographed and published on a newspaper front page was 21-year-old English window-dresser Sally Cooper, who streaked across Kingston Bridge near London with four friends on 17 March 1974. She was pinned to a wall by a patrolman and nipped on the behind by a police dog for her efforts, but she did escape. She passed away in 1994.

Streaking arrived in the Antipodes on 24 March 1974, during a New Zealand vs Australia Test at Eden Park, Auckland, and in Australia when Allana Kereopa and David Cook streaked down the straight and across the finish line at Randwick racecourse during the Doncaster Handicap on 13 April. They were fined $200 and $150 respectively; during her hearing, Kereopa invented what became known as the Streaker's Defence: 'It seemed like a good idea at the time.'

The first Academy Awards streaker was Robert Opel, who caused an international sensation by streaking across the stage at the 1974 Academy Awards, flashing a peace sign as he ran. At first oblivious to the record-making event taking place behind him, host David Niven recovered in time to make jokes about Opel's 'shortcomings'. Opel wasn't arrested at the time. It has since been proposed that the streak had previously been arranged and Niven knew about it in advance.

Michael Angelow, a navy cook, was probably the first English cricket streaker when he raced onto the pitch at Lord's in 1975 and hurdled the stumps before the bobbies caught up with him. Angelow said later that he waited until the end of Dennis Lillee's over to make his own run because he didn't want to disrupt the game.

Greg Chappell, who managed to get in a stroke at Angelow with his bat, later blamed him for making cricket streaking a fad and went on to have something of a career sideline in bagging streakers. He tackled a streaker in Christchurch, giving him 'a whack or two' when the man wouldn't be led to the police quietly. At another New Zealand game, he paddled a young streaker across his naked bottom with the cricket bat, and in another incident held onto a male streaker by the hair for several minutes while he marched him to the fence and the waiting police.

The first known female streaker at a major European football match was Variana Scotney, who ran onto the pitch at Highbury during an Arsenal vs Tottenham Hotspur match in 1981.

The very well-endowed 24-year-old bookshop assistant Erica Roe was the first English female streaker to become a national newspaper celebrity when she had her turn at displaying her charms to Twickenham spectators, which included the Queen, after a few beers during the England–Australia Rugby Test in January 1982. This time the policeman's helmet covered a breast. She made such an impression that a *Guardian* newspaper poll in 2001 voted her streak 71 in a list of 100 greatest sporting moments.

The most prolific serial streaker in the world is generally recognised to be Mark Roberts from Liverpool, England, who has performed some 380 streaks so far at a number of international venues.

PART V
TRANSPORT

THE MISSILE AND THE MONORAIL

Louis Brennan and his life of invention

Firsts

- Inventor of the first practical guided missile, the wire-guided torpedo
- Inventor of the first gyroscopically balanced monorail and tilt-train system, and thus the inventor of the first gyroscopic land vehicle

The young South African boy found himself a seat under his favourite baobab tree on a slight rise overlooking the rail line as the setting sun neared the hills on the horizon. There would be just enough time to see the train and then run back to the family homestead before dark. As dusk came on, it was so quiet he could hear a lion cough somewhere out on the veldt. Suddenly, a bright beam of light was shining along the single rail that stretched away in the direction of Victoria Falls, and then on across the continent to far-distant Tangiers. A faint hum began to vibrate the air. Then there was a rush of wind, a burst of light and the six long carriages of the *African Streamliner* monorail were hurtling soundlessly by him at their usual speed of around 320 kilometres per hour, the polished aluminium of the carriages gleaming in the light of the setting sun. In less than a minute it had vanished into the oncoming night, and the boy was away and happily running for home.

Unfortunately, that young boy never did actually see the *African Streamliner* hurtle by, but if the dream of Louis Philip Brennan and a South African railway company had become reality then it might well have happened. Speeding monorails were still many years away when the Irish-born nine-year-old Brennan came to Australia with his parents and younger siblings in 1861. He showed an early interest in mechanical puzzles and toys, taking them apart and experimenting with reassembling them in different ways to discover how they worked, and he eventually became 'articled' (or apprenticed) at the Carlton Foundry in Melbourne to owner Alexander Kennedy Smith, a renowned civil and mechanical engineer, mayor, politician and officer in the Victoria Volunteer Artillery Regiment, which had close connections to the Victorian Torpedo Corps.

Brennan was a man who evidently thought as he worked, often about how he could improve on or make use of what was in front of him; he exhibited prototypes of an improved sliding scale, a window-latch, a mincing machine and a billiard marker at the Victorian Juvenile Industries Exhibitions in 1872 and 1873. However, these were only intimations of what was to come. While working at the foundry, Brennan often operated a belt-driven planing machine. After a while, he noticed that even if the belt became worn to a single leather thong, it would still power the machine as effectively as a new belt. He'd also observed that if he pulled a cotton sewing thread away from its spool from underneath, the spool would move away at a corresponding speed. Over the next few years, substituting wire for leather and winding drums for cotton spools, Brennan experimented with combining these two sets of observations into the development of a wire-guided and -powered torpedo, a weapon that could be steered towards its target across or under water with an option of recovery if unused. The concept of torpedoes was not new, but successful propulsion and guidance systems had yet to be developed, so there was room for Brennan's creativity.

By 1877, assisted by William Culvert and Professor W.C. Kernot, lecturer in civil engineering at the University of Melbourne, Brennan had built a half-scale working model, 9 feet (2.7 metres) long, that he demonstrated in July to a pair of Royal Engineers officers who had arrived from England. Brennan's nineteenth-century innovation was, of course, slightly different from what we currently think of as 'wire-guided' weaponry. His torpedo was actually propelled by wires as well as guided by them. Connected to a huge steam winch, a pair of wires was pulled from two drums inside the torpedo as it moved through the water, the unspooling action of each wire powering one of twin contra-rotating propellers. In other words, as the wires were pulled backwards from each drum at greater or lesser speed, so the torpedo was propelled forwards faster or slower. The speed at which the wires unspooled could be governed independently by an officer in an elevated position using a pair of binoculars on which was located an electronic control key. As the speed of one wire was increased or decreased, the speed of the corresponding propeller increased or decreased. To the amazement of observers, this meant that the weapon could actually be steered towards a moving target, even turned across a current. Not only that, it could be recovered if it missed the target and didn't explode. The running depth of the torpedo was governed by two planes at its bow. At a speed of 6 knots, it had an excellent range at the time of 600 yards (about 550 metres) and the officers were profoundly impressed.

The following year, Brennan began carrying out tests with a 15-foot-long (4.6-metre) prototype in the Graving Dock at Williamstown, near Melbourne, which demonstrated that he had the steering concept right but depth control was going to be more complicated. Nevertheless, the weapon clearly had potential. The British Admiralty commissioned reports and expressed interest after the favourable tests, and so the Victorian colonial government evidently thought it should be seen to be doing something. To facilitate and finance further development, Brennan formed the Brennan Torpedo Company, in which he was a major shareholder, and was duly awarded a £700 government development grant. Rather ironically, even though it put up that original seed money for the project, the government's subsequent request for some torpedoes was rejected on the basis that Brennan's weapon was needed for the defence of home ports in Britain. Brennan duly patented his torpedo in London.

Brennan's first public test of his weapon was carried out offshore from Williamstown on Hobsons Bay on 21 March 1879, in the presence of the state governor, military and press representatives, and selected civilians. The experimental wire-guided torpedo ran true for just over a minute at 11 knots to strike a target boat at 400 yards (365 metres) range. It was the first and last time the Australian public would ever see the torpedo; within three years it was a classified secret weapon.

Brennan originally and rather prophetically envisioned his torpedo being fired from specially built fast boats, armoured but lightly gunned, that would be able to move at speed among a fleet of battleships and wreak havoc. However, invited to England in 1880 to present his invention to the War Office, Brennan found that although it liked his concept, the War Office remained unconvinced it would work effectively from on board ship. Even a short run of 350 yards (320 metres) used 1125 yards (1030 metres) of thin wire wound onto drums by steam winches, all of which took up space. Perhaps, too, having spent vast sums on those very battleships, the thought that this weapon would just turn them into huge floating targets probably didn't go down well with the War Office either, and so it chose to see Brennan's torpedo primarily as a land-based coastal defence weapon.

In 1883, the Brennan Torpedo Company signed a three-year development contract with the British government. An experimental station was established at Garrison Point Fort, Sheerness, at the mouth of the Thames River, while the workshop would be at the nearby Chatham Barracks, the base of the Royal Engineers. Trials took place over the next two years before the weapon was officially recommended for use as a harbour defence weapon in 1886. Three years later, on

26 June 1889, Brennan's torpedo was conclusively demonstrated in the Solent of the Isle of Wight in front of the Secretary of State for War, Edward Stanhope, as well as the Adjutant-General to the Forces, General Garnet Wolseley (Viscount Wolseley), members of the Ordinance and Defence committees, assorted generals, admirals, politicians, members of the press and even the poet Lord Tennyson. In its finished form, it was 6.7 metres long, weighed about 1000 kilograms, had a warhead containing 100 kilograms of guncotton and had a range of about 2 kilometres with a speed in excess of 20 knots (37 kilometres per hour). Launched down a slipway and successfully steered to a moving target, it convincingly sank an old paddle-steamer a mile (1.6 kilometres) away across the water.

By then, Brennan had happily accepted the wildly extravagant tax-free sum of £110000 (well over £5 million today) from a British government anxious to ensure he didn't sell this advanced weapons technology to someone else. After all, it had paid only £15000 for the Whitehead torpedo a few years previously. This self-propelled, unguided torpedo fired from an underwater tube, invented by Robert Whitehead and Giovanni Luppis in 1866, was the forerunner of modern torpedoes. However, the British had only been able to buy rights to use and reproduce the torpedo while Whitehead had retained the ownership of it, and his large factory in Fiume, Italy, continued to fill orders for a number of countries. The British were not about to make the same mistake twice, and paid Brennan the largest amount up to that time paid by any government to a weapons inventor for the sole ownership rights. The money was paid to Brennan's company over five years with an initial £30000 first payment; every year, Brennan would drive up to the Bank of England in his carriage and collect the equivalent of his next instalment in gold bars. He was also officially appointed superintendent of the new Brennan Torpedo Factory at Gillingham in Kent on £1500 a year, and in 1892 was awarded the Companion of the Most Honourable Order of the Bath when only forty years of age. Meanwhile, in September 1892 Brennan had married Anna Mary Quinn, a childhood sweetheart from his home town of Castlebar in County Cork. The ceremony was in Dublin, but they returned to a large house named Woodlands built for them in Gillingham, Kent, near the torpedo factory, overlooking the River Medway. There they raised two daughters and a son. In 1895, he was appointed Torpedo Adviser to the War Office and Admiralty.

For a number of years, the Brennan torpedo was regarded as the most important coastal defence weapon that Britain possessed, and a series of eight torpedo forts was erected to house Brennan's weapon and its required delivery system around England's coastline, at Cork in Ireland, on the island of Malta, and overlooking Victoria Harbour in Hong Kong. Each fort had twelve torpedoes and was manned by an officer, a mechanic, eight NCOs and two engine drivers. However, by 1906 control of coastal defence had passed into the hands of the Admiralty from the War Office and the former was not a fan of Brennan's invention, instead favouring long-range guns, submarines and mines. In January of the following year, the torpedo factory was closed on the basis that supply had now exceeded demand, that the torpedo's range was too short and that they were difficult to launch at night.

By then, however, Louis Brennan was a rich man who was working on another project: a new type of train. The traditional concept that trains needed a pair of rails on which to move created some inherent problems. One rail could wear more than the other, for example, or they could spread, sag or warp so that rather than running smoothly, a train jolted, bucked sideways, swayed and even sometimes derailed. Such problems would be considerably reduced, Brennan theorised, if there was only one rail. He initially considered suspending a car from an overhead rail, but the supporting structure would consume a large amount of the budget. Besides, he was aware that the Germans were already working on overhead rail systems. So Brennan decided that it would be more economical and effective to have the rail under the vehicle, but then the really tricky part would be designing a train that could balance on only one rail, especially when rounding corners.

Once again, Brennan was inspired by everyday objects. He noticed that a child's spinning top had a propensity to right itself as long as it kept spinning, and this led him to the possibilities of the gyroscope, at that time regarded as only an interesting movable model with which to demonstrate the laws of revolving bodies. Brennan observed that once a gyroscope starts whirling, it will resist any attempt to change its plane of rotation. If he fixed a gyroscope in a square metal frame and set the wheel turning on the same plane, the gyroscopic persistency would hold the frame upright. He successfully experimented with placing the frame on two legs and substituted two wheels in line with each other, but these initial experiments only worked as long as the wheeled gyroscope travelled in a straight line. Once it reached a curve, it leaned and fell over.

It took twelve years of trial and error before Brennan found a solution to the problem of the curve. To cut a very long story short, he discovered that by using dual electrically driven balance wheels, or twin gyroscope wheels, mounted within a frame in the car and spinning in opposite directions to each other on axles above the truck wheels, the car would balance itself. As one side of the car rose as it entered a curve, it would contact the axle and the friction would act the same as friction on the point of a leaning child's top, turning the gyroscope into an automatic balancing machine for the vehicle. So, even when unevenly loaded or being pushed by a side-wind, the monorail car's equilibrium could constantly be restored, even when stationary.

First patenting his concept in 1903, Brennan took his idea to the Army Council, which awarded him a £2000 grant with which he built a rough wooden structure fitted with his gyroscopic stability mechanism. When he requested more money, the War Office told him in January 1906 to build a bigger model that could be tested in trials. Judging by photographs taken at the time, and by the surviving chassis currently exhibited in the National Railway Museum in York, his second model was a beautifully detailed and engineered working example of Brennan's concept. Clad in aluminium, it was built to one-eighth scale, 6 feet (1.8 metres) long and 18 inches (45 centimetres) wide, weighing 128 pounds (58 kilograms) and able to carry 140 pounds (64 kilograms). The two gyroscopes, each wheel only 5 inches (12 centimetres) in diameter and spinning in opposite directions to each other at 8000 rpm, were mounted at the front within the cabin. The control mechanism accelerated or retarded the precession of the gyroscopes, so allowing the vehicle to always be returned to a horizontal plane. The model ran on two pairs of inline wheels coupled together, with one in each pair being driven by electric motors carried on two pivoting bogies, each mounted in the middle of the underside at either end, allowing the vehicle to lean into a curve like a modern tilt-train. Accumulator cells stored power in batteries mounted at the rear which drove the motors.

For the purposes of demonstrating the capabilities of his train under every conceivable condition, Brennan constructed his own 800-metre model monorail test track using 13-millimetre gas pipe around the spacious grounds of Woodlands, complete with hills, sharp curves, a complete circle, a bridge over a valley with a wire cable span of 15 metres and a length of the wire cable laid on the ground without sleepers. He even included a section of track that was bent and severely twisted as if damaged by an earthquake.

Finally, after some pressure from the War Department, Brennan gave a demonstration to the War Office Committee of his model running on the track at Chatham on 23 July 1907. The committee members were duly impressed and recommended Brennan be funded for further work, but their superiors were not as visionary and notified Brennan in November that the department was no longer interested in the monorail. However, having had prior experience with the War Department, Brennan had pre-empted their decision and was already in discussions about building a monorail with the Indian government through Lord Morley, Secretary of State for India, and the government's committee duly viewed trials later in November.

The War Department quickly decided it would lend Brennan and the torpedo factory to the Indian government, cleverly letting itself off the financial hook while the colonials funded further experiments.

Brennan's first public demonstrations of the model away from his custom-built track were held in a large room at the Royal Society building in London in early May 1907, on a track constructed 2.5 metres above the floor so the monorail could run around the room above the heads of the audience. The impact was as dramatic as the demonstrations, which were so popular, as H.G. Wells rhapsodised in his book *The War in the Air*, 'that celebrated demonstration room was too small for its exhibition'. Wells visualised the monorail in action as part of a travel network, both on the ground and running along a cable suspended between pylons, so accurately that it seems highly likely he actually attended one of those demonstrations. Brennan gave further exhibitions later that year for the Royal Society and for the Savage Club, at which another well-known literary figure, Mark Twain, was present.

At the beginning of May, Brennan held an open demonstration of his model monorail at Woodlands for the general public, members of the press, railway men and leading engineering authorities. To the amazement of them all, the monorail's two electrically powered gyroscopes enabled it to remain upright not only when moving but also when standing motionless, entirely unsupported. Reporters marvelled at how they could feel the resistance of the vehicle if they pushed against one side, almost as if it was pushing back, and how it followed even a sharp curve of the pipe or cable along which it was travelling. At one point during the demonstration, Brennan stopped his model at one end of the cable suspension bridge. After reversing it into the middle, Brennan then demonstrated the car's stability by taking hold of the cable and swaying it back and forth, then smacking the car on the side. The car remained upright and motionless on the cable, held there by the action of the gyroscopes. He shifted the weights in the car from one side to the other, equivalent to forty passengers suddenly jumping up and running to one side. The car still held steady on the cable. Finally, he rolled the car across the bridge to the bank, where his daughter climbed into it and sat down. Then Brennan ran the car out to the middle of the bridge again and stopped it, where it remained perfectly balanced. In short, it was a remarkable demonstration of advanced railroading that could not be performed anywhere else at that time.

Brennan predicted that each full-scale car would be about 200 feet (60 metres) long and 30 feet (9 metres) wide and would weigh 100 tonnes empty. A full train, he said, would have five or six such cars built of enamelled steel with flush windows, each fitted out in ocean-liner-type luxury, each with their own gyroscopes spinning at 3000 rpm. Even if the electric power failed, he claimed, the lubricated and vacuum-chambered wheels would continue to spin for two or three days with their own momentum. If lubrication failed, the engineer would be warned and the train run into a safety siding with support walls; if sidings couldn't be built, then the cars could be fitted with emergency legs. If one gyroscope wheel failed, the other would hold it steady. Driven by electricity or steam or gasoline, these frictionless 1200-foot (365-metre) trains could attain speeds of 200 miles (320 kilometres) per hour.

All this publicity had the desired affect. After another demonstration at the end of May before Lord Morley and American steel baron Andrew Carnegie, the Indian Council awarded Brennan £6000 towards the building of a full-scale monorail car. Brennan in turn granted the Indian government the use of the invention at a royalty of 5 per cent on the cost of the rolling stock ordered. They planned to construct 200 miles (320 kilometres) of track just as soon as Brennan could build the rolling stock at the converted torpedo factory. The War Office put in another £2000. A South African railway company also expressed interest in laying a monorail track from Johannesburg to Victoria Falls, then from there around Lake Chad through Morocco to Tangiers, from where people could board ship to London, shortening travel time over that distance from twenty-one to six days. By July 1908, Brennan was negotiating with the Deakin government in Australia with hopes of laying track in New South Wales but, in typical Australian government fashion, the Commonwealth and the states were still passing the buck about it four years later, blaming each other that nothing had been done.

Brennan had actually begun work on a full-size prototype before he was forced to stop while he built his second demonstration model, and now with money in hand he moved ahead quickly and the prototype was demonstrated on 10 November 1909. This was a 22-tonne mono-rail car 40 feet (12 metres) long, 10 feet (3 metres) wide and 13 feet (4 metres) high, with a cabin at one end, carrying around forty people on a flat tray at the rear. The monorail ran backwards and forwards along a straight single rail section and then around a circular track. The electric power to drive the gyroscopes was generated by a 20-horsepower Wolseley petrol engine while another 80-horsepower engine drove the running wheels. This time, the car's balance could be tested by actually moving people from one side to the other and, just as with the earlier model, the car remained perfectly stable and upright.

In December 1909, Brennan transferred his interest in the rights to the monorail to the British army and navy in consideration of the funding they had given him, and in February 1910 he sold the German rights to his competitors there who expected to be able to build a 200-kilometre-per-hour version of his system within eighteen months, running between Berlin and provincial towns. In May 1910 it was reported that Brennan had sold the American rights to a syndicate that would lay 110 miles (34 kilometres) of track in Alaska, of all places, from the Matamiska coal fields towards Fairbanks.

That same year, Brennan took his prototype to the Japan–British Exhibition in London where it won the highest award, the Grand Prize. Winston Churchill, then Home Secretary, was so captivated by it that he not only insisted on riding in it, but on driving it himself. The general public queued up to pay sixpence a ride. Churchill persuaded Prime Minister Herbert Asquith and the Chancellor of the Exchequer,

David Lloyd-George, to ride in it as well, saying it would revolutionise the world's railway systems. Notably, however, the War Minister had declined an invitation to see it, and it was a portent of things to come. Concerned about the weight and safety of the gyroscopes, the government refused further funding. Brennan had actually been paying his torpedo factory employees out of his own pocket since 1907 to work on his monorail cars, and now even his money was gone. Having invested everything in his dream, he had to sell his beloved house in 1912. A surviving prototype carriage ended up as a park shelter. It would be 70 years before anyone would again ride on a high-speed tilt train.

Brennan went back to work in the inventions department of the Ministry of Munitions until he was engaged by the Air Ministry in 1919 to carry out design and testing of his Brennan helicopter at the Royal Aircraft Establishment, Farnborough. He'd been toying with this idea since 1884 and now that he carried sufficient weight with the government, finance became available to build a full-scale rotary-wing prototype. Brennan's concept was a propeller-driven rotor, a single 18-metre-long rotor blade with small propellers at each tip driven by a 230-horsepower Bentley engine within a triangular weighted frame sitting on four feet, looking a little like a lunar landing module. Construction progressed in great secrecy, with tethered tests inside a hangar beginning in 1921, and outdoor tethered flights in May 1924. By then it was said to have cost £40 000 to develop. By the following year, the helicopter was making short flights of 18 to 27 metres at heights of 1.5 metres, but in October the machine crashed and broke up. The government baulked at sinking more money into the project, especially now that Spanish engineer Juan de la Cierva had arrived in England with his much more advanced and flyable autogyro, and it closed Brennan's project down in early 1926.

There would be no more great ideas. Brennan died on 17 January 1932, after being hit by a car while on holiday in Montreux, Switzerland. Sadly, tragedy had gradually overtaken his previously triumphant life; his wife, Anna, had died and he had also lost one of his two daughters in the 1918 influenza epidemic. His outstanding contributions to weapons and transport had largely been forgotten because of the secrecy that surrounded them and so, forgotten like his work, Brennan was buried in an unmarked grave at St Mary's Cemetery in London. Among his thirty-eight patented inventions were: a two-wheeled gyrocar; a pocket-size, five-key silent stenographer's typewriter known as the Brennanograph, similar to those later used in law courts; a mini-lift for stairs known as the Helping Hand that he had designed for his wife who had a heart condition; and mechanical starting devices for engines. Although England and Ireland also claim him, Australia too was home for this brilliant man who was so far ahead of his time.

★

The rest of the world

The first passenger-carrying monorail, the Cheshunt Railway in Cheshunt, Hertfordshire, England, was opened on 25 June 1825. Powered by a horse that pulled cradle boxes slung below a cable, it was built to carry bricks but at the opening ceremony spectators climbed into the cars for the ride.

General LeRoy Stone designed the first steam-powered monorail. The ornate single car, demonstrated at the United States Centennial Exposition in 1876, had a narrow external verandah deck on each side as well as seating inside. The first commercially viable steam-driven monorail line, known as the Sonoma Prismordial, was also constructed in 1876. Originally intended to connect the Northern California city of Sonoma with the harbour at San Pablo Bay, barely half of the planned 11.3-kilometre route was eventually built.

The Enos Electric Railway, the first suspended monorail, was tested on the grounds of the Daft Electric Company in Greenville, New Jersey, in 1886. It was an elevated steel girder construction that, though never actually constructed for public use in America, bears a close resemblance to Eugen Langen's Wuppertal Schwebebahn (Floating Tram) that went into operation in Wuppertal, Germany, in 1901 and is still running.

Right behind Brennan came August Scherl, who by 1910 was demonstrating his own gyroscopic monorail. Though quite similar in concept, the prototype was smaller than Brennan's and was powered by electricity through trolley wires alongside the track.

Perhaps the two most famous modern monorails are the Disneyland Monorail System, the first daily operating monorail in America, and the short-lived French suspended SAFEGE Monorail test track built in 1958 near Orleans, featured in the 1960s science-fiction classic *Fahrenheit 451* directed by Francois Truffaut. Although the track was demolished in the 1960s, the cars still existed in storage in 2000. The Disney monorail opened as a sightseeing attraction in Tomorrowland on 14 June 1959. Originally three-car trains, they were increased to four cars in 1961 when the track was lengthened, and then five cars in 1968. There have been a number of refurbishments since then, and the latest version of the train began operating in 2008.

Like many other cities now, Sydney has its Metro Monorail that runs along a single-loop 3.6-kilometre track through eight stations, connecting the city with major attractions and facilities. First conceived in the 1980s as the Darling Harbour Monorail, it was designed and constructed in twenty-six months in a failed attempt to open in time for the 26 January 1988 Australian Bicentennial celebrations; it did eventually open in July that year. Originally intended to be automatic, the seven-car, forty-eight-seat, trains are now manually driven. Expensive to build, operate and ride, the system has never quite lived up to expectations. In March 2012, the New South Wales government announced they had purchased Metro Transport Sydney and that the monorail would be scrapped and removed.

HER SKILL AND ART ARE
WONDROUS RARE

Florence Mary Taylor, glider pilot, architect and town planner

Firsts:

- First known woman to pilot a glider
- First woman to qualify and practise in Australia as an architect, and as a structural and civil engineer
- First qualified female town planner in Australia

Looking down at the sand flashing by beneath her, Florence Taylor must have felt an incredible weightlessness totally unknown to people of that era before flight was a common experience. The ground silently fell away beneath her, the air rushed into her face and for those brief few exuberant minutes she would have felt like a bird looking down on the upturned faces beneath her, hearing their shouts drifting away on the wind. Then suddenly the lines pulled taught and the glider touched down onto the beach sand with a soft thump and she was surrounded by people laughing and shaking her hand. Whether she knew it or not, Florence Taylor had just become one of the first women in the world to pilot a winged aircraft.

Born to working-class parents in Bristol, England, in 1879, the sixth of eight surviving children, Florence Mary Parsons emigrated from England to Australia with her family in 1883, living first in a home built of kerosene tins in Rockhampton, Queensland, before moving to Sydney where her father, John, became a draughtsman for Parramatta Council. For a few years, the large family was moderately comfortable, but then tragedy struck. In 1893, their mother, Eliza, died, followed only three years later by John, from tuberculosis. Suddenly the children were orphaned with no inheritance, and nineteen-year-old Florence had two younger sisters to look after.

Having had some education—at a time when women often had little or none—and probably demonstrating an interest in engineering and drafting because of her father's early influence, she found work as a clerk at Francis Ernest Stowe's architectural practice while she studied architecture at night at Sydney Technical College (STC), the first formal architecture course to be offered in Australia. It was practically unheard of for a woman to venture into this profession at the time, and consequently Florence found herself the only woman in her class of two hundred (she would later claim she was harassed by other students and ignored by some lecturers). In 1900, Stowe arranged for her to become articled to architect Edmund Skelton Garton, who had been impressed by her work and was a good mentor. She eventually gained a senior drafting position there, meanwhile completing her formal architecture training at STC in 1904 and then moving on to night classes at Stowe's Marine Engineering College. Still looking after her sisters, she didn't have the luxury of forsaking work for full-time study. The following year she became chief draughtsman in J.B. Clamp's architecture practice, also encountering in that workplace the same resistance from her male colleagues to a woman in the practice that she had found at Stowe's.

Finally, Florence completed her qualifications as a structural and civil engineer from the University of Sydney in 1906. By then, Clamp had developed such a high opinion of her that his practice formally nominated Florence for associate membership of the Institute of Architects of New South Wales. Not surprisingly, considering the prejudice she had faced so far, her nomination met such a groundswell of hostility from the all-male institute membership that it was defeated. The vote was later declared illegal and she was offered another chance to apply on passing an entrance exam but Florence didn't take them up on it, perhaps because of injured pride. When the institute eventually caught up with changing times in 1919 and formally agreed to accept women members on the same terms as men—provided they pass an oral exam—Florence was once again the first woman to apply and to finally be accepted as the first female member of the institute. But she had been successful in her career without the institute and so she subjected herself to this process, which she labelled persecution, for the sake of the women who would come after her.

Refusing to allow her life to be restricted by the attitudes of her male peers, Florence won design awards and later claimed to have designed between fifty and one hundred houses around Sydney, although little specific record remains connecting her to existing buildings. Because of her expertise in civil engineering, Florence also developed a number of town planning schemes during her life, some of which have since become reality, such as a harbour tunnel, an Eastern Suburbs freeway, construction of 'double-decker' streets, increased apartment building, and the need to conserve and plant more trees. She was a supporter of widening the top end of Sydney's Martin Place to form a civic square, continuing the street to the Domain and then on as a tree-lined boulevard to Woolloomooloo and through tunnels under Potts Point and Darling Point to form a gateway to Sydney. However, she also wanted to demolish the convict-built Hyde Park Barracks and declared that the Sydney Opera House would be a white elephant—but you can't be right all the time.

In 1907, Florence astounded those who knew her—as she would so often do during her life—by suddenly getting married. While studying at the STC, Florence fell in love with one of her part-time lecturers, George Taylor. They were married at St Stephen's Presbyterian Church during their lunch hour, returning to work afterwards. George would have a profound influence on Florence's life and she would eventually leave her architectural practice to co-found a publishing empire with him. She became involved in many of his interests, and together the Taylors made both a powerful and romantic couple. George wrote a poem for Florence every day, presenting it to her with breakfast. They never had children, a decision which may have been influenced by George's epilepsy—the popular belief was that epilepsy could be inherited.

Born in Sydney in 1872, George Augustine Taylor was the second of nine children, five of whom would die in childhood as a result of epilepsy. His younger brother was Vincent Patrick Taylor, who would become internationally famous as a balloonist and parachutist under the name of Captain Penfold and the man responsible for first demonstrating aerial bombing to the US Navy. The family were proprietors of a King Street, Sydney, shop that sold cut flowers, fruit and confectionery. They later developed a catering business based in a Darlinghurst factory, supplying racecourses, sporting fixtures and beach resorts with cut sandwiches, pies, cakes and soft drinks. George had a wider vision, however, and he found work with an architect's practice before joining the New South Wales Department of Mines. From 1897 he contributed cartoons to *The Bulletin* and then founded his own short-lived comic paper, *Ha-Ha*, after which he returned to work as a freelance cartoonist for the *Sunday Times*, Melbourne *Punch*, *Steele Rudd's Magazine* and others. A personal friend of Norman and Lionel Lindsay, he was the first Australian cartoonist to have his work published in the London *Punch* magazine and his cartoons became so popular that many were made into comic postcards. A fluid lightning sketch artist, George was such a high achiever that when he wrote *Those Were the Days: Being reminiscences of Australian artists and writers* in 1918, many of his colleagues disputed that he could have been involved with so many events.

While doing coloured poster work at the John Sands company in the 1890s, he invented a method for casting posters in high relief

Dr Fiona Wood at Royal Perth Hospital. Courtesy of Dr Fiona Wood

Charlie Samuels in a Sheffield standing start pose, c. 1887. Courtesy of Colin Tatz

The Alexander Patent Racket Factory in Launceston as it looks today.

A newspaper advertisement for Alexander racquets in the Adelaide *Register*, February 1928.

A newspaper advertisement for Alexander racquets in the Brisbane *Courier-Mail*, May 1937.

Jack Brabham on the Brands Hatch track in his BT19 during the British Grand Prix, July 1966.

Jack Brabham photographed in 1968, looking very relaxed despite finishing only one race of eleven starts that year.

Michael O'Brien is escorted out of the Twickenham Stadium by British constabulary, followed at the run by Mr Grundy with coat in hand, 20 April 1974. Courtesy of Ian Bradshaw

The Brennan monorail car being demonstrated for the first time at Brennan's torpedo factory site in Gillingham, Kent, UK, 10 November 1909.

Florence and George Taylor with pigeons in St Mark's Square, Venice. Courtesy of Mitchell Library, State Library of NSW PXA 218

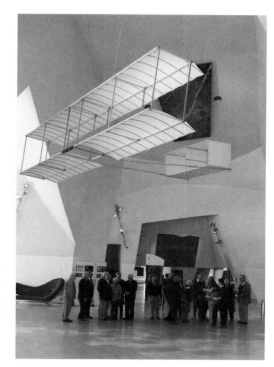

A replica Taylor glider constructed by the Australian Gliding Museum, on display in the National Museum of Australia in 2010. Courtesy of Russell Darbyshire

The cross–Channel steamer *Paris* c. 1913, the first ship to use Michell thrust bearings. Courtesy of Ian Boyle Collection

Anthony George Maldon Michell.

Portrait of Private Lancelot Eldin de Mole, 10th Battalion AIF, c. 1917.
AWM P09319.001

The model of de Mole's tracked vehicle that was lost by the British and now resides within the Australian War Memorial collection. AWM J00300

The Summit car that currently resides within the National Automobile Museum collection in South Australia. Courtesy of National Automobile Museum

Bill Lancaster and Jessie Keith Miller relax with their plane on the ground at Darwin, 1928.
Courtesy of M. Goodale Collection, Northern Territory Library PH0345/0020

A view of the *Empress* showing the stern loading door at Burnie, Tasmania, November 1966.

rather than printing them. He then adapted his casting method to using 'bagasse', a type of cement plaster mixed with sugar cane fibre that could be sawn, nailed and worked like timber, and patented it in 1900 with Alexander Knox, prominent Sydney merchant and president of NSW Rugby League, exhibiting samples all over the world. It was an ideal medium for working Australian fauna and floral motifs into ceilings—a popular idea at the time—and it won him a gold medal at the 1897 Queensland International Exhibition. The massive sculpted 1901 Commonwealth Federation Arch in Sydney at the intersection of Park and Elizabeth streets was a wooden frame clad in bagasse composed to imitate marble. By 1903, George Taylor had formed the Bagasse Company Ltd with a factory in Little Bourke Street, Sydney.

A true polymath and lateral thinker, George made up in energy for what he lacked in height and health. Having developed an interest in the military uses of radio and telephony, George co-founded the Wireless Institute of New South Wales (now the Wireless Institute of Australia) in 1910, and helped found the Institute of Local Government Engineers of Australasia in 1909, the Town Planning Association of New South Wales in 1913 and the Institute of Australian Engineers in 1919. It was largely due to his work that the first government wireless station was set up in Australia, and he was a pioneer in wireless transmission of drawings, both in black and white and in colour.

Inspired by the work of Lawrence Hargrave, who in 1894 had been the first man in Australia to be airborne via a tethered box kite, and by the Wright brothers' 1903 flight at Kitty Hawke, North Carolina, George founded the Aerial League of Australia in April 1909, which eventually had some five hundred members. Branches of the Aerial League were formed in Queensland and Victoria, and a landing ground was developed at Penrith, near Sydney, for use by members, who lobbied the government to establish an aviation corps and flying school as part of the defence department.

After experimenting with building various types of model aeroplanes and flying them from the roof of his home, he set up Australia's first aircraft factory in Surry Hills in September 1909. Known as the Aeronautics Supply Company, the factory began to build several full-scale gliders, or 'war kites', capable of carrying a military observer into the air, and a powered monoplane with a wingspan of 8 metres, which was said to be only waiting the delivery of the engine to be flown. Some of the construction work was carried out by fellow league member and furniture manufacturer Edward Hallstrom. No doubt George had his eye on the imminent arrival in Australia of Bleriot machines and the Wright aeroplane, and wanted an Australian product to be in the air first. It was the largest one of these winged kites—in fact the largest one in Australia—that took to the air on the end of a cable on 22 October 1909, outside the Garden Palace Exhibition Building in Sydney.

By the end of that year, George was ready to publicly test his glider, and so on Sunday, 5 December 1909, he and Florence and about a hundred friends, spectators and press reporters gathered at the northern end of the wide stretch of beach at Narrabeen Heads, some 20 kilometres north of central Sydney, on land owned by Charles and Emma Schultz behind their house, Billabong. The glider, disassembled for its journey from Sydney and stored in the Schultz boatshed, had been reassembled and may well have been test-flown before this particular day. On the Sunday, a number of short tethered flights were made until the trim of the glider had been balanced to enable stable flight while it carried the weight of a person. The glider was 18 feet (5.5 metres) long with 4-foot (1.2-metres) planes and a box-kite tail for balance, built from coachwood covered with oiled calico. There was no rudder; the pilot steered by shifting their body weight while lying prone in the middle of the lower wing, leaning over the front spar with most of their body weight and hooking their shins over the rear spar, much like steering a modern hang-glider.

Then, early in the day, the glider was brought around to face into a stiff south-east wind, which would grow stronger as the day went on. Launched from the beach into the wind, George's glider was pulled along by men hanging onto guide-lines attached to the corner of each wing until it had achieved sufficient elevation. Taylor successfully lifted into the air on his first flight, covering a distance to the water's edge of 98 yards (90 metres), achieving the first piloted flight of a winged heavier-than-air machine over distance in Australia. By late afternoon, with the wind freshening to a 30-kilometre-per-hour easterly, Taylor was achieving distances of 253 yards (231 metres). On the last of the twenty-nine flights, the guide-ropes were released and George Taylor made the first untethered heavier-than-air flight in Australia.

Not all of the flights were piloted by George, though. At one point Florence naturally climbed aboard for her turn, flying out over the beach into that stiff breeze for about 90 yards (82 metres) to become the first recorded female glider pilot in the world and the first female Australian flyer. She was not apparently aware of her place in history, but she was worried her dress might blow up and reveal her bloomers, so she made sure her skirts were securely tucked in.

George continued manufacturing gliders and light aircraft, mainly with a view to their military use, and claimed he was trying to persuade Florence to get a pilot's licence. Establishing the Lilienthal Camp at Narrabeen, named after the German pioneer flier Otto Lilienthal, George and Florence and their friends continued flying the glider through that December and into January, gathering experience and achieving further free flight and soaring flight, although there were some inevitable injuries due to the pilots being so exposed. It was claimed the glider was the first full-size Australian aeroplane and the first heavier-than-air device to fly in the Commonwealth.

Florence once commented that if two architects met they were destined to start a publishing business, and so it happened. In 1907, George and Florence launched a publishing venture with the monthly trade journal *Building* as their flagship. They were so successful that five years later they became incorporated as the printing and publishing company Building Limited, and in 1917 they acquired their own building at 20 Loftus Street, near Circular Quay, with the financial assistance of Florence's old mentor, Francis Stowe. There were two apartments on the top floor; the Taylors moved into one and Stowe into the other. By now their publications had multiplied: they launched journals such as *Construction* (1909), the *Australasian Engineer* (1910), *Town Planning and Housing* (1915), the *Radio Journal of Australia* (1927) and *Commonwealth Home* (1925), which claimed to be the first magazine in the world to print naturally coloured photographs from original plates. For ten years, George and Florence worked alongside each other every day in a seemingly equal partnership, something that Florence claimed was important. However, once George became involved in military intelligence work and as he grew increasingly unwell due to epilepsy, Florence assumed more of the workload. No doubt to remove the workaholic George from the stresses of the office, they began to travel widely overseas, mingling with the rich and famous, visiting exhibitions and meeting with their peers, even talking with royalty.

Then suddenly on 20 January 1928 George was gone from her life, drowning in the bath at their Sydney home, most likely as the result of an epileptic seizure. He was eulogised widely by many, certainly by Florence, who spent the rest of her life in 'grande dame' widowhood. George left her £10000 and the business; she promptly bought out Stowe's interest and became one of the very few female publishing company owners and CEOs in the world. Consequently, she encountered a lot of prejudice in her day-to-day running of what was now known as the Building Publishing Company, but she persisted. Florence was a vocal supporter of equality in the workplace, encouraging women to be employed in the company not only as journalists and secretaries but in responsible positions; her magazine *Harmony* had an all-female editorial team. A supporter of free enterprise and a great believer in the work ethic, saying that too many Australians had developed a 'gimme' complex, she remained actively involved in her company, which survived both the Depression and World War II intact when others failed. In 1950, for reasons of her own, she sold the business while remaining as managing director and editor-in-chief.

Even while busy with her company, Florence had continued to produce town planning schemes, travelling the world as far afield as China to gain new ideas. George and Florence had been founding members of the New South Wales Town Planning Association in 1913, and Florence continued as an active member for many years. Widely respected, and sometimes disliked, for her energy, determination and forthright views, the tall and striking Florence left a vivid personal impression with her long sweeping skirts and outsize picture hats, often decorated with ostrich feathers. Her politics were as interesting as her achievements; the intensely patriotic Florence keenly opposed public housing because she considered deregulation a better solution to the housing shortage, opposed trade unions, considered Labor politicians incompetent bunglers drunk with their own power, and supported the right-wing anti-communist New Guard in the early 1930s. She applauded Captain Francis de Groot's now infamous slashing of the ribbon at the opening of the Sydney Harbour Bridge ahead of Labor Premier Jack Lang in 1932 and established a women's auxiliary of the New Guard that year.

Honoured with an OBE in 1939 for her contribution as an Australian businesswoman and the CBE in 1961, she finally conceded to retirement at the age of 81, and passed away eight years later, after a number of years as a recluse due to illness. During her life, she was formally connected to over twenty-five organisations, many in a founding or administrative capacity, including the Arts Club, the Australian American Association, the Royal Aero Club of New South Wales, the Society of Women Writers and the Australian Institute of Building, not to mention the various trade organisations associated with her publications. She was a fellow of the Royal Society of Arts in London and in 1919 was the second woman accepted for membership by the English Society of Architects, automatically becoming a member of the Royal Institute of British Architects when the two societies merged in 1925. The Canberra suburb of Taylor was named in her honour, as well as a number of professional industry awards such as the Florence M. Taylor Award of the Master Builders Association of New South Wales. A three-storey portrait of her adorns an apartment building facing the railway on the southern approach to Sydney's Central Station.

It would be a disgrace, she once said, for a woman to marry, be confined to the home and never to be articulate in public affairs.

★

The rest of the world

In 1898, the Royal Institute of British Architects had accepted its first female member, Ethel Mary Charles, while the Americans had accepted Louis Bethune in 1888.

With such matters lagging behind as usual in Australia, it wasn't until 1916 that the Queensland Institute admitted Beatrice Hutton. New South Wales followed in 1919.

To celebrate the centenary of the Taylor glider flight at Narrabeen, the Australian Gliding Museum built three full-size replicas of the glider at its Bacchus Marsh, Melbourne, facility. The project took three years, culminating in a re-enactment of the event at Rat Park, Pittwater, close to where the original flight took place, on 5 December 2009. One of the replicas is now hanging at the Moorabbin Air Museum, Melbourne, one is in storage at the Australian Aviation Museum in Bankstown, west of Sydney, and the third is on display at the National Museum in Canberra.

British engineer Sir George Cayley, regarded by many as the first aeronautical engineer, experimented with aerodynamics from the late eighteenth century, and in the 1840s designed the first successful glider to carry a human being (a young boy) in flight. He then built a larger-scale glider that was successfully flown in 1853, a replica of which is on display at the Yorkshire Air Museum.

Otto Lilienthal, often referred to as the 'glider king' and consid-ered to be the originator of modern hang-gliding, was the first to make repeated successful glider flights and the first to recognise the importance of lift from rising air and to use it in prolonging flight. Starting in about 1867, he is thought to have made some two thousand flights until his death in a crash in 1896. The Wright brothers would later publicly acknowledge his work as one of their greatest influences.

John Duigan was the first Australian to design and build his own powered aeroplane, flying at Mia Mia in Victoria in July 1910. Seven years later, Victorian pilot Basil Watson would make the first airmail flight from Melbourne to Mount Gambier, South Australia, in an aeroplane that he had built himself inside his parents' house in St Kilda Street, Elsternwick. Using Albert Park as his airfield, he was in the process of planning the first non-stop flight from Melbourne to Sydney when he was killed at Point Cook, Victoria, when his plane broke up during aerobatics.

The first Australian to formally qualify for a pilot's licence was Lieutenant Arthur Longmore from New South Wales, then serving in the Royal Navy, who gained Licence No. 72 on 25 April 1911, in England. On 28 March 1927, Millicent Bryant became the first Australian woman to be awarded a pilot's licence. Within two years, a further eighteen Australian women had qualified.

'THEORY IS THE CAPTAIN, PRACTICE THE SOLDIERS'

Anthony George Michell, Australia's James Watt

Firsts

- Holder of the first patent for the tilt-pad thrust bearing
- Holder of the first patent for the cross-flow water turbine
- Inventor of the crankless engine
- Inventor of the Michell Workshop Viscometer
- The first Australian to be awarded the James Watt International Medal, the highest award for mechanical engineers

Anthony George Maldon Michell, usually either known as George or simply as A.G.M., took his motto about theory and practice from Leonardo da Vinci, another great engineer, and it said a great deal about his approach to his life's work. He was born in 1870, the youngest of five children, in London, where his parents were visiting relatives. Michell's second middle name was that of the small gold-mining town in Victoria where the family actually lived. His parents, John Michell and Grace Rowse, had emigrated from the mining village of Mary Tavy, outside of Tavistock in Devon, to join the gold rush in Creswick and then Maldon after their marriage in 1853. The Wheal Friendship Mine in Mary Tavy was at one time the largest copper mine in the world, and John was an experienced miner descended from generations of copper miners dating back more than a century to Cornwall. Knowing that not all money came from personally digging in a mine, John eventually accrued some four hundred profitable mine shares in Maldon that bolstered the family income.

After George was born, his family eventually returned to Maldon where he grew up surrounded by mine engineering and ore-crushing machinery. Fortunately, John and Grace were parents who had a great respect for knowledge and learning, and were quick to recognise the potential in their two boys. When George was seven, they moved to Melbourne to enable his older brother John Henry to begin school. Seven years later, they returned to England so that John could study at Cambridge University on the advice of his professors at the University of Melbourne, from where he had graduated with first-class honours. George attended Perse Grammar School at Cambridge and then studied at the university, where he showed talent in mathematics, physics, chemistry, mechanics and engineering. When the family returned to Australia in 1890, so that John could take up the newly created mathematics lectureship at the University of Melbourne, George resumed study there in architecture, civil engineering and mining engineering, finally graduating with his Masters in Civil Engineering in 1899.

George Michell became interested in pumps and hydraulics while working as an assistant for hydraulics engineer and teacher Bernhard Alexander Smith, with whom he went into business and jointly patented a pump design. Perhaps that work sparked Michell's interest in patents themselves, because in 1902 he became an examiner of patents for the Victorian Patents Office. The following year he established his own engineering consultancy for irrigation, water supply and sewerage projects, in which capacity he did the initial 1911 designs for the Lake Margaret hydro-electric scheme for Mount Lyell Mining in Tasmania, one of the first Australian hydro-electric installations; designed the pumping machinery for the Murray Valley irrigation project which included designing the Grant-Michell water meters at Cohuna; and investigated hydro-electric power possibilities on the Kiewa River for the Victorian government. In 1903, he also patented the cross-flow water turbine, in which water passes through the turbine transversely, across the turbine blades. Ideal for small hydro-electric plants, the low-maintenance turbine unit cleans itself and can be left unattended for long periods.

Michell had an abiding interest in the physics of hydraulics and lubricative fluids used to reduce friction between moving mechanical parts, mostly through his early experience with centrifugal pumps and turbines in which the rotating shaft commonly has to be supported against longitudinal thrust. Without sufficient lubrication and thus too much metal-to-metal contact, a lot of energy could be lost due to friction, and parts could wear out quickly and fracture due to overheating. Aware of earlier theories concerning lubrication, Michell theorised that if a constant supply of lubricant could be maintained at pressure within a sealed unit, then not only could friction be reduced but the lubricant itself would actually be able to bear a load.

On 16 January 1905, Michell patented his tilt-pad thrust bearing in Australia and England. Initially it was used primarily in land-based machinery, and by 1916 it was estimated that over eight hundred thrust-bearing units were in service in Australia and the United Kingdom within a range of machinery from high-speed steam turbines to low-speed grinding machines. They were fitted to the giant pumps at the Newport Power Station in Melbourne. However, Michell's invention would become best known for its use in marine engineering, but that didn't happen without a fight on two fronts.

The first front was concerned with the traditional method of securing a spinning propeller shaft to the ship so that the thrust energy being generated was transferred to the ship's hull. At that time, this was achieved through a series of ring collars around the shaft. The outside of these collars consisted of a series of planes that made direct contact with corresponding 'shoes' mounted in massive housings bolted to the ship's frame. That contact transferred the energy developed by the engine-driven propellers through the spinning shaft to the hull of the ship, and so generated thrust that drove the ship through the water. But with metal parts in direct frictional contact with each other, there were severe overheating and wear problems that limited allowable load bearings and thus limited the size and speed of shipping.

The second front was concerned with changing technology. The traditional reciprocating steam engines of the nineteenth century were being replaced with direct-drive steam turbine engines that did not need heavy-duty thrust bearings. Just when it looked like Michell's invention might become redundant before it had even had serious use on water, geared turbines that would need thrust bearings to take the loads of their relentless drive began to replace direct drives after 1912. Michell was back in business.

Unlike the traditional collars then in use, Michell's collar bearing contained a series of tilting slipper pads arranged around the propeller shaft that trapped wedges of self-pressurised oil inside the spinning bearing, not only absorbing the thrust of the shaft but eliminating direct contact between metal surfaces and so enabling more direct thrust. Instead of the load being taken by the metal, it was being taken by the film of oil. Michell's bearing could operate at speeds up to thirty times faster than the old type and was only a tenth of the size. In short, his invention revolutionised thrust technology and was particularly important for the development of new turbine-powered ships. Now a ship could be driven faster without having to increase the size of the engines or propellers, thus making possible the development of the type of warships, tankers, container ships and cruise liners at sea today.

Unfortunately, to Michell's bitter disappointment he did not achieve a worldwide patent for his bearing; a rival patent was granted in the United States in 1911, where it is known as the Kingsbury thrust bearing. Neverthless, Michell and his English friend Henry Newbigin, with whom he had gone into business partnership, set out to market his invention to the large shipbuilding companies, especially those with contracts for the Royal Navy. The first installation of the Michell bearing on a British ship was in the cross-Channel steamer *Paris* in 1913. Built at the Dumbarton yard of Denny Bros, she was claimed to be the fastest passenger steamer of her size in the world. (The *Paris* was sunk at Dunkirk during World War II while acting as a Red Cross rescue ship for wounded soldiers.) That installation was such a success that Michell thrust bearings were then included in the first geared-turbine destroyers, HMS *Leonidas* and HMS *Lucifer*, the following year. However, British marine specialists remained sceptical about this innovative thinking from a colonial until a German U-boat was captured early in World War I that, when examined, was found to be fitted with a version of Michell's lubricated thrust bearings designed by the Krupp company. Suddenly, the British Admiralty had an epiphany and quickly adopted Michell's technology. The largest of his bearing units made during World War I went into the battle cruiser HMS *Hood*. Launched in 1918 as the largest warship in the Royal Navy, the massive *Hood* visited Melbourne in March 1924, seventeen years before its demise under the guns of the *Bismark* in World War II. You have to wonder whether Michell went to have a look at her.

Within a few years, Michell's invention completely revolutionised steam turbines and marine propulsion. Applying for a seven-year extension to his patent after the war, which was granted in 1919, Michell estimated that his bearings had saved the Admiralty £500 000 in coal just during 1918 alone. Even his American rival, Albert Kingsbury, credited the use of Michell bearings by the Royal Navy with influencing the US Navy to adopt his similar bearing in 1917. By the time World War I ended, the dominance of Michell's tilt-pad bearing within nautical engineering was complete. Ship-owners were now clamouring for them to be fitted to vessels new and old.

However, even with the extension of the patent, it was apparent to Michell and his business partner Newbigin that royalty income would not support their work much longer, and so a more permanent and lucrative business arrangement was formulated in a meeting with leading shipbuilders. In May 1920, Michell Bearings Ltd was established in Newcastle in England to take over the existing patents and have a manufacturing role as well. Half the shares went to Michell and Newbigin and the other half was divided between the four shipbuilding companies of Vickers, Fairfield Shipbuilding and Engineering, John Brown & Co. and Cammell Laird & Co. The company struggled for a few years until it was restructured in 1925, after which it remained successful and profitable, supplying marine bearings. When the *Queen Mary* was launched in 1934, four Michell thrust blocks and forty-six Michell self-lubricating bearings supported the shafts that drove the four great 35-tonne propellers in excess of 30 knots. In 1969, Vickers Ltd took over sole operation of the company and in 1994 a joint operation was set up in India; then, when Rolls-Royce acquired Vickers in 1999, the company became a member of Rolls-Royce Marine Systems and continues today as Michell Bearings.

Perhaps Michell's most ambitious business venture was the formation in 1920 of Crankless Engines (Australia) Pty Ltd in Fitzroy, Melbourne, to commercialise his invention in 1917 of an engine without a crankshaft. Sometimes also known as a swashplate engine, in which the piston movement turned a shaft by means of obliquely set collars and Michell lubricated slipper bearings, it was an early version of what we now generally refer to as a rotary engine. With the oil film taking the load, absolutely no metal-to-metal contact took place and the engine was completely balanced at all speeds. Michell had one of the engines successfully fitted to his Buick. His leading designer was Queenslander Louis Sherman, who became the company's representative in England and America, and one of the company's co-directors was future Governor-General Richard Casey, later Lord Casey of Berwick. Casey took an eight-cylinder, 4-litre version of one of the crankless engines to the United States in 1922, where it was tested extensively at the General Motors research facility in Dayton, Ohio, and then by Ford in Detroit. Both companies reported to Casey that their bench tests had demonstrated the crankless engine was at least 10 per cent more efficient than the car engines Ford and GM were building at that time. However, in their opinion that 10 per cent was not enough to compensate for the extensive and expensive re-tooling they would have to carry out in order to manufacture the radically different Michell engine.

So although a crankless five-cylinder automobile was developed by 1927, it was never put into large-scale commercial use. However, a number of aero engines and gas engines for pumps and compressors were produced for use in Australia, England and the United States up to the early 1970s. In more fortunate economic times, Crankless Engines Ltd might have had a better chance of overcoming financial hurdles and the market's traditional views about mechanics, but eventually the company was defeated in Australia in 1928 by the oncoming Depression. Two engines, an 800-horsepower petrol engine and a 2000-horsepower diesel, are held by the Smithsonian Institute in Washington DC. The crankless auto engine that Casey took to the United States was obtained by the National Museum of Victoria (now amalgamated into Museum Victoria) in 1976 and is currently housed at the University of Melbourne. A 1927 70-horsepower eight-cylinder gas engine is in the Sydney Powerhouse Museum collection, as is an example of a Michell thrust bearing.

Michell travelled extensively throughout Europe and the United States between 1925 and 1933, lecturing on and publicising his crankless engine, and becoming acquainted with a number of fellow scientists and engineers, including Albert Kingsbury. When he returned to Australia, he once again became involved in the field of patents, this time as a registered patent attorney and a member of the Institute of Patent Attorneys of Australia. During his life, Michell was granted some sixty patents for a wide range of inventions, including the Michell Workshop Viscometer for measuring the viscosity of fluids; the Smith-Michell regenerative centrifugal pump (1901); a telegraphic cypher encoding and decoding system (1907); a system of hydraulic power transmission that could be fitted to cars (1912); a new type of roof guttering (1916); and the Michell–Seggel floating-pad bearing in 1935—but it is his work on lubrication for which he mainly is remembered today.

In 1934, he was elected as a Fellow of the Royal Society on his first nomination; his brother John, who had become a distinguished mathematician, University of Melbourne professor of mathematics and founder of the Mathematical Association of Victoria, was also a Fellow. They were the only known siblings to have been elected from Australia and possibly even England. Four years later, Michell received the Kernot Memorial Medal from the University of Melbourne, awarded for distinguished engineering achievement in Australia, and in 1943 his work was recognised with the honour of the James Watt International Medal by the Institution of Mechanical Engineers in London. His weighty 1950 tome, *Principles of Lubrication*, published when he was 80, became the standard text on the subject for many years. His thrust-bearing design is still standard equipment on ships.

Few families were as close-knit as the Michells. Of the five children, only Elizabeth—the eldest—married. George, who was shy, very modest and slightly built, lived with his brother and two sisters, Grace and Amelia, in their home with its exotic tropical forest garden in Prospect Road, Camberwell, in Melbourne, until his death at the age of 88 in 1959, the last of his family. Their garden included Lord Howe Island palms, an orchard of cumquats, guavas, feijoas and a 9-metre-high mulberry tree. In 1911, he purchased a property that he named Ruramihi at Bunyip, Victoria, in order to protect the native flora and fauna and to which he could retreat from the pressures of his busy schedule, believing that it was essential to have such a place to achieve a balance in life. Over the years he added acreage to it, while in May 1927 he had it officially proclaimed by the Governor of Victoria to be a native wildlife sanctuary, which it remained until 1959 after his death. The beautiful timber homestead was later destroyed by fire and the original 1000 acres (400 hectares) have now been subdivided, but something of his spirit still remains in that beautiful countryside. Today, the four children who lived together are as close in death as they were in life, buried together in the Boroondara Cemetery in Kew.

Although the extensive libraries of both brothers were presented to the University of Melbourne, they were not retained as collections in their own right and Michell's private papers were destroyed after his death. Fortunately, an AGM Michell Prize in Mechanical Engineering was created by the Australian Institute of Engineers to be awarded to the top final year Mechanical Engineering student at the University of Melbourne, and an AGM Michell Medal has been awarded annually since 1978 by the Mechanical College of Engineers Australia in recognition of outstanding service to mechanical engineering. So in some way the memory of this man of great intellectual discipline, absolute standards and inventive power, who has been described as probably the most versatile engineer in this country's history and as Australia's James Watt, lives on.

★

The rest of the world

Michell did not, of course, invent in a vacuum, but built on and developed the earlier theories of a number of people. Beauchamp Tower, who was the inventor of the Tower spherical rotary steam engine, had discovered hydrodynamic lubrication in about 1844 and theorised that friction in bearings was least when the intervening film of oil was continuous. Professor Osborne Reynolds, the first full-time professor of engineering in England in 1868, theorised about the circumstances in which a film of oil could be maintained against external pressure. His theoretical model of fluid dynamics is still the standard mathematical formula used today. The third main influence on Michell was the work of Sir George Gabriel Stokes, nineteenth-century mathematician, physicist and natural philosopher, who made important contributions to the field of fluid dynamics with work on fluid motion, friction and viscosity.

Then there is Albert Kingsbury who, though seven years older than Michell, was very much Michell's American alter ego. With a mechanical engineering degree from Cornell University in New York State and much practical experience in machine shops, Kingsbury became interested early in his career in bearings and lubrication. By 1890, he was a professor of mechanical engineering at the University of New Hampshire, where he continued his research into developing a tilt-pad thrust bearing. His first test models there were successful but after he joined Westinghouse Electric Company as a general engineer, his tests failed and the company declined to use his bearings, as did the Pennsylvania Water and Power Company initially. However, Kingsbury persisted and his work eventually was successful.

His first patent application in 1907 was rejected due to Michell's patent having been granted in 1905, but he was granted an American patent five years later on the dubious basis that his 1898 experimental tests at the University of New Hampshire pre-dated Michell's work. That premise was never accepted in Australia, the United Kingdom or Europe. Kingsbury went on to manufacture his bearings with the Westinghouse Machine Company and to actively pursue further patents. Like Michell, his bearings came to be used extensively by the navy during World War I, and he received a number of awards for his contributions to mechanical engineering.

Michell's cross-flow turbine was later further developed by Hungarian Donat Banki and by the German Fritz Ossberger in 1933. Michell worked with Ossberger to develop a steam turbine in the early 1920s, and the Ossberger company remains the leading manufacturer of this turbine type today.

TANKED

Lancelot de Mole and his tracked vehicle

First

- The first designer and builder of a working model of a practical, continuously tracked armoured military vehicle

Out of the smoke of the Somme Offensive battlefield of Flers-Courcelette on the morning of 15 September 1916 lumbered a group of huge, lozenge-shaped armoured vehicles moving forward on continuous tracks, spitting bullets from machine guns mounted on their sides and terrifying the enemy. The Germans would probably not have been quite so terrified if they had known that these new British 'tanks' were so mechanically unreliable that only fifteen of the forty-nine available had finally gone into battle, that they could be knocked out by artillery, needed carrier pigeons in order to communicate and had such poor visibility that they frequently gunned down their own troops. If the British had only listened to an Australian engineer with the intriguing name of Lancelot de Mole, this new weapon might have been safer, more effective, more reliable and introduced much sooner, thus saving countless lives.

Born in 1880, Lancelot Eldin de Mole moved when he was young with his family from Kalgoorlie, Western Australia, to Renmark in South Australia, where his father William Frederick de Mole was an architect and surveyor. Lancelot de Mole eventually trained as an engineering draughtsman.

He worked on surveying and mining projects in various states, and while working in rugged country in Western Australia in 1911 he became tired of his buggy frequently sticking in the soft and stump-cluttered ground. He concluded that what was needed for the job was a vehicle fitted with caterpillar tracks, but at that time such vehicles couldn't be steered easily. So he set to work to design a type of tractor that could be steered and turned accurately and quickly. He then saw that the tractor could be adapted for military purposes into an all-terrain vehicle that could move as easily backwards as forwards, would be raised at both ends to enable it to climb over obstacles, and would be propelled by a flexible continuous metal track running under four bogies.

The next year he submitted a design to the British War Office for an armoured tracked vehicle that would be 37 feet (11 metres) long with a wheel base of 25 feet (8 metres), travelling on a continuous caterpillar track of steel plates mounted inside the armour (not completely exposed as in the future Mark I tanks). The vehicle would be capable of crossing a trench 16 feet (5 metres) wide, either forwards or backwards, as it had a double climbing face enabling it to reverse over rough ground out of trouble, something the early British tanks that would come later were not able to do. De Mole pointed out to an interviewing journalist for the *West Australian* on 14 February 1920 that while his tank had a front and rear climbing face, the British tanks had only one at the front and that there was a lot of difference in the steering mechanism. Rather than having to be crabbed around by driving one tread forward and the other in reverse, his tank could be driven around a curve just like a long-wheelbase car. The chain rail track of de Mole's tank could be moved laterally to form a curve that, as the vehicle proceeded, would alter the direction of travel. If the vehicle was reversing, it could be steered by pressing the bogie nearest the rear to one side by means of a screw gear operated by the driver. The size of the tank would be governed by the weight and horsepower of the engine. It might sound complicated, but it was actually a very efficient vehicle and de Mole's plans mapped out what would later take the British a considerable period of trial and error to achieve. According to a letter he wrote in 1919, de Mole built the first prototype model of his tracked vehicle in 1912 but evidently didn't send it to England with this set of plans.

Despite the advantages of de Mole's proposal, it was rejected in 1913 by the War Office, which commented that it was no longer experimenting with chain rails. Although he was urged by some of his friends to sell his idea to the German Consulate in Perth, he wasn't comfortable with that suggestion, and the outbreak of war soon after proved him right. His attempt to enlist in the Australian Imperial Force (AIF) was rejected on the grounds that he was too tall and delicate, and so he continued to work as a draughtsman for the Engineering Department of the South Australian Government. In July 1915, he married Harriet Walter in Adelaide.

Many years later, *The Argus* revealed on 9 August 1924 that a letter was sent to the British Minister of War in September 1914 by G.W.D. Breadon, a civil engineer in Western Australia who later became Commissioner of Munitions in India, informing the minister about de Mole's invention of two years before and recommending that it be placed before a committee of experts. Describing de Mole's concept as 'travelling caterpillar forts' that could travel across broken ground, climb embankments and span ditches and streams with ease, Breadon claimed that 'no deadlier or more efficient war engine could be used' and that, once armed, a line of these vehicles supported by artillery could 'carry everything before it and save the infantry'.

By the time de Mole put forward a subsequent proposal around the middle of 1915, duly considered and rejected by the Committee of the Panel of Advisory Scientific Experts, Winston Churchill and the Landship Committee—established to look into armoured trench-crossing vehicles—had already begun development of an armed military tracked vehicle, given the name 'tank' after water tank to keep its real purpose secret. De Mole's technically superior proposal, which at that time was far ahead of anything the committee had then developed, was never passed on to them. An opportunity to shorten the war and save many lives was lost.

De Mole then submitted a proposal to the Australian Inventions Board early in 1916, who evidently could not be bothered attempting to understand the plans. Their rejection ignored de Mole's plan for a fleet of five hundred to one thousand armed and armoured vehicles attacking the enemy and they justified their rejection on the grounds that one vehicle could fall into a hole.

When those first British tanks went into battle on the Somme in 1916, de Mole must have realised that his proposals had been ignored, even though his plans had been for a technologically superior vehicle, and so he became determined to take a working model of his tank to London. Although he claimed in 1919 that he made his model himself while living in Geraldton, Western Australia, this was not the case. With financial help from his friend Lieutenant Harold Leslie Boyce, later Lord Mayor of London Sir Harold Boyce, he had a one-eighth-scale working metal model of his tank concept manufactured by the Melbourne mechanical and engineering firm of Williams & Benwell. He then went on a fitness program and was finally accepted for enlistment in 1917 as a private in the 25th Reinforcements, Tenth Battalion, AIF. Boyce had de Mole assigned to him and they departed with the model for England on the troopship *Aeneas*.

Arriving in Plymouth in January 1918, de Mole obtained leave and took his model and proposal personally to the Munitions Inventions Office. The model passed its first test at the end of the month, and he was asked to present it to a second committee. He was to be notified when the committee was to convene, but his luck turned against him again when he fell ill. Six weeks later, when he had recovered but hadn't received news, he investigated and found his model had been consigned to the Experimental Tank Corps cellar without ever being unpacked, while the letter from the first committee recommending his concept to the second committee had never been sent. Before he could locate the model and put together a second demonstration, he was recalled to active service when the Germans launched their massive spring offensive on the morning of 21 March. He fought at Merris, Meteren and Villers-Bretonneux, and was still in France when the Armistice was signed. When he returned to London, he was attached to the ammunition workers' depot at AIF headquarters. There, he heard the news of a Royal Commission being convened to compensate inventors whose concepts had been used by the Allies during the war and filed a claim for his contribution to tank development.

De Mole appeared before the British Royal Commission on Awards to Inventors on 20 and 21 October 1919. Mr Justice Charles Henry Sargant was initially cautious in connecting de Mole and the eventual tanks used in combat, but during the hearings the British government admitted that Mole's plans and model had been found gathering dust in a neglected War Office cellar. On 3 November 1919, the commissioners stated their opinion that de Mole had 'made and reduced to practical shape, as far back as 1912, a very brilliant tank invention which anticipated, and in some respects surpassed, that put into use in the year 1916'. Trevor Watson, counsel for the Ministry of Munitions, admitted that Mole's suggestions 'would have made a better article than those that went into action'. The commissioners stated that it was the claimant's misfortune and not his fault that his invention was in advance of its time and had not been appreciated. Justice Sargant summed up that de Mole had 'the higher satisfaction of being ranked a latter-day Leonardo among the signal few who have earned the distinction of being ahead of their times'. The following day, the London *Daily News* suggested the war could have ended in the spring of 1917 if the War Office had used de Mole's tank design.

However, although de Mole had gained belated recognition for his invention, at the end of November the commission clarified that it could only offer full financial compensation in cases where it could be proved that the actual invention had been used by a government department. Unfortunately, due to the official rejections of de Mole's proposals, no connection between the tanks that finally went into battle and his early proposals could ever be proved. The credit and the £15 000 reward were divided between Major W.C. Wilson and Sir William Tritton. Major Wilson, secretary of the Tanks Designs Branch of the War Office, was the officer whose critical report on de Mole's invention was responsible for it being rejected in 1918, a report later described by the officer in charge of tank experiments, Colonel Philip Johnson, as unjustified and neither reasoned nor proper. All the commission finally offered to de Mole was £985 as a reimbursement of his expenses.

De Mole wasn't the only one greatly disappointed with that result. An irritated Andrew Fisher, former prime minister and by now Australian High Commissioner in England, promptly fired off a letter from Australia House to British Prime Minister David Lloyd George on 18 December, referring to Breadon's 1914 letter and demanding the matter be investigated. It seemed incredible, he wrote, that the War Office's neglect of de Mole's invention should have been used as justification for the commission's finding. Of course, nothing eventuated. However, the matter was also raised in the House of Representatives by Mr William Mahony, the Labor member for Dalley in New South Wales. On 15 April 1920, he asked Prime Minister William Morris Hughes a series of questions referring to the need for de Mole to receive a suitable grant by way of recognition from his homeland. Sounding just like contemporary counterparts, the prime minister replied that the matter was being looked into. Having done that, his answer the following week finally revealed the reply by British Prime Minister Lloyd George to Australian High Commissioner Fisher's letter. In short, Lloyd George had backed the

Royal Commission's verdict that de Mole's invention had not actually contributed to the tank that was used during the war; therefore, in his opinion, the commissioners had been generous in compensating the expenses.

Having returned to Australia, de Mole was living at Bondi in Sydney when he refused what had to be for him a deeply ironic approach from the British Imperial War Museum and instead presented his model to the new Australian War Memorial, where it remains to this day. On 3 April 1920, Lancelot de Mole was created a Commander of the Order of the British Empire for his services in connection with the invention of tanks. This was no small honour, as a CBE was the next rank down from a knighthood, but it was undoubtedly an official attempt to compensate for the bureaucratic mistakes that had been made. His investiture by Governor-General Lord Forster took place in the Government House drawing room in Sydney on 29 July the following year.

De Mole continued inventing after World War I and is known to have held at least three American patents: one for a ten-wheel all-terrain vehicle with multiple-wheel drive and steering; another for a differential or balanced gear; and a third for a keyboard-operated advertising sign and display mechanism, which he took to England. In 1936, de Mole became an engineer in the design branch of the Sydney Water Board, and in 1940, during World War II, he gained the support of the Army Headquarters Invention Board and Prime Minister Robert Menzies for the concept of an artillery shell fired from the ground or from an aircraft that would eject a fence or screen of suspended wires as a defence against enemy aircraft. Once again, however, the British authorities—who had the last word in those days—dismissed another of his ideas as impracticable. He died ten years later in Sydney, aged 70.

One is left wondering how different World War I might have been if the British had taken up de Mole's invention and tanks had been ready to go into action when war broke out in 1914. Perhaps the war could have been shortened and thousands of lives saved, not to mention the substantial sums of money invested in the slow evolution of British tanks during that war. When in 1915 Winston Churchill, then Lord of the Admiralty, wrote to Prime Minister Herbert Henry Asquith about the need for steam tractors fitted with armoured shelters and caterpillar tracks to cross the open spaces between the lines, de Mole's model and letters had been gathering dust in the War Office for two years.

★

The rest of the world

Like any other invention, what we think of today as a military tank is the product of a series of ideas over a considerable period of time. The development of a continuous track propulsion system or 'caterpillar' track began with Richard Lovell Edgeworth in the 1770s and progressed through the nineteenth century, mainly associated with tractors and other agricultural machinery. The first commercial manufacturers in the early twentieth century were Alvin Lombard and Benjamin Holt in the United States and the Hornsby company in the United Kingdom. The Holt Manufacturing Company eventually became the Caterpillar Tractor Co. in 1925.

In 1902, Frederick Simms built the only prototype of his 'motor war car', a wheeled armoured vehicle powered by a 16-horsepower Daimler engine fitted with two Maxim guns and a 360-degree traversing turret; another version was built by the French in the same year, but they were wheeled vehicles rather than tracked.

Having ignored de Mole, British Army officer Colonel Ernest Swinton and the Secretary of the Committee for Imperial Defence, Maurice Hankey, proceeded, with the official encouragement of Winston Churchill, to develop a tracked tank (or 'landship' as they originally termed it) for the British army. The first tank, 'Little Willie', weighed 14 tonnes, travelled at just under 5 kilometres per hour and couldn't cross ditches.

Known as the Mark I, the first combat tank that could climb out of a ditch was ready by 16 January 1916. Tanks were rolling off the production line by June of that year. Beginning with the battle at Delville Wood in September 1916, increasingly larger numbers of tanks were put into action until the entire British Tank Corps of 474 tanks took part in the Battle of Cambrai on 20 November 1917, with great success.

The French had tanks fighting on the front by April 1917, and the American forces adopted French Renault tanks in late September. The Germans finally brought their vehicles into the field in April 1918, at Villers-Bretonneux, in the first battle in which tanks on both sides engaged each other.

WIRED FOR SOUND

William T. Kelly, the Summit car and the first factory-installed car radio

First

- First car radio to be fitted by a manufacturer in the factory as an integral part of an assembled vehicle model and powered by the car battery

We take audio sound in our cars now so much for granted, but it was certainly not a standard inclusion in vehicles for many years. If you wanted music while you drove in the early days of motoring, you pretty much had to build and install the radio yourself and mount a very visible wire aerial on the roof or the hood. Then along came a very astute Australian car manufacturer and salesman, William Thomas Kelly, who in 1924 started a whole style trend by offering the customer his Summit car, which came with a radio already installed in the factory.

As is the case with many successful inventions, Kelly's was the culmination of some earlier experiments. The first known person who attempted to take his music with him was, unsurprisingly, Guglielmo Marconi, who in 1922 fitted a Daimler with an eight-valve receiver in a rear compartment, powered by a separate battery, with a large frame aerial on the roof. A one-off prototype was exhibited at the Olympia Motorshow in England. That same year, George Frost, president of the Lane High School Radio Club in Chicago, installed a radio in the passenger door side-pocket of his Model T Ford, and Mr and Mrs J.C. Davenport had a radio they called a Dashboard Special fitted to their car with a loop aerial on the hood and took it on a 40 000-mile (64 000-kilometre) journey around the United States. But it was William Kelly who took what until then had been a hobbyist's speciality and transformed it into an integral part of motor car design and history.

Kelly had the experience to back his idea, having risen rapidly through the ranks of the burgeoning Australian motor industry. Starting out as a hire car driver in a 15-horsepower Star in 1910, he'd graduated to become the manager of Bondi Taxi Cabs the following year. As the owner of the Eastern Suburbs Taxi Cab Company in 1914, he invested that year in Elliott's Motors in Phillip Street, advertised as the most modern garage in the city, with an up-to-date repair workshop and a fleet of hire cars. He also invested in racehorses, but unfortunately he couldn't pick horses as well as automobiles, once losing £600 on his horse Moving Picture when it failed to win at Victoria Park. Somehow, Kelly managed to persuade Hugh Denison, a politician and tobacco manufacturer, to become his business partner in a car dealership. Denison, who had formed Sun Newspaper Ltd and would later found the Macquarie Broadcasting network, was also a racehorse owner so it's possible that was their connection. In November 1914, Kelly registered the public company of Kelly's Motors Limited with himself as managing director and with capital of £5000 in £1 shares. Originally a one-fifth shareholder while Denison held the rest, Kelly later increased his holdings to two thousand shares and acquired the agency rights for Chevrolet throughout New South Wales and Queensland, travelling through those states appointing agents on a salary of £1000 a year.

By the early 1920s, Australians were taking to the wide-open road as if it was theirs to own: from one vehicle for every 370 people in

1910, there was one for every seventy-one within ten years. At this time, there was really no such thing as an entirely Australian-made car; the country had neither the manufacturing nor parts industries to support one. All vehicles were in some way imported; either they were shipped out to Australia assembled or unassembled, or a locally made body was fitted to an imported chassis with an imported engine and running gear. Even so, manufacturers dreamed of a wholly locally made vehicle, and the highway of Australian car manufacturing was already littered with the wrecks of unsuccessful attempts. As is still the case, it was very difficult in a relatively small market to compete economically against larger numbers of cheaper imported vehicles.

In 1920, Kelly visited the United States while on an international marketing tour for the Acme patent spring, at the same time closely observing the American system of assembling a vehicle from components manufactured by specialist companies. In other words, even though the badge might say 'Duesenberg', the engine, brakes, instruments and seats might have been made by other companies and brought together in the factory to become part of the finished product known by the one name. After giving it some thought, and no doubt talking it over with Denison, he couldn't see why the same idea wouldn't work back home. A man who believed in Australian product, Kelly worked out that building a car in this way would save him 2.5 per cent on import duty and 50 per cent on freight compared with the cost of importing a complete chassis; more importantly, he could still call it an Australian-built car because it had actually been constructed here.

Putting words into action, Kelly and Denison sold up the Chevrolet business and decided to establish themselves as an entirely independent Australian vehicle manufacturer and dealer, free of connection to any overseas car manufacturers. With Denison as the company chairman, Kelly organised a dealership network across all states and a component supply network of some fifty-five manufacturers. It was no wonder that the Premier of New South Wales himself, Sir George Fuller, accepted the invitation to personally open the Summit factory at Alexandria in Sydney on 15 August 1923, when a new, efficiently organised production line that would be able to turn out the impressive number of five finished Summit cars a day, was on display. Although the factory was touted as one of the largest car plants in the country, it was very polite of Fuller not to elaborate too much in his opening speech on his own recent visit to Ford's vast Highland Park factory in the United States, where fifty thousand workers were turning out nearly two million Model Ts a year.

However, the Summit's selling strength was not its production numbers but that it was an Australian car, built by Australian workmen using Australian materials. Patriotically, the radiator badge was the original pre-1912 Commonwealth of Australia coat of arms, complete with Advance Australia motto, and the body frame was of Queensland maple clad in Australian-made steel, built entirely in the factory. Of course, among all the Australian-made hype, Kelly was quiet about the fact that while the car was built in Australia, many of the components were not. The Summit's engine was the proven and reliable American four-cylinder 3375cc, 21-horsepower Lycoming motor with a five-bearing crankshaft that drove the car at around a steady 50 miles per hour (80 kilometres per hour) maximum speed in top gear. At that time Lycoming, which later became renowned for its aircraft engines, was the principal supplier of engines for Auburn, Cord and Duesenberg automobiles, so it was one of the finest engines of its time. Other quality American components included Timken bearings, a 6-volt electrical system by Delco, Brown-Lipe gears, and a clutch by Borg & Beck, which would soon merge to become Borg-Warner. Four models were offered: a five-seater tourer and two-seater roadster, with 'Dickie' (or rumble) seat, for £450, and a non-folding California Top tourer and roadster for £495—all with a one-year written guarantee, and the money spent by the customer would be an investment in Australia.

Not surprisingly, the Summit's advertising emphasised that this Australian car was built for Australian conditions and so fulfilled the needs of Australians. Now, where have we heard that slogan before?

With this kind of appeal, the Summit was way ahead of its time. The cost-saving benefits during manufacture would be passed on to Australian buyers, Kelly claimed. Not only that, he added with more than a touch of patriotism, money spent buying his car would not be enriching the pockets of American shareholders. By way of proving his point about the suitability of the car for Australian conditions, Kelly had a Summit driven in August 1923, for 832 miles (1339 kilometres) around Victoria on a six-day test, advertising that it had covered the distance at 25.2 miles per gallon (11.2 litres per 100 kilometres) and a pint (about half a litre) of oil. He then entered two Summits in the *Daily Guardian* and *Smith's Weekly* Three Day Reliability Trial in February 1924. The 607-mile (977-kilometre) route judged reliability, punctuality and petrol economy, along with tests for braking, acceleration and hill climbing. Although it turned out that climbing steep hills with any speed was not the car's forte, the Summits scored the best fuel consumption figures in their class of 22 miles per gallon (12.8 litres per 100 kilometres) and one of them lost no reliability points at all, a record achieved by only four other entries in the entire trial. Both Summits were among the fifteen out of twenty-six entries in their class to complete the event.

Kelly's secret weapon for these trials, rather like an equivalent of Ben Lexcens's winged keel, was the Summit's unique Australian innovation of the Acme Patent Spring Suspension. This leaf-spring system, designed by Christian Frederickson in 1920, consisted of three cantilever sets of springs connected together at their ends on each side of the car. The centre springs were fixed in the middle of the base to the chassis while the front and rear sets were pivoted from the centre of the bow with one end of the front spring sliding within a copper box. When the car went over a bump, the action of one spring against the other absorbed the rebound through the pivots into the middle spring. Instead of the body of the car being thrown upwards, the effect in the car was more like a slight forward surge, similar to being in a rowing boat. The car didn't even have body roll on corners.

While the Summit was not, of course, the first car built in Australia, it was the most successful of the early cars built before the 1930s. Some five hundred were produced in two years, whereas the notoriously slow Australian Six factory in Ashfield, Sydney, took six years to turn out the same number. With much successful publicity, there was a quick boom in Summit sales. By the end of 1923, agents could be found throughout most states. There was a Summit Motors in Melbourne at 197 La Trobe Street; Glassford & Avalcot Motors in Castlereagh Street were the distributors in Sydney; Central and Northern Queensland were served by Comfort Motors in Mackay and F.G. Locke in Lake Street in Cairns; the General Motor Co. in Hobart's Collins Street stocked the 'Sensation of 1923'; in Western Australia it was the Westralian Auto Syndicate operating from the Tivoli Garage in Hay Street, Perth; and in Adelaide, May's Motor Works in Victoria Square reported sales of seven Summits in one week.

Reviewers and customers alike heaped praise on the car, in terms of its reliability, fittings, comfort, mileage, and ease of handling in both city traffic and rough rural road conditions. For the time, it was a very well-equipped car. There were rubber mats on the running boards, glass wind-deflectors on both sides, a manual windscreen wiper (known as a 'rain-clearer'), a motometer or external engine temperature gauge mounted on the radiator cap, an eight-day clock, a cigar lighter, a rug rail along the back seat, an interior light built into the back seat, a stop light, a tool kit, and that practically unnoticed innovation—the car radio. You didn't hear the music through speakers, though; you had to use headphones that were stored in side pockets attached to the inside of the top. The aerial was fitted in the hood. Powered from the vehicle battery, the radio was made by New System Telephones P/L of Melbourne, Sydney and Adelaide, a subsidiary of the Telephone Manufacturing Co. Ltd of London that later became part of Email Limited (Electricity Meter and Allied Industries Ltd) in 1934.

Unfortunately the boom was short-lived; despite the Summit's quality and popularity, it started to lose ground within a few years.

The car may have been value for money, but it was still more expensive than its fully imported American competition. After all, a Studebaker Six could be bought for £455, a Chevrolet for £275 and a Model T for £205. In desperation, dealers lowered Summit prices. By the middle of 1924, the five-seater roadster or touring model was being offered for £395, or you could have the deluxe model for £20 extra, still with a twelve-month guarantee. Sales were higher in rural and outback areas than the city, perhaps the best comment on the Summit's ruggedness and reliability, but in the end they were not enough to keep the company afloat. Kelly and Denison were forced to give up their dream in 1925 and close the factory. They lost some £50 000, but Denison covered the debts. Kelly went back to selling cars, although they were other people's cars from then on. By later that year he was a licensed auctioneer for Kelly's Motor Auctions in Elizabeth Street and the following year he registered Kelly's Motor Sales Ltd in Parramatta Road, Camperdown, with capital of £1000, before moving on to Riley Street Motor Auctions in 1930.

At least one Summit is still known to be alive and well today. In 1925, John Trescowthick of Angaston in South Australia bought a Summit and was so impressed by it that he kept the car until his death in 1964. His family presented it, still virtually complete, to the Birdwood Mill National Motor Museum at Birdwood in the Adelaide Hills in 1970. For many years it was preserved just as it was until in 1988 the museum was given a $32 500 Bicentennial Grant for its restoration. The Summit was completely dismantled and fully restored as closely as possible to the condition it was in on leaving the factory, a job that was sometimes frustrating but in the end enormously satisfying. A search for authentic parts revealed that ten complete Summits still existed in Australia at that time. In December 1988, the restored Summit was driven from the Birdwood Mill to the original Trescowthick house where it was 'redelivered' to John's grandson by the youngest son of George May of May's Motors, from whom the car had been purchased back in 1925.

★

The rest of the world

In 1921, British police fitted voice radios into two ex-army trucks with huge frame aerials on the roof that became known as the 'Flying Bedsteads'. Five years later, the first broadcast receiver radio was installed in a British car behind the dashboard with a speaker in the ceiling, but this model, weighing about 45 kilograms, still needed a separate group of batteries for power. The first English car manufactured with a radio was the 1934 Hillman Melody Minx. As radios were all licensed in England, customers also had to have a separate paid-up licence for their car radio.

In the United States, by the end of the 1920s, various radios were being manufactured for post-production installation. Police forces had also been experimenting with radio there, and in 1928 the Detroit Police Department was the first to fit dispatch radios, albeit one-way, to their patrol cars. When they started testing in 1927, so the story goes, they had no designated band on which to broadcast and so they began as licensed radio station WKOP. To meet federal requirements, they had to be listed as an entertainment station and so they played music in between lists of stolen cars and descriptions of missing children.

In 1927, the Automobile Radio Corporation was formed in the United States by C. Russell Feldman to produce Transitone radios for cars, but they were bulky and expensive and didn't sell well until the Philco company took them over in 1930 and set up the successful Transitone Automobile Corporation. That same year William Lear, Elmer Wavering and Paul Galvin were responsible for the first mass-produced affordable car radio in the United States, the Motorola, although it was still powered by its own separate battery. It cost $110 installed when you could buy a new car for $650. It was not until 1933 that Henry Ford began offering Motorolas pre-installed. They were quickly followed by Crossley, which brought out a car radio known as the Roamio. Lear went on to hold over 150 patents, including for radio-direction finders for planes and the auto-pilot; he also designed the first fully automatic aircraft landing system, eight-track tape players and in 1963 the Lear jet.

In Europe, the Ideal company, later Blaupunkt, brought out the first German car radio in 1932, a 15-kilogram model mounted in the rear of a Studebaker with a remote control next to the steering wheel.

Meanwhile back in Australia, Ferris Bros Pty Ltd, founded in Sydney in 1932, was probably the first Australian company to mass-produce a specifically designed car radio for sale and installation, the Fultone, in 1938. Ferris Bros has always claimed to be the first in the world to manufacture an all-transistor car radio in 1959, operating from its own dry battery and/or car battery, but the Delco Radio Division of General Motors claims to have got there in 1957 and Chrysler in 1955, so that's a debate the radio technicians and historians can continue at their leisure. The car radios most memorable for many Australians, though, were probably those manufactured by Amalgamated Wireless (Australasia) Ltd for installation in Volkswagens, Holdens built in Sydney, and Ford Falcons.

AVIATRIX

Jessie Miller, Australia's first long-distance airwoman

Firsts

- First woman to complete a flight from England to Australia
- First woman to fly 14000 miles (22500 kilometres), at that time the longest flight made by a woman
- First woman to cross the equator by air
- First Australian to compete in a national American air race, the 1929 National Women's Air Derby (the 'Powder Puff Derby') and the only Australian to be a charter member of the 'Ninety-Nines' female pilot organisation
- The holder in 1930 of the American transcontinental aerial speed record for women in both directions between the east and west coasts

The French Foreign Legion officer couldn't believe his eyes. Raising his binoculars, he could see an object in the distance ahead of him where there should be nothing but sand in an area of the Sahara Desert where even camels feared to tread. On this February day in 1962, the motorised desert patrol was some 60 kilometres off the main trans-Sahara track in a rarely visited waterless area of desert known as the Tanzerouft or, as the local Bedouin called it, the 'Land of Thirst'. As they drew closer, the officer could see this was the crumpled skeleton of an old biplane lying on one side. Jumping out of the truck to inspect the wreck, they found the mummified body of the pilot lying under one wing. Tied to a strut was a package that included a logbook diary, passport, a lucky horseshoe and a wallet containing two photos of a small, smiling woman wearing a flying helmet and goggles. The diary revealed that the airman was Captain Bill Lancaster, who had crashed during the night of 13 April 1933 while flying from England to Cape Town. Injured, with no means of attracting attention, he'd lasted eight days until his water ran out. One of his last entries read, 'Chubbie darling, give up flying and settle down.' By the time she read those last words from a man she'd once loved more than thirty years before, Jessie 'Chubbie' Miller, the smiling young woman in the photographs, was 61 years old and hadn't flown for years, but this petite woman saddled for life with an ironic childhood nickname for her cheeks had packed a lifetime of achievement into her slight frame.

'Chubbie' Miller was born Jessie Maude Beveridge in the Western Australia town of Southern Cross in 1901, where her father was the manager of the local branch of the Commercial Bank. She grew up in Broken Hill a competition swimmer as well as an accomplished pianist with a reputation for achieving her goals. She married Melbourne *Weekly Times* newspaper journalist George Keith Miller at Christ Church, St Kilda, when she was eighteen. Nine years later, bored and restless, she left Australia for a six-month holiday in England.

During that summer of 1927, she was invited to a party in London where she fell into conversation with a distinguished former Royal Air Force pilot, Captain William Newton 'Bronco' Lancaster. They had geography in common: the dashing public-school-educated athlete, horseman and flier had been living in Australia at the outbreak of World War I, whereupon he'd enlisted with the Light Horse, eventually transferring to the Australian Flying Corps and then becoming a captain in the RAF in England by the time he was twenty. Now no longer in the air force and married with two children, the strain of trying to manage a family on little income was showing in his worn features and thinning hair but, inspired by Charles Lindbergh's recent non-stop flight across the Atlantic, Lancaster had come up with a dramatic plan that would solve his problems. He would become the first to fly a light plane solo from England to Australia. Brothers Ross and Keith Smith with two mechanics had made the trip first in 1919 in a Vickers Vimy bomber, followed by Ray Parer and John McIntosh in their De Havilland DH9 in 1920, but the journey had yet to be made in a small plane.

Any flights on this scale were expensive and required careful planning; not only did a pilot need a plane that would get them there in one piece but, with the limited fuel capacity of early planes, a series of refuelling stations had to be organised along the route. Sponsorship was necessary to fund all this, and Lancaster was having problems finding it. Enthralled by his élan and adventurous spirit, Miller immediately offered to help Lancaster raise the money, but on one condition: she would come along as a co-pilot and crew member. Hardly believing his luck, Lancaster readily agreed; in those days an aviatrix, as the press loved to call female fliers, was a rare bird indeed and the public relations potential was enormous.

His instinct was correct. This petite young lady who was so determined to be the first woman to travel in an aeroplane to Australia impressed everybody she met, and so within a short time Lancaster and Miller's joint venture attracted the interest of Sir Sefton Brancker, Director of Civil Aviation, and the financial support of several wealthy London-based Australians such as the pastoralist Sir Sidney Kidman. Shell and BP promised to supply fuel, and Miller was also able to obtain advances on contracts with Australian and English newspapers for regular stories about the flight. Aircraft manufacturer Avro even sold them their new small, twin-cockpit Avian biplane at a reduced price as a publicity venture. They named it *Red Rose*, the traditional Lancastrian flower, after Lancaster's mother who was known as Sister

Red Rose by the Mission of the Flowers charity with which she worked. Lancaster gave Miller some preliminary flying instruction, but on arriving late one morning for lessons he found his impatient student had taken off without him for her first successful solo flight. Miller had found her element.

After modifications to the plane that included fitting dual flight controls—so the plane could be flown from both cockpits—and larger fuel tanks, they were finally ready to take off from Croydon Aerodrome on 14 October 1927. Lady Ryrie, wife of the Australian High Commissioner Sir Granville Ryrie, christened the plane and presented Miller with a bunch of white heather for luck. Miller and Lancaster then lifted off into the sky to the cheers of a huge crowd towards far-distant Australia carrying a letter from the Australian High Commissioner to Prime Minister Stanley Bruce. With only nine hours' flight per tank of fuel, their trip would require some forty stops, taking them south through France into Italy and across to Malta, then to Egypt and the Sudan, Iraq, Persia (Iran), India, on across Burma to Singapore and then dropping down through what was then the Dutch East Indies (Indonesia) to Darwin. Right behind them, aviator Bert Hinkler would leave England in early November on his attempt to fly much the same route, only faster, with fewer stops. As he was flying solo, he had room to store extra fuel and that weight would, of course, decrease as he flew on.

The weight of the *Red Rose*, on the other hand, would remain constant. With its 80-horsepower engine, the biplane had a maximum speed of about 80 to 90 miles (128–44 kilometres) per hour. Any adverse weather conditions would put them on the ground. Without radio, if anything broke and they managed to land safely and find a telegraph station, then there was a chance of help. Otherwise, they'd have to fix it themselves. If they crashed somewhere remote, which much of the world was in 1927, the odds were high they would be added to the rapidly lengthening list of vanished aviators. On the other hand, flying a plane like this could be much like driving a car; if you saw someone's campfire you could land for a cup of tea or ask at a farmhouse for directions.

Caught in a sandstorm between Giza and Baghdad, Miller and Lancaster were forced to land at a desert outpost of the RAF in Iraq, where the officers shared their ration of bully beef and onion stew. Leaving Baghdad on 8 November, they reached Basra only to be quarantined for a week because of a cholera outbreak. By the end of November, they were stranded at Bushehr on the Persian Gulf (now in Iran) when their magneto gear wheel was stripped and Lancaster had to make another by hand. Finally, they were able to fly on to Karachi (now in Pakistan) where the engine was overhauled, then to Calcutta and after that Rangoon in Burma where on 22 December they were forced to land in rice fields due to more engine trouble and were forced to remain there until the New Year. By then, they had set a new official record for long-distance travel in a light plane.

Just after they took off from Rangoon on 2 January, Miller found she was sharing her cockpit with a poisonous snake, which she promptly beat to death with the joystick and threw over the side. Five days later they reached Singapore. They were on the last stage of their journey, only a week from Australia, and Lancaster was already planning to fly the *Red Rose* back to London over the same route. As they flew between Singapore and Muntok, Miller became the first woman to cross the equator in an aeroplane. Then disaster struck. As they were taking off from Muntok on the island of Bangka on 9 January, the engine cut out. The biplane fell out of the sky and smashed into the ground. Lucky to be alive, Lancaster was slightly concussed; Miller had two black eyes, lots of bruises and a broken nose. Their journey was perilously close to being over.

Lancaster, Miller and what was left of the *Red Rose* were all shipped back to Singapore, where they were delayed for just over two months while the plane was rebuilt. While they waited, Bert Hinkler overtook them to claim the record for which Lancaster and Miller had striven so hard, reaching Darwin on 22 February, having flown from England to Australia in sixteen days' flight time in the same type of light plane as Lancaster and Miller were using. To their credit, they had been there to meet him in Singapore and to wish him well.

After winning a fight with their insurance company and taking delivery of parts shipped out to them by the Royal Navy, the intrepid couple eventually resumed their own interrupted flight on 13 March, continuing on via Timor to finally arrive unexpectedly in Darwin after 156 days on 19 March 1928. Because they had been reported delayed due to bad weather, there was no one to meet them when they landed except the wife of the gaol governor who lived next to the landing field, but within a short time they were being mobbed by well-wishers. Jessie Miller became instantly famous as the first woman to complete a flight from England to Australia, during which she had acted as co-pilot and mechanic as well as recording the flight and being their public relations person. No woman had flown so far before.

After much celebration, Lancaster and Miller took off from Darwin on 22 March on a triumphal progress south. They landed at Newcastle Waters, then Camooweal, before flying into Longreach escorted by a Qantas plane to be feted at a dinner hosted by the managing director of Qantas, Hudson Fysh. Then they flew to Brisbane, where once again they were honoured and celebrated, finally arriving in Sydney at the end of March where they were met at Mascot by a crowd of a hundred thousand. From there they flew to Canberra and then on to Melbourne, where they landed at Essendon on 7 April to be met by another large crowd. After remaining there for a few days, they flew across Bass Strait to Tasmania, reaching Hobart on 30 April 1928, finally completing their epic journey to become the first aviators to fly from England to Tasmania.

By then, both their lives had become complicated and not just by fame; somewhere under the Persian stars they'd fallen in love. Miller and Lancaster had met every challenge together, forging a close partnership in which her courage and cheerfulness in the face of danger had endeared her to him. Lancaster decided to leave his family, but his wife, Kiki, refused to divorce him, preventing him and Miller from marrying. After visiting some of the main Australian cities on a lecture tour, Lancaster was contracted to fly a photographic mission for the arrival of Charles Kingsford Smith's trans-Pacific flight in the *Southern Cross* at Brisbane in early June 1928, and naturally he and Miller met 'Smithy' and the crew. They became particularly close friends with the American navigator Harry Lyon, and began to make plans with him for other long-distance flights. Consequently, when Lyon and *Southern Cross* radio operator James Warner returned to San Francisco later that month on the steamer *Sonoma*, Miller and Lancaster went with them.

Once they arrived, Lyon quickly announced his plans for a trans-Atlantic non-stop flight between England and America in the spring of the following year, with Lancaster and Miller as pilots in a tri-motor radio-equipped Fokker, followed by a round-the-world flight. By September, Lyon had expanded his transatlantic plans to also be trans-continental; their flight would depart from Los Angeles for New York and London and then return to Los Angeles with only one stop each way.

With all these plans happening around her, Miller apparently decided it might be a good idea to take the written test and do the twelve hours of solo flying required for her formal pilot qualification, and so in April 1929 she became only the third woman in the state of New York and one of only thirty-four women in the United States to be granted a private pilot's licence. Although Miller announced that she and Lancaster were about to fly the Lyon tri-motor from Los Angeles to New York to London and back, Lancaster was severely injured a few days later when his plane crashed as he took off from Trinidad. He was hospitalised in New York for four months, and that was the end of the duo's long-distance flying ventures.

Instead, now that she was qualified, Miller set out to enhance her own solo flying career. At the beginning of August, she announced that she would compete in the first transcontinental National Women's Air

Derby (later christened the 'Powder Puff Derby' by comedian Will Rogers) from Santa Monica, California, to Cleveland, Ohio, then the centre of air racing. Miller, the only Australian in the race, would fly a Fleet biplane after the cockpit had been rebuilt for her small body. Contestants for the 2700-mile (4300-kilometre) nine-day race against the clock, navigating only by dead reckoning and road maps, had to have a hundred hours of solo flight and be qualified for three different pilot licences. With $8000 in prize money at stake, the shortest elapsed time would win. Almost every competitor was a record-holder or former record-holder and many were known internationally for their flying feats.

Miller flew her own plane from New York to start in the derby at Santa Monica on 18 August 1929, with nineteen of the world's leading female aviators, including Amelia Earhart and Florence Lorre 'Pancho' Barnes. During the race, some fliers drifted into Mexico, there were numerous crashes, some incidents that provoked fears of sabotage and one death—all of which prompted hysterical calls by some media commentators to stop the race because the women had proved they couldn't fly; but these women pressed on through dust, sandstorms and forest fires. Miller was forced to land in Arizona after she mysteriously ran out of fuel, only to find that cactus spikes had ripped up the fuselage, delaying her badly. Then she was forced down and delayed again in Xenia, Ohio, because of engine trouble. The overall winner of the derby was Louise Thaden of Pittsburgh in 20 hours and 19 minutes, but Miller was awarded third prize of $325 in the light plane division, proving an Australian aviatrix could compete with the best.

She made up time immediately afterwards by winning the 50-mile (80-kilometre) closed-circuit pylon race for women at Cleveland against the two favourites, Phoebe Omlie and Amelia Earhart. These races, for which Cleveland became famous, were flown by high-speed planes around a tall chequered pylon at either end of a long field. Depending on the type of plane and the length of the race, a group of pylon racers could be flying at anywhere from 100 miles an hour (160 kilometres per hour) up to 300 miles an hour (482 kilometres per hour), banking into the tight pylon turns while flying as low as 30 feet (9.1 metres) off the ground. Needless to say, pilot fatalities and aircraft wrecks were not uncommon. Miller came third in the women's pursuit handicap race on 2 September. Before the Cleveland races were over, the Fairchild Aircraft Company was so impressed by her flying that it approached her to fly its new KR–34 in the 5000-mile (8046-kilometre) Ford National Reliability Air Tour in October. As one of only three women among thirty-eight starters, she made quite a fashion statement in white kid jodhpurs, white silk shirt and white leather flying helmet with black boots and tie, as she stood alongside her sleek plane that was also white with a single black line down the fuselage. But her flying wasn't just about fashion. Against some of the toughest pilots then in the air, she came eighth overall and was the only woman to finish. That year she was also engaged for a publicity stunt to race the *Blue Comet*, the Jersey Central Railroad's new high-speed passenger train to Atlantic City. In November 1929, Miller's ranking among her peers was recognised when she was accepted as a charter member of 'The Ninety-Nines', the first organisation formed for women pilots. It still honours her today.

By March 1930, having gained her commercial pilot's licence in Ottawa, Canada, Miller was working as chief test pilot for the Victor Aircraft Corporation in New Jersey. Although she announced a plan to fly solo from Newfoundland to England, instead she took off from Curtis-Wright Field, New York, on 13 October in an Alexander Bullet to try to break the transcontinental record of thirty-one hours set by Laura Ingalls the previous week. While the Bullet had been flown successfully by Edith Folz in the 1929 Derby, it was by no means an easy plane to fly and had killed two test pilots, so Miller had to stay focused all the way. On 16 October, she landed in Los Angeles in a flight time of 25 hours 44 minutes. Two days later, she heard that her rival Ingalls had left Los Angeles and set a new west–east flight record to New York of 25 hours and 35 minutes, so she in turn took off to beat it, landing again at Curtis-Wright Field on 26 October after a flight time of 21 hours and 47 minutes.

Within a week, Miller was announcing an attempt on the 2000-kilometre non-stop flight from Pittsburgh to Havana, Cuba. After being delayed by fog, she took off on 22 November and landed in Havana the next day. However, when she failed to arrive on her return journey, it was feared after a prolonged air search that her Alexander Bullet had gone down in the sea. Just when all hope had been lost, Miller stepped off a boat at Nassau on 1 December. She had been blown off course and forced to land on remote Andros Island in the Bahamas. Guided by locals, she walked 25 kilometres through the jungle to where the only four white residents of the island were living. One of them was fellow Australian Percy Cavill, one-time champion swimmer of the world, who until his death there ten years later would still swim every day from one end of the island to the other. A fishing boat took Miller to Nassau.

Fate wasn't finished with her yet, though. After her plane was fixed, she took off again for Washington but crashed at Jacksonville in Florida on 14 December. This time the damage was irreparable. Miller was damaged too, and was hospitalised in New York for some time. To add insult to injury, her sponsors refused to pay her for the uncompleted flight. In early June 1931, she announced her intention to apply for US citizenship and that apparently was the last straw for her long-suffering husband, who promptly and successfully filed for divorce in Melbourne on grounds of desertion. Lancaster's wife, on the other hand, still refused to divorce him.

On 30 July, Miller heroically roused hotel guests and management by running through smoke-filled corridors and banging on doors when her hotel in Fort Plain, New York, caught fire. By Christmas, Miller and Lancaster were living in Miami, barely able to scrape the rent together and occasionally stealing food. There they met Charles Haden Clarke, a young and handsome reporter for the *New Orleans-Picayune* who also had a wife who wouldn't divorce him; despite this,

Clarke was engaged to marry a young lady named Peggy Brown. The trio hatched a plan whereby Clarke would ghost-write a book about Miller and Lancaster's experiences that would hopefully make them all some money. In return, Clarke could have room and board with the couple while they worked on the project.

All went well until Lancaster had to leave to help investigate a new airline route in the south-west. Once he was gone, Miller felt abandoned. She had no money, her flying career was going nowhere and she no longer loved Lancaster, who after all these years still couldn't make the break to get a divorce. He was a true and close friend, but the fire had gone out. Clarke had seen that, and with Lancaster out of the way he moved right on in. Miller was swept completely off her feet and before long was madly in love with him. Lancaster never saw it coming. The first inkling he had of trouble was when Miller didn't write and was distant when he called. His fears seemed founded when one of his colleagues on the airline trip received some letters from his wife describing the drunkenly amorous behaviour of Miller and Clarke at parties. Then, to his shock, he opened the long-awaited letter from Miller only to read that she and Clarke were engaged and about to marry. He promptly abandoned the airline project and flew home, buying a pistol and ammunition on the way.

That night, 20 April 1932, there was a heated discussion around the dinner table that took some odd turns; at one point, Lancaster proposed that he crash his plane so Miller and Clarke could collect his $1000 life insurance as a 'wedding present'. They eventually agreed to postpone the wedding for a month and then they went to bed, Miller in her room while the other two were in another. Lancaster later claimed Clarke had then confessed things to him that would have been revealed to Miller the next day and would have caused her to call off the wedding altogether.

At about 2 a.m., Miller was awakened by Lancaster pounding on her door and calling out that Clarke had shot himself with Lancaster's pistol. The police arrived to find a blood-stained Miller cradling a terribly injured Clarke in her arms; he'd been shot in the head and died about noon that day. State Attorney N. Vernon Hawthorne was not persuaded by the suicide story and Lancaster was arrested in May 1932 and charged with Clarke's murder. The sensational trial before a packed courtroom revealed drama and romantic tragedy of which headlines are made.

Poor Clarke had obviously fallen heavily for Miller, with whom he'd been intimate. She, in turn, testified she had been totally infatuated with him to the extent they had considered a suicide pact as a solution to their dilemma. Unable to defend himself, Clarke was characterised by the defence as an immoral, poverty-stricken, depressed drunk and suicidal hashish addict. Clarke's body was exhumed so that his skull could be examined for powder residue and to determine the bullet trajectory. It was duly produced in court by the defence ballistics expert Albert Hamilton, a charlatan with a fake doctoral degree, to help him make a case for Clarke's suicide. Despite the acknowledged absence of close-contact powder burns, the presence of an exit wound clearly indicating the gun was held almost vertically above Clarke's head and angled backwards, and mistaking cotton fibres in the gunsight for human hairs, Hamilton confidently stated that it had been suicide. Even Miller didn't stand up for Clarke in the end, claiming at the trial that she no longer cared for him because she'd since discovered he'd lied about such things as his age, his career and his love life.

On the other hand, six famous aviators, including a Congressional Medal of Honor holder, were there to testify as character witnesses for Lancaster who, despite being a rival for Miller's affections, was known to be in possession of a gun and ammunition at the time, was overheard to say he'd 'go back and get rid of the S.O.B.', was the only other person in the room at the time of the shooting, and who admitted forging Clarke's suicide notes, was acquitted on the first ballot after the all-male jury deliberated for barely five hours on 17 August. Fashionably dressed women in the courtroom shrieked and wept. He had been successfully portrayed as a hero and a man of honour, whose great love had been stolen by a treacherous friend. 'I feel that Haden's committing suicide was the culmination of a beautiful love,' he said at the trial, 'and that the suicide itself was a beautiful thing.' It was certainly a convenient thing. But fate had her own plans for Mr Lancaster.

Despite the verdict, the pair were seen by the authorities as trouble, and they left the United States separately in October for England in exchange for the dropping of deportation charges. Speculation was rife at the time of their departure about whether they would marry, but Miller had asserted on the stand that she hadn't been in love with Lancaster for the previous two years. She remained very fond and supportive of him, though, as he prepared to embark on his next challenge: an attempt to beat the recent England–Cape Town flight record set by Amy Johnson Mollison of 4 days, 6 hours and 54 minutes. It was a plan put together too quickly by a man desperate to restore his reputation and clear his name.

On 11 April 1933, Lancaster was waved off by his parents and some journalists from Lympne Airfield in England. His plane was a blue, single-seat Avro Avian biplane, christened *Southern Cross Minor* by Sir Charles Kingsford Smith, who in 1931 had unsuccessfully attempted to break the Australia–England record in it. Carrying no survival supplies other than 8 litres of water to cover over 10 000 kilometres of visual navigation, including 2300 kilometres of desert, he reached Oran in Algeria behind schedule. With his eye on the clock, he flew all night, reading a map by torchlight, to land at Adrar—still in Algeria—the next morning in a sandstorm. He was so tired by now that he flew in a circle trying to reach Reggane and landed at Adrar again. When he finally did land at Reggane, officials begged him to rest, but he was too far behind schedule and took off again for Gao in Mali on 12 April. He never made it and, although an extensive search took place, he was never seen alive again. In 1933, Lancaster's will that he'd made on 8 April was opened. He'd made Miller sole heir of everything he had: £170.

In July 1934, Miller was reported as planning to participate in the Centenary Air Race to Australia in an Airspeed Courier that would be piloted by her and co-piloted by Mrs Neil Fergusson. However, she was unable to persuade anyone to back her financially, despite public appeals for help in newspapers. The following year, she was appointed manager of the Heston Aerodrome office of the Commercial Air Hire Company. Heston Aerodrome, which ceased operation in 1947, was situated near what is now London Heathrow Airport. Broke, Miller was now paying off debts incurred when the small Robinson Redwing biplane she was flying from England to West Africa and then Cape Town, taking orders for British manufacturers on the first known international commercial traveller's flight to Africa, had crashed while making a forced landing just outside of Cotonou, on the coast of Benin. This latest in a long line of misadventures was the final straw for Jessie and she retired behind a desk; it was probably small comfort that her Robinson Redwing had flown further than any other Redwing.

In 1936, Jessie married her former boss at Commercial Air Hire, Flight-Lieutenant John Barnard Pugh, who was now a chief pilot for the original British Airways. Although she still had to be around aeroplanes, she said, there would be no more flying stunts for her, and she was right. Miller quietly faded into history until the discovery twenty-six years later of Lancaster's body out there in the desert. Because his will had stipulated Miller as his sole beneficiary, the last words that he'd written were finally read by the one for whom they'd been intended. Jessie Miller died in England in December 1972.

The *Southern Cross Minor* was recovered from the Sahara in 1975 and is now in the warehouse of the Queensland Museum in Brisbane.

★

The rest of the world

The first woman known to have flown in a powered aeroplane was American Edith Hart Berg, who went up with Wilbur Wright when he demonstrated the Wright Flyer at Le Mans, France, in September 1908. French sculptress Thérèse Peltier was the first European woman in the air when she flew with fellow sculptor Leon Delagrange on 8 July 1909.

The first woman known to pilot a powered aeroplane in controlled flight was French Baroness Raymonde de la Roche (aka Elise Raymonde Deroche). Formerly a balloonist, she was the first woman to qualify for a fixed-wing pilot's licence, in March 1910. On 22 October 1909, she flew a Voisin aeroplane at Chalons in France. She was also the first holder of a women's flight distance record (323 kilometres). She died in a crash in 1919 while attempting to become the first female test pilot.

The first woman known to have piloted a full-scale glider was Australian Florence Taylor, on 5 December 1909.

The first woman to design, build and fly her own aeroplane, the *Mayfly*, was Lilian Bland of Ireland, who took flight across Lord O'Neill's estate at Randalstown in August 1910. She was quickly followed by American Bessica Faith Medlar Raiche, who built her own aeroplane in her drawing room and backyard in Mineola, New York, and flew it at Hempstead Plains, New York, on 16 September 1910.

The first American woman to pilot an aeroplane in controlled flight was Blanche Stuart Scott who, perhaps inadvertently, took off in her Curtiss biplane on 6 September 1910, while training at Hammondsport, New York. She went on to become the first female stunt pilot to fly at public events, the first woman in America to fly long distance, the first female test pilot, and in 1948 the first American woman to fly in a jet. However, Harriet Quimby was the first American female licensed pilot; she died in a crash three months after she gained her licence in 1911.

On 15 June 1921, Elizabeth 'Bessie' Coleman became the first qualified female pilot of African-American descent. She gained her qualification in France because no flight school in America would admit a black woman.

Millicent Bryant was the first Australian woman to gain a pilot's licence, in 1927. She had little time in which to use it, however, drowning in a ferry accident later that year. In 1932, Maude Rose 'Lores' Bonney OBE was the first woman to circumnavigate Australia by air and to fly solo in 1933 from Australia to England, and in 1937 from Australia to South Africa. Freda Thompson became the first woman in the British Empire to obtain an instructor's licence in 1933 and in 1934 was the first Australian woman to fly solo from England to Australia.

SAILING THE SEA ROAD

The Empress of Australia

Firsts

- Largest purpose-built ROPAX (roll-on, roll-off, passengers) ferry of its kind in the world when built
- Operated on the longest ROPAX ferry route in the world when built
- Largest passenger vessel constructed in Australia when built

When I was a young man working in Melbourne, my family lived in Tasmania and so I would frequently travel between Melbourne and Devonport on the Australian National Line ferry *Empress of Australia*. The weather for the Bass Strait crossing would sometimes be appalling, but as I'd been raised on small boats and had worked on fishing trawlers it never bothered me and I'd sometimes be one of the handful of hardy souls who turned up for breakfast. The *Empress* actually had an open walkway forward just below the bridge that was an extension of the bridge deck and, as even the strongest stomach can only handle the smell of violent seasickness for so long, a friend and I were standing up there one night getting some fresh air. Really, we were getting a lot more than that because the *Empress* was nosing into waves that were breaking right over the bows and drenching us with spray. Suddenly a window on the flying bridge above us flew open and a voice shouted down: 'If you're so keen on this weather, at least come up here where you can watch it and be dry!' And that was how two young men during a much more innocent period of history came to spend a fascinating and unforgettable hour or two on the darkened bridge of the *Empress* that night.

While never quite as popular as her predecessor, the *Princess of Tasmania*, and not a very lucky ship, the *Empress* nevertheless served Tasmania well for many years, and contributed much towards the development of the tourist industry on which the island now largely depends. The Australian National Line, which had taken over the passenger service across Bass Strait between Melbourne and Devonport in Tasmania in 1959, originally ordered the construction of the *Empress* to supplement the highly successful service of their first ferry, the *Princess*. One of the earliest purpose-built ROPAX (roll-on, roll-off, passengers) ferries in the world and the first in the southern hemisphere, the 3964-gross ton, 113-metre, diesel-powered *Princess of Tasmania* was built by the New South Wales State Dockyard at Newcastle and launched on 15 December 1958. She had twin rudders and a bow thruster for added manoeuvrability, and reputedly was the first Australian coastal vessel to be fitted with fin stabilisers, although you wouldn't have been able to tell this as a passenger. The *Princess* developed a legendary reputation for her corkscrew roll in a heavy swell.

After fitting-out and sea trials, she left Melbourne on her maiden voyage to Devonport on 23 December 1959. Some eight thousand people lined the banks of the Mersey River to see her arrive at Devonport the next day. The *Princess* would make three round-trips a week, each leg being a fourteen-hour overnight voyage. She was originally fitted out for sixty-seven crew and 334 passengers: 156 in aircraft-style reclining seats and the rest in a range of cabin accommodation. The vehicle deck, accessed through a stern door, reached almost the full length of the hull and could hold 142 cars with room for a few more in a lower hold accessed by a lift.

Advertised as the 'Searoad' service, the *Princess* was soon smothered by her own popularity. In her first year alone, she carried nearly sixty-five thousand passengers and over twenty-four thousand vehicles. It was soon obvious she could not meet demand and so the 104-metre, 4129-ton RORO (roll-on, roll-off) ferry *Bass Trader* was built in 1961 to carry sixty semi-trailers and cargo between northern Tasmania and Melbourne. She was the first vessel in the world constructed in such a way that her twin 18-cylinder Deltic diesel engines by Napier & Son of Liverpool could be repaired by replacement, and thus the vessel would not have to be taken out of service. Each engine weighed only 5 tonnes and when needing mechanical servicing or repair could be lifted out and replaced within a few hours with a spare engine stored onshore.

Both these ships were so successful that plans were drawn up in 1961 for a third vehicle and passenger ferry to be built for ANL to operate between Sydney and Tasmania. She would be the largest purpose-built ROPAX vessel of its kind then in operation in the world, and the largest passenger vessel ever built in Australia. Constructed at a cost of £2.6 million by the Cockatoo Docks and Engineering Company at Cockatoo Island Dockyard in Sydney, the diesel-powered 'Ship 220' was 12 037 gross tonnes with a length of 136 metres, and was able to hold up to ninety-one cars or fifty-one cars and thirty-three semi-trailers on a vehicle deck accessed by a stern door, and 250 passengers in a range of air-conditioned cabin accommodation. There were also lounges, a dining room, a writing room and children's playrooms. She was fully air-conditioned and stabilised, and fitted with a unique combination of twin screws and side thrusters.

New terminals were built for her in Sydney and in Hobart, Bell Bay (Launceston) and Burnie in Tasmania, and she was launched as the *Empress of Australia* on 18 January 1964 by the Honourable Catherine Sidney, daughter of Governor-General Lord de L'Isle. The ship was named in a proud tradition; there were two previous ships by that name operated by Canadian Pacific (CP). The first *Empress of Australia* in 1922 was originally the 1913 Hamburg-Amerika Line's 21 860-ton, 55-metre liner *Tirpitz* that was handed over to CP after World War I. She had a distinguished career that included rescuing 3000 survivors of the 1923 Yokohama earthquake, becoming the royal yacht for the 1939 visit of George VI to Canada, and then an armed troopship during both World War II and the Korean War, until 1952 when she was scrapped. Her successor was launched in 1924 as the French Line's *De Grasse*. After being sunk by gunfire in Bordeaux in 1944, she was raised, refitted and returned to service until she was purchased by Canadian Pacific in 1953 to replace the *Empress of Canada*. Renamed the *Empress of Australia*, she operated on the Liverpool–Montreal route for only three years until she was sold to Grimaldi–SIOSA. Rebuilt with a graceful raked bow as the *Venezuela* for the Italy–Venezuela service, she sank off Cannes in 1962.

The Australian National Line originally planned that the new *Empress of Australia* would make three return trips from Sydney every two weeks to Hobart, Bell Bay and Burnie respectively. The minimum fare was £17 to share a four-berth cabin and £27 per car. At that time, the 1006-kilometre Sydney–Hobart route was the longest being serviced by a ROPAX ferry in the world and was a two-night voyage. On her maiden voyage from Sydney to Hobart on 16 January 1965, she averaged 18 knots and broke the travel time record by over eleven hours.

The *Empress* was immediately embraced by the travelling public. Her arrival into Sydney was always spectacular, as she passed under the Harbour Bridge and around Goat Island to turn 180 degrees in her own length, using the bow thruster, so that she could glide smoothly into the berth stern-first until she gently nudged the vehicle ramp. However, from early in her life a series of incidents dogged the *Empress*, and she slowly but surely developed the reputation of being a 'jinxed' ship. Apart from various disruptive industrial disputes, a fire broke out in the engine room on 13 January 1966 while she was docked at Bell Bay, putting her out of service for a week, as did another fire almost exactly twelve years later. In 1968, someone stole $10 000 from the purser's safe and got clean away. The notorious Bass Strait weather was also a constant hazard; in June 1976, a huge wave struck the ship so hard that the captain was knocked unconscious and the load on a semi-trailer collapsed, flattening a neighbouring campervan down on the vehicle deck. In July 1978, she ran aground in the Mersey River while arriving from Melbourne and it took four tug boats to pull her off in the midst of very bad weather. Then in March 1984, a piston seized in one engine and she drifted for five hours before engineers could raise power again.

Even by 1972, despite an annual federal government subsidy of around $2 million, ANL was in economic trouble and compelled to completely overhaul its operations. It decided to retire the *Princess* and replace it with the *Empress* on the Melbourne–Hobart run. The company's newer ship, *Australian Trader*, would take over the Sydney route. After thirteen years carrying over a million passengers for nearly 4000 voyages, the *Princess* left Tasmania on her final voyage to Melbourne on 27 June 1972, farewelled by thousands of people. She was quickly sold and began operating with the same name on the eighteen-hour overnight service between North Sydney, Nova Scotia and Argentia in Newfoundland from September 1972 until 1975, when she became the *Marine Cruiser*, operating between Yarmouth, Nova Scotia and Portland in Maine for eight years. Then she was sold again and, as the *Majorca Rose*, began operating in 1984 between Port Vendres in France and Alcudia on the island of Majorca. For a number of years she then sailed between Greece and Italy under various names and owners, until moving to Saudi Arabian ownership in 1991, carrying Muslim pilgrims across the Red Sea as the *Shahd Fayez*. In 2005, as the *Tebah 2000*, she was scrapped.

In April 1972, the *Empress* went into dock in Newcastle for extensive refitting, which included installation of 190 reclining seats in what had been the lounges, increasing passenger capacity to 440. Beginning on 30 June, she sailed three return trips a week on the fourteen-hour overnight voyage to Devonport, and continued to do so for many years. After 1976, when the *Australian Trader* was withdrawn, the *Empress* became the sole passenger vessel connecting Tasmania to the mainland of Australia.

However, the *Empress* was an ageing ship and the swelling demand for a service that could carry larger numbers of passengers and vehicles across Bass Strait motivated discussion about replacements. During 1982 and 1983, at least five companies put forward proposals for alternatives, including new European-style ferries and a high-speed catamaran service that would carry 300 passengers and fifty cars between Devonport and Melbourne in five hours. Finally, with no decisions made on any of these projects, ANL announced in June 1984 that it could no longer justify the unprofitable Tasmanian operation and would be withdrawing the *Empress* from service. Faced with the prospect of being cut off from the mainland of Australia and major sources of revenue, the Tasmanian government was at last galvanised into action and persuaded the federal government to establish a new section of the Tasmanian Department of Transport, to be known as Transport Tasmania or the TT Line, which would run a new ferry service. It would be funded as part of a compensation package from the federal government for not allowing the destructive hydro-electric scheme on the Gordon River to proceed.

The TT Line's first task was to find a suitable second-hand ferry as soon as possible, as there was no time to build a new one, and after an international search the Tasmanian government announced in August 1984 that it would be purchasing the West German ferry *Nils Hogersson*, built in 1974 for the Baltic Sea route. Able to carry 850 passengers in full cabin accommodation and 470 cars on two vehicle decks with bow and stern door access, the ship was officially handed over after refitting on 21 April 1985. Renamed the *Abel Tasman*, she went into service between Melbourne and Devonport on 1 July.

Six months after her twentieth anniversary of service along the Australian coast, the *Empress* left Devonport on her final voyage to Melbourne on 2 June 1985. She was quickly sold to a Cyprus-based shipping subsidiary and renamed simply MV *Empress*. She left Melbourne towards the end of July for the Mediterranean, where she eventually entered service on a regular ferry run between Larnaca in Cyprus and the Lebanese port of Jounieh. In 1989 she was re-registered by new owners and by 1991 had been completely rebuilt as a 13176-gross ton, 143-metre cruise ship for 623 passengers. The rebuilding included extending her superstructure, raking of the bow and construction of a new stern, installation of more cabins, and the additions of a two-deck show lounge, a casino, swimming pool, library and observation lounge. She thus became one of the first cruise ships to have twin rudders and screws, and side thrusters.

Still known as the MV *Empress*, but now bearing no resemblance to the original ship, she operated for a brief period as a high-standard cruise ship for Starlite Cruises between San Diego and Mexican ports. But in December 1991 she became the Nassau-registered MV *Royal Pacific*, just another casino ship sailing out of Singapore to Indonesia on three- and four-day gambling cruises. Coincidentally, a number of the croupiers on board were Australians recruited from the casino in Adelaide. However, whatever little luck the old *Empress* had left was about to finally run out. In the early hours of 23 August 1992, while proceeding through the Straits of Malacca into the Andaman Sea, she was rammed at full speed by an 800-tonne Taiwanese fish factory vessel, punching a gaping hole in the hull near her stern. Perhaps the old *Empress* was just tired of it all by now; for some mysterious reason that was never identified, her watertight doors refused to close and she flooded and sank quickly. Fortunately, the experienced Captain Tasos Papayannis was able to get almost everyone off in the lifeboats and only nine people lost their lives; although it was not his fault, the incident haunted him until his death in 2005.

Thus ended the career of a landmark ship in the maritime history of both Australia and the world. Some indication of how quickly ROPAX ferry construction had developed since she was launched can be seen in the capacity of her successor, *Abel Tasman*, which could accommodate 850 passengers and about five hundred vehicles, and had three restaurants, multiple lounges, shops, a sauna, swimming pool and two vehicle decks that could be accessed by stern and bow doors.

But the *Empress* still sails in my memory.

★

The rest of the world

The first purpose-built RORO ferry to operate in British waters was the MV *Princess Victoria*, built in 1947 by William Denny & Bros Ltd in Dumbarton. She was employed by British Railways on the crossing from Stranraer in Scotland to Larne in Northern Ireland. On 31 January 1953, she sank during a severe storm in the North Channel with the loss of 133 lives, including all the ship's officers and the deputy prime minister of Northern Ireland. It was at that time the deadliest maritime disaster in UK waters since World War II, and an annual memorial service is still held on both sides of the North Channel on every anniversary of the sinking.

Britain's first drive-through RORO ferry was the cross-Channel *Viking I*, built for Thoresen in Norway in 1964 to operate between Southampton, Cherbourg and Le Havre. Cruise-liner car ferries were also in service along the Southampton–Lisbon–Tangier (and later Algeciras) route, the first British vessel of which was P&O's 11 500-tonne *Eagle*, which entered service in 1971.

The first purpose-built RORO ferry for the Baltic Sea was the 1000-passenger *Skandia*, built in 1961. It went into service between Helsinki and Stockholm.

In Japan, these vessels are known as long-haul car ferries and the first of these was the 4979-gross ton ferry *Hankyu*, which began service in 1968 between Kobe (Honshu) and Kokura (Kyushu). New Zealand's first RORO ferry was the *Aramoana*, which began crossing the Cook Strait between Picton in the South Island and Wellington in the North Island in August 1962.

The first modern RORO vessel in the United States was the *Comet*, a motorised vehicle carrier built for the US military in 1957 with stern and interior ramps allowing vehicles to drive directly from the dock into place; an adjustable chocking system locked vehicles into place. However, the United States had vehicle ferries from as early as 1913 when the *Leschi* became the first purpose-built drive-on ferry to carry cars across Washington State's Puget Sound.

Irish Ferries' *Ulysses* is now claimed to be the ROPAX ferry with the greatest vehicle capacity in the world. Operating between Dublin and Holyhead, Wales, since 2001, the 50 938-gross ton ship is 209 metres long and carries 1342 cars or 240 semi-trailers, and two thousand passengers and crew. The largest ROPAX vessel in size is the MS *Color Magic*, a 75 100-gross ton cruise ferry built in Finland in 2007. It is 224 metres long and carries 550 cars and cargo.

ACKNOWLEDGEMENTS

I'd like to express my special thanks to the former editor of the arts magazines *The Melbourne Report* and *The Melburnian*, Phil Pianta, to whom I've dedicated this book. For a number of years, Phil was my writing mentor and gave me encouragement while I gathered a wide variety of experience for work that he then published. I suspect I am not the only person involved in 'the artz' in Australia who could thank him for a similar start. Phil taught me the discipline of producing a certain number of words by a deadline and believe it or not, writers-to-be out there, that's a very valuable lesson to learn. That Great Australian Work will never appear in a bookstore if you don't finish it and send it to the publisher. So, all these years later, 'Thank you, Phil.'

This kind of book inevitably leaves a writer with a head full of facts with which you bore everyone except your long-suffering wife and even her eyes glaze over sometimes, so Marci deserves a big vote of thanks for putting up with the complexities of Michell tilt-pad thrust bearings, gyroscopic monorails, glider construction and why so many people took their clothes off in 1974.

I would also like to thank the wonderful team at Allen & Unwin, including Foong Ling Kong, Stuart Neal, Jo Lyons and John Mapps, for their belief in and contributions to this book.

The stories in this book could not have been gathered without the willing assistance and contributions of many people, not all of whom were located in Australia. My thanks and appreciation go to the following organisations and individuals.

Organisations

The Alexander Turnbull Library, National Library of New Zealand; the Australian Aviation Museum, Sydney (Trevor Dean, Curator); the Australian Gliding Museum, Bacchus Marsh, Victoria (Bruce and Judith Hearn); the Australian Museum, Sydney (Mark McGrouther, Collection Manager, Ichthyology); Heritage Tasmania, Hobart (Ester Guerzoni, Senior Executive Officer); the History of Medicine Library, Royal Australian College of Physicians, Sydney (Liz Rouse, Librarian); the Ian Boyle Collection (Ian Boyle); the Launceston Historical Society, Tasmania (Dr Marita Bardenhagen); the Malvern Historical Society, Melbourne (Jane Nigro, Vice President); the MS Bullet Project, Jackson Hole, Wyoming (Jim Baughman); the National Library of Australia; the National Motor Museum in South Australia (Allison Russell, Senior Curator; Matthew Lombard, Curator; Darryl Grey, Research Volunteer); the National Museum of Science and Industry, UK (Rory Cook and Sarah Norville, Corporate Information); the Newhaven Maritime Museum, UK (Richard Beckett); the Ninety-Nines, Inc. International Organization of Women Pilots, Oklahoma City, OK (Laura Ohrenberg, Headquarters Manager); the Northern Territory Archives Service, Darwin (Francoise Barr, Archivist); the Northern Territory Library, Darwin (Ines Autiero); the Regional Council of Goyder, South Australia (Leonie Fretwell); the Royal Engineers Museum, Library and Archive, UK (Amy Adams, Assistant Curator); the Sound Preservation Association of Tasmania, Bellerive, Hobart (Lindsay McCarthy, President); the Stonnington History Centre, Victoria (Di Foster, Local Historian); the State Library of New South Wales (Diane Jackson, Manuscripts & Original Materials); the University of Nevada

Las Vegas Library (Su Kim Chung); the Telstra Museum, Hawthorn, Melbourne (Stefan Nowak, Museum Manager); the West Adams Heritage Association, Los Angeles (Flo Selfman and Jim Childs); the White House, Westbury, Tasmania (Chris and Jude Clemons).

Individuals

John Angove AM, for kindly sharing his photos, memories and information about Thomas Angove.

Ian Boyle at Simplon Postcards (www.simplopc.co.uk), for his permission to publish the photo of the *Paris*.

Ian Bradshaw, for permission to use his photo of Michael O'Brien and for information about it, and Andrew Kener for permission to use the manuscript of his study of the photograph carried out at the University of Pennsylvania.

Lorayne Branch, for her friendship and for kindly sharing her detailed knowledge about her famous relative, Henry Sutton.

Robert Caldwell, for sharing his unique and detailed knowledge about streakers everywhere.

Kay Cottee AO, for her willingness within her busy schedule to help with information about her voyage.

Russell Darbyshire, for permission to use his photos of the reproduction Taylor glider.

Lonnie Dupre and John Hoelscher, for sharing their experiences and photos about their Greenland expeditions.

Gus Green, for sharing his research about Alfred Alexander, published in May 2011 as *What a Racket! The story of the Alexander Patent Racket Co.*

John Hipwell, for his information about Sir Hubert Wilkins.

Andrew Lancaster, for assistance with the story of his great-uncle, Bill Lancaster.

Rosemary Madigan and John Wollaston, for kindly sharing their knowledge and family photos of Tullie Wollaston.

Donna J. Neary, for her willingness to share details of her career as a war artist.

Cr Bill Pearson, for sharing information about A.G.M. Michell's property at Bunyip.

Peter M. Silcock, for sharing his knowledge of Dr Lidwill's black marlin.

Colin Tatz, for sharing his encyclopaedic knowledge of Aboriginal sportspeople.

Mary Jane Terenzi, at the Revere Society for Cultural and Historic Preservation, Revere, Massachusetts.

Dr Fiona Wood FRACS, AM, for her support and assistance.

BIBLIOGRAPHY

Books

Acierno, Louis J., *The History of Cardiology*, Parthenon Publishing Group: Pearl River, New York, 1994.

Barker, Ralph, *Verdict on a Lost Flyer: The story of Bill Lancaster and Chubbie Miller*, Fontana/Collins: Sydney, 1986.

Bevan, Scott, *Battle Lines: Australian artists at war*, Random House Australia: Sydney, 2004.

Encel, Vivien, *Australian Genius: 50 great ideas*, Atrand: Crows Nest, NSW, 1988.

Brabham, Sir Jack, and Nye, D., *The Jack Brabham Story*, Minidi-Chrysalis: Windsor, NSW, 2004.

Cottee, Kay, *First Lady: A history-making solo voyage around the world*, Macmillan: South Melbourne, 1989.

Craddock, David A., *Feeling the Air: The famous names and colourful personalities who pioneered Australia's first flights*, D.A. Craddock through Book House at Wild & Woolley: Sydney, 1999.

Crawford, Elizabeth, *The Women's Suffrage Movement: A reference guide 1866–1928*, Routledge: London, 2001.

Dowson, D., Taylor, C., Godet, M., Berthe, D. (eds), *Fluid Film Lubrication—Osborne Reynolds Centenary*, Elsevier Science: Amsterdam, 1987.

Dundy, Elaine, *Finch, Bloody Finch*, Michael Joseph: London, 1980.

Dupre, Lonnie, *Greenland Expedition: Where ice is born*, Northwood Press; Minnetonka, Minnesota, 2000.

Eckert, Allan W., *The World of Opals*, John Wiley & Sons: New York, 1997.

Evans, Colin, *A Question of Evidence: The casebook of great forensic controversies*, John Wiley & Sons: Hoboken, NJ; 2003.

Faulkner, Trader, *Peter Finch: A biography*, Taplinger Publishing Company: New York, 1979.

Freestone, R. and Hanna, B., *Florence Taylor's Hats*, Halstead Press: Sydney, 2008.

Gilltrap, Terry and Maree, *Gilltrap's Australian Cars from 1879: A history of cars built in Australia*, Golden Press: Sydney, 1981.

Gray, Edwyn, *Nineteenth-century Torpedoes and Their Inventors*, Naval Institute Press: Annapolis, MD, 2004.

Gwynn-Jones, Terry, *Heroic Australian Air Stories*, Rigby: Sydney, 1981.

Harrison, Dennis, *The Summit: The story of an Australian car*, Dennis and Margaret Harrison: Malvern, South Australia, 1989.

Harrison, Ian, *The Book of Firsts*, Cassell Illustrated: London, 2003.

Idriess, Ion L., *Lightning Ridge: The land of black opals*, Angus & Robertson: Sydney, 1940.

Ingpen, Robert, *Australian Inventions and Innovations*, Rigby: Sydney, 1982.

Irwin, Sally, *Between Heaven and Earth: The life of a mountaineer, Freda Du Faur 1882–1935*, White Crane Press: Hawthorn, Victoria, 2000.

Jeffrey, Kirk, *Machines in Our Hearts: The cardiac pacemaker, the implantable defibrillator and American health care*, Johns Hopkins University Press: Baltimore, MD, 2001.

Jessen, Gene Nora, *The Powder Puff Derby of 1929: The true story of the first women's cross-country air race*, Sourcebooks Inc: Naperville, ILL, 2002.

Klepak, Lou, *Nora Heysen*, The Beagle Press: Sydney, 1989.

Lamberton, Kathryn (ed), *Mari Nawi: Aboriginal Odysseys 1790–1850*, State Library of New South Wales: Sydney, 2010.

Lang, W.R., *James Harrison: Pioneering genius*, Neptune Press: Melbourne, 1982.

Lenburg, Jeff, *Who's Who in Animated Cartoons: An international guide to film and television's award-winning and legendary animators*, Applause Theatre & Cinema Books: New York, 2006.

McIver, Stuart B., *Murder in the Tropics: The Florida chronicles, Vol. 2*, Pineapple Press: Sarasota, FL, 2008.

Nasht, Simon, *The Last Explorer: Hubert Wilkins, Australia's Unknown Hero*, Hodder Australia: Sydney, 2005.

Plowman, Peter, *Ferry to Tasmania*, Rosenberg Publishing: Sydney, 2004.

Robertson, Patrick, *The Shell Book of Firsts*, Ebury Press and Michael Joseph Limited: London, 1974.

Sears, Edward Seldon, *Running Through the Ages*. McFarland: Jefferson, NC, 2001.

Speck, Catherine, *Painting Ghosts: Australian women artists in wartime*, Craftsman House: Melbourne, 2004.

Sullivan, James E., *How to Become an Athlete*, American Sports Publishing Co., New York, 1916.

Sussex, Lucy (ed.), *The Fortunes of Mary Fortune*, Penguin: Ringwood, 1989.

Tatz, Colin, *Obstacle Race: Aborigines in sport*, UNSW Press: Sydney, 1995.

Tatz, Colin and Paul, *Black Gold: The Aboriginal and Islander Sports Hall of Fame*, Aboriginal Studies Press: Canberra, 2000.

Thomas, Lowell, *Sir Hubert Wilkins: His world of adventure*, Readers Book Club: Melbourne, 1963.

Throsby, Margaret, *Talking with Margaret Throsby*, Allen & Unwin: Sydney, 2008.

Walker, Mike, *Powder Puff Derby: Petticoat pilots and flying flappers*, Wiley: Chichester, 2003.

Waterworth, Eric and Cassidy, Jill, *Eric Waterworth: An inventive Tasmanian*, Queen Victoria Museum and Art Gallery: Launceston, 1990.

Wild, J.P. (ed.), *From Stump-Jump Plough to Interscan: A review of invention and innovation in Australia*, Australian Academy of Science: Canberra, 1977.

Williams, Cicely, *Women on the Rope: The feminine share in mountain adventure*, Allen & Unwin: Sydney, 1973.

Wilson, Gwen, *One Grand Chain: The history of anaesthesia in Australia Vol. 1, 1846–1934*, Australian and NZ College of Anaesthetists: Sydney, 1995.

Wollaston, T.C., *Opal: The gem of the Never-Never*, Thomas Murby & Co.: London, 1924.

Articles

Arthur, Ian, 'Shipboard refrigeration and the beginnings of the frozen meat trade', *Journal of the Royal Australian Historical Society*, June 2006.

'A Bag O' Wine, Please', *Australian Packaging*, November 1985, p. 85.

Cherry, T.M., 'Anthony George Maldon Michell 1870–1959', *Biographical Memoirs of Fellows of the Royal Society*, vol. 8 (Nov. 1952), pp. 91–103.

Drane, Robert, 'Innovators: Race Cam', *Inside Sport*, October 2008.

Fullagar, Kate, 'Bennelong in Britain', *Aboriginal History*, vol. 33, 2009, pp. 31–51.

Gray, E. Dwyer, 'Story of the tanks', *The Argus*, 9 August 1924, p. 6.

Gregory, Max, 'The inventive genius of Henry Sutton', *Restored Cars Magazine*, 1989, pp. 5–6.

Gwynn-Jones, Terry, 'Bill Lancaster: Lost in the Sahara after attempting to break the England–Cape Town flight speed record', *Aviation History*, January 2000.

'Gyroscope car runs with forty passengers', *New York Times*, 11 November 1909.

'The gyroscope and its promise for the future', *New York Times*, 12 December 1909.

McIntyre, John, 'The first marlin', *Blue Water*, February/March 2002, pp. 67–9.

Moffett, Cleveland, 'Transportation and the gyroscope: Louis Brennan's mono-rail car', *Munsey's Magazine*, 1907.

Mond, Dr Harry, 'The first pacemaker', *Modern Medicine of Australia*, October 1987, pp. 75–6.

Mueller, S. and Umberger, W., 'Myth busting: who is the Australian cask wine consumer?' *Wine Industry Journal*, Jan/Feb. 2009, vol. 24, no.1, pp. 52–8.

Nugent, Ann, 'Nellie Alma Martel and the Women's Social and Political Union, 1905–9', *Hecate*, May 2005.

Sawer, Marian, 'The right to stand but not to sit', *About the House*, July–August 2003, pp. 20–3.

Smith, Keith Vincent, 'Bennelong among his people', *Aboriginal History*, vol. 33, 2009, pp. 7–30.

Sunter, Anne Beggs, 'Henry Sutton: The Eureka Man', *Australian Heritage*, November 2005, pp. 36–8.

'Wine now sold in bags!', *The Australian Exporter*, January 1966, p. 15.

Wright, Charles, 'Newham Waterworth 1867–1949', *Australian Journal of Optometry*, 1980, vol. 63, no. 4, pp. 145–8.

Wright, Ken, 'The design was not passed on', MilitaryHistoryOnline. com, accessed 7 August 2006.

Other

Heritage Tasmania, Tasmanian Heritage Register Datasheet, 'Alexander Patent Racket Company', 2009.

Kener, Andrew, 'The Streaker', unpublished paper, University of Pennsylvania, Fall, 2010.

INDEX